Ben Campkin is Director of the UCL Urban Laboratory and
in the Bartlett School of Architecture. He is co-editor of *Dirt: New Geographies
of Cleanliness and Contamination* (I.B.Tauris, 2007, paperback 2012).

'An important and much-needed corrective, full of fascinating insights, which exposes the myths of regeneration.'

Anna Minton
author of *Ground Control: Fear and Happiness in the Twenty-First Century City*

REMAKING
LONDON

DECLINE AND REGENERATION IN URBAN CULTURE

BEN CAMPKIN

I.B. TAURIS

LONDON · NEW YORK

Published in 2013 by I.B.Tauris & Co. Ltd
London • New York
Reprinted 2014, 2017
www.ibtauris.com

International Library of Human Geography: 19

ISBN: 978 1 78076 307 1 (HB)
ISBN: 978 1 78076 308 8 (PB)
eISBN: 978 0 85773 416 7
epdf: 978 0 85772 272 0

A full CIP record for this book is available from the British Library
A full CIP record is available from the Library of Congress

Library of Congress Catalog Card Number: available

Designed and typeset by 4word Ltd, Bristol
Printed and bound by CPI Group (UK) Ltd, Croydon, CR0 4YY

CONTENTS

List of Illustrations   vii
Acknowledgements   xi

Introduction   1

1   Slum Spectacle   19
2   Life in the Ruins   37
3   Regeneration ad nauseam   57
4   Sink Estate Spectacle   77
5   Crisis and Creativity   105
6   Ornament from Grime   127
7   Burial and Bioremediation   149

Conclusion   163

Notes   169
Bibliography   215
Index   237

ILLUSTRATIONS

Figures

0.1 The Women's Library, London, 2012. © Ben Campkin   3

1.1 'The Devil's Architecture. A typical crumbling and vermin-   22
ridden staircase'. *House Happenings*, London, St Pancras House
Improvement Society, Christmas 1931

1.2 'Mrs Fry and her baby in her old house in Gee Street', *c.* 1920s.   23
Reprinted from Malcolm J. Holmes: *Somers Town: A Record of
Change*, London Borough of Camden, 1989

1.3 Somers Town – cockroach, rat, flea and bedbug set alight, 1929   29
– site of St Christopher's Flats, Werrington Street. Courtesy of
Camden Local Studies and Archives Centre, St Pancras Housing
Association collection

1.4 Fumigators sealing a fumigation van, *c.* 1930. Courtesy of   34
Camden Local Studies and Archives Centre, St Pancras Housing
Association collection

2.1 Bert Hardy, 'The Emblem of the Cockney World', 'Life in the   38
Elephant', 1948, *Picture Post* collection. © Getty Images

2.2 Albert L. Lloyd, 'Life in the Elephant', with photographs by   46
Bert Hardy, *Picture Post*, 42, January 1949, double page spread
showing layout and image-text relationships, *Picture Post*
collection. © Getty Images

2.3 Bert Hardy, 'Maisie', 1948, *Picture Post* collection. © Getty   49
Images

2.4 Philip Michael, Elephant and Castle shopping centre as seen   52
from the London College of Communication, 'Life in the
Elephant, 2005'. Courtesy of the Cuming Museum, London
Borough of Southwark. © Philip Michael

3.1 Optimistic view of the redevelopment of the Elephant and   58
Castle in 1962 with sunburst. Reproduced from Leonard Reilly,
Southwark: An Illustrated History (London, 1998), p. 86

3.2 Ernö Goldfinger, Alexander Fleming House, Elephant and   60
Castle, *c.* 1967. © Architectural Press Archive/RIBA Library
Photographs Collection

3.3 Metro Central Heights, 2009. © Ben Campkin   66

3.4 Elephant and Castle shopping centre, photograph taken from   68
outside Metropolitan Tabernacle, *c.* 1965, photographed by
Roy Brooke © Southwark Local History Library

3.5 Willett Group public relations and marketing brochure,   69
Elephant and Castle shopping centre, transport links, 1962.
© Southwark Local History Library

4.1 The Aylesbury Estate, Aylesbury Redevelopment Area,   78
Opening Ceremony brochure, 1970. © Southwark Local
History Library

4.2 The Aylesbury Estate, architect's drawing, Aylesbury   83
Redevelopment brochure, *c.* 1966. © Southwark Local
History Library

4.3 Stills from John Mansfield (dir.), *Horizon: The Writing on the*   87
Wall, 1974, BBC video, 50 minutes approx. © BBC

4.4 Prime Minister Tony Blair with Police Constable Kevin   98
Holland, Aylesbury Estate, photographed by Stefan Rousseau,
1997. © Press Association Images

5.1 King's Cross from the air, 1963, photographed by Simmons   107
Aerofilms from a light aircraft. © English Heritage, NMR
Aerofilms Collection

5.2 King's Cross Railwaylands, 1987, photographed by British Rail   109
Property Board. © Unknown

5.3 Derek Jarman, stills from Pet Shop Boys' 'King's Cross', tour   114
video, 1989. © Becker Brown

5.4 View of the scene at King's Cross on the evening of 18   116
November 1987, photographed by John Downing, Hulton
Archive. © Getty Images

5.5 Photograph of King's Cross Underground Station Piccadilly   117
Line escalator mechanism, showing accumulation of grease and
detritus on undamaged part of running track of escalator 4,
taken 20 November 1987. From Desmond Fennell, *Investigation*

into the King's Cross Underground Fire, Department of Transport: Her Majesty's Stationery Office (1988), plate 12. Courtesy of Camden Local Studies and Archives Centre

5.6 King's Cross Partnership hoardings, King's Cross, 2001.   120
© Ben Campkin

5.7 The Almeida at King's Cross, temporary theatre, external view   121
of site before conversion, 2001. © Haworth Tomkins Architects

6.1 The Dirty House, general view of the exterior, 2007.   129
© Tim Wray

6.2 The Dirty House, 2002. © Adjaye Associates Ltd   137

7.1 Cover of *Buried*, 2006. © Stephen Gill   152

7.2 Extract from *Buried* series, 2006. © Stephen Gill   155

Plates

1 Sidney Street Estate, St Pancras, View from the Air, 1931, back cover of *House Happenings*, Christmas 1931. Courtesy of Camden Local Studies and Archives Centre, St Pancras Housing Association collection

2 Bert Hardy, 'A Ghost Strayed from Old Greece', 'Life in the Elephant', 1948, *Picture Post* collection. © Getty Images

3 Ernö Goldfinger, Alexander Fleming House, Elephant and Castle, *c.* 1967. © Architectural Press Archive/RIBA Library Photographs Collection

4a Elephant and Castle Shopping Centre, artistic impression by A. J. Middleton, 1962. © Southwark Local History Library

4b Willett Group public relations and marketing brochure, Elephant and Castle Shopping Centre, drawing by A. J. Middleton showing the centre as conceived, 1962. © Southwark Local History Library

5 Elevated view of the Aylesbury Estate, Walworth, photographed by Mike Seaborne, 1997. © Museum of London

6 London Borough of Southwark, Department of Architecture and Planning, 'Looking east along a first floor walkway' and 'Arriving by car', concept drawings, *Heygate redevelopment*, 1969. © Southwark Local History Library

7 Stills from *Mona Lisa*, dir. Neil Jordan, 1986, showing a depiction of King's Cross. © Handmade Films

8   Haworth Tomkins Architects, The Almeida at King's Cross, temporary
    theatre 2001 (demolished 2002), external view at night, photographed
    by Philip Vile, 2001. © Haworth Tomkins Architects, 2001
9   The Dirty House, 2002. Photographed by Lyndon Douglas
    © Lyndon Douglas
10 Stephen Gill, extract from *Buried* series, 2006. © Stephen Gill

ACKNOWLEDGEMENTS

I have benefited enormously from the support and insights of many friends and colleagues as I have researched and written this book. I am particularly grateful to Johan Andersson, Michael Edwards, Matthew Gandy, David Gissen, Barbara Penner, Jane Rendell, Rebecca Ross and Timothy Wray, who have all generously shared ideas that have shaped my approach and arguments, as well as providing friendship, encouragement and careful commentary at various stages.

I am lucky enough to work in a university where critical urban scholarship is in good shape, and I would like to thank colleagues and students of the Bartlett Faculty of the Built Environment and of the UCL Urban Laboratory for their inspiration, and their specific contributions in developing my research, especially Pushpa Arabindoo, Matthew Beaumont, Nick Beech, Sarah Bell, Iain Borden, Richard Dennis, Adrian Forty, Murray Fraser, Penelope Haralambidou, Andrew Harris, Jonathan Hill, Chee Kit Lai, CJ Lim, Yeoryia Manolopoulou, Louis Moreno, Alan Penn, Hilary Powell, Peg Rawes, Luis Rego, David Roberts, Jennifer Robinson, Myfanwy Taylor, Mark Tewdwr-Jones and Susan Ware.

In the process of the book's completion, I have benefitted from meticulous assistance with image research from Brent Pilkey. Huge thanks also to Laura Hirst for her support during the protracted final stages, Kate Ahl for providing great comments on a draft, David Stonestreet at I.B.Tauris for being a patient editor, and to 4word Ltd and Cecile Rault for managing the production process. Particular thanks to David for commissioning the book and encouraging me along the way.

Across UCL and beyond, many other friends and colleagues have offered expertise and motivation for which I am very grateful, including Sam Ashby, Caroline Bressey, Victor Buchli, Rosie Cox, Elizabeth Darling, Alberto Duman, Tim Edensor, Peter Gibbs-Kennett, Adrian Glasspool, Victoria Grimwood, Tony Hallam, Max Hill, R. Justin Hunt, Jane M. Jacobs, David John,

Iain Low, Issac Marerro-Guillamón, Mariana Mogilevich, Anna Minton, James Paskins, Ian Scott and Paul Watt.

I would also like to acknowledge the financial support of the Bartlett School of Architecture Research Fund for image reproduction costs and teaching cover to help me finish the manuscript.

Finally, thanks to my parents, David and Judy Campkin, and family – this book is for you.

The city is a jewel fed by lowly operations.

Dominique Laporte

As long as people have lived in cities, they have been haunted by fears of urban ruin.

Marshall Berman

INTRODUCTION

In autumn 2002 I attended a talk given by the sociologist Paul Hirst (1947–2003) on 'Modernism's fear of dirt'.[1] Delivering his lecture in London's East End, in a mid-nineteenth-century Victorian bathhouse that had been recently 'regenerated' and now housed The Women's Library, Hirst asked: 'in attempting to remove grime and disorder from the urban environment, did modernist planners and architects also inadvertently wash away the spirit of the city?'[2] This rhetorical question singled out a pervasive debate in modern urban culture, policy and theory over how ordered cities should be, and the role of degradation and disorder in propelling and legitimising certain forms of change, or stimulating imagination, creativity and 'spirit'. Through a survey of three canonical Western modernist 'utopian' architect-urbanists – Ebenezer Howard, Le Corbusier and Frank Lloyd Wright – Hirst came to the conclusion that the answer to his question was resoundingly 'yes' – though there was nothing inadvertent about this act of cleansing the 'cityness' of cities. Rather, these men were fundamentally anti-urban in conceiving of the city as having a 'natural' predisposition to disorder that architecture and planning needed to address. Furthermore, though the history of modern architecture repeatedly presented visions of efficiently organised, sanitised cities, for Hirst, as a sociologist, the pursuit of an ultra-regulated urban environment constituted a delusional and undesirable project. These key figures in the history of the modern city had failed to acknowledge, he argued, the myriad ways that dirt, degradation and disorder (or at least, informality) were themselves a product and fundamental part of the city. Cleanliness and order, the argument went, can be taken to excess in a certain ideal of civilisation, at the expense of risk, sociability, imagination and creativity.

Hirst was speaking in a building that had recently become the home of a cultural and educational institution, with space for collections, exhibitions and events, but that had originally been built in 1846 as a washhouse, designed as part of a concerted programme of urban sanitation.[3] Given the historical

1

context of the building, his arguments, delivered from the centre of its former washrooms, resonated with particular intensity. The setting evoked the grand public health agendas that underpinned urban improvement in the Victorian period, and that had continued to drive change in the twentieth century as part of the modernist project, and through the establishment and expansion of the Welfare State. This building had originally been intended to bring functional and symbolic hygiene to the East End's 'great unwashed'. However, sand-blown and sanitised, reconfigured by Wright and Wright architects, it had been transformed into a rarefied cultural institution, aided in 1998 by a grant from the UK's state-directed Heritage Lottery Fund.[4]

In millennial London, and in other UK cities, there had been a massive drive led by the state, and by the Urban Task Force established by the New Labour government in 1998, to 'identify the causes of urban decline' and achieve an 'urban renaissance'.[5] The foundation of the Urban Task Force and the Commission for Architecture and the Built Environment (CABE), the government's adviser on architecture from 1999 to 2010, marked a feverish new appetite for the regeneration of cities, and one continued by successive governments and local authorities ever since.

The Women's Library (see Figure 0.1) stands as an example of such heritage- and culture-triggered millennial regeneration, the aesthetic of which conforms to a trope of gritty contextual architectural recycling typical in the reuse of buildings in London's former industrial areas. On a surface reading, this example suggested that the anxious pursuit of urban order and cleanliness, as a physical and moral public health imperative, had been replaced by a different, yet in some ways comparable, zest for regeneration. Here, however, development and design had been decoupled from the grand narratives of public health improvement for the poor. A facility originally established to deal directly with material dirt, dangerous conditions and unhygienic bodies had fallen into disuse, later being acquired by a university and revalued as heritage, with a new purpose to accommodate and symbolise cultural capital. Hirst's interest was in architecture as a civilising and disciplining instrument, put to use to reorder disorderly spaces such as the slums of the Victorian East End. How, I wondered, did the architecture and urbanism of more recent regeneration respond to urban dirt and disorder?

In this book we shall examine different phases and examples of urban renewal in London by focusing, in particular, on the forms of decline and degradation they have purportedly set out to counter. Our examples will be taken from some of the most hotly contested sites in modern and late-modern London,

Figure 0.1: The Women's Library, London, 2012.

with fine-grained analyses of the processes and discourses of transformation to which they have been subjected. The first four chapters focus on various forms and representations of housing in the twentieth century, while thereafter the book pays particular attention to the aesthetics of degradation and regeneration in late twentieth- and early twenty-first-century art and architecture.

The locales on which we shall focus are contested to different degrees, and the book aims, even where controversies appear to have long passed, to scrutinise them closely in order to understand them better. These are places that were key to London's functioning as a modern city, and that, over a long period and increasingly in the late twentieth century, have been subject to major reconfigurations and projections of future improvement. Since their earliest development, they, and their communities, have been stigmatised through reference to base conditions, and diverse forms of spatial and social disorder. At certain times, these neighbourhoods, and specific sites within them, have become entangled with negative associations, in which material degradation has been inextricably intertwined with ideas of social decline. In response, counter-narratives, challenging stereotypical representations, have also emerged.

The discussion will centre on two problems: first, how today's 'dysfunctional' regeneration zones can be situated in relation to a longer-term history and through a better appreciation of changing approaches towards urban 'improvement'; second, how to understand the ways in which in its various material and symbolic forms urban degradation drives, and is actively produced within, urban change, and how it appears in a range of cultural artefacts directly associated with different phases of urbanisation. The following introductory remarks frame these two emphases: first contextualizing the book in relation to recent debates about regeneration across a number of related disciplines; then suggesting some theoretical reference points, drawing particularly on psychoanalytic theory and neo-Marxian approaches to the material presence, and representation, of urban squalor.

Regeneration and its contradictions

'Regeneration' has recently become a pervasive metaphor for urban change in London. Yet evocative as it might be, this is by no means a straightforward concept. The word itself is Latin, and has an interesting etymology, originally referring to spiritual rebirth.[6] In Anglo-Norman English a new definition extended the meaning to biological improvement, and specifically the formation of new cells. Its use in reference to place can be traced back to the mid-sixteenth century, but it is not until the late-nineteenth century that 'urban regeneration' begins to feature, referring to the reconstruction of slum districts.[7] 'Regeneration' also appears in the twentieth century in the repertoire of socio-biological metaphors through which the renewal of the post-war city was conceived. In that context there was a sense that properly functioning neighbourhoods would self-regenerate, meaning that radical reconstruction was necessary where regeneration did not occur spontaneously. Even considering these historical usages, however, it is striking that this word and concept have such widespread currency in present-day London, with the discourse and practice of regeneration gaining momentum from the 1980s to the 2000s.

The *London Plan* (2011) is the capital's current strategic plan, written by the directly-elected Mayor of London and published by the Greater London Assembly, the city's governing body since 2000.[8] The word 'regeneration' features heavily in this document, which identifies great swathes of London as 'opportunity areas'. The Plan has an extensive glossary of key terms, yet the meaning of 'regeneration' is not spelt out. Even if the Mayor does not define what regeneration is specifically, in another sense it is possible to glean its various meanings through the contexts in which it occurs. These oscillate between social and economic aspirations, but with the emphasis on economic growth and a more intensive use of land. The Plan defines regeneration areas as those 'in greatest socioeconomic need', on the basis of the UK's 'Index of Multiple Deprivation', a statistical dataset published by the government and focused on income, employment, health deprivation, disability, education, skills and training, barriers to housing and services, and crime.[9] There is an assumption that business and property-led redevelopment and the housing market will cause a 'trickle down' effect, ultimately raising the quality of life and income levels of communities living in such areas. In practice, however, in London and elsewhere, the neoliberal strategies the Plan promotes have been widely criticised for working directly against such objectives: increasing inequality, reducing the amount of genuinely affordable housing, instigating the demolition of estates rather than their renewal, alienating communities instead of engaging with them, and so on.[10]

There are some striking similarities between those areas identified as 'regeneration areas' in the 2011 *London Plan* and those identified as 'opportunity areas' in the 1943 *County of London Plan*, as well as a common mode of large scale, *tabula rasa* redevelopment. The latter was commissioned by the London County Council (LCC), and written by John Forshaw and Patrick Abercrombie, as an ambitious collective vision for post-war London, focused on reconstruction, and on a more controlled pattern of urban order and development.[11] As a strategic plan for London, this was followed only by the *Greater London Development Plan*, in 1972, produced after the LCC had been replaced by the Greater London Council (GLC) in 1963. The GLC was itself disbanded in 1986, leaving the city with no strategic governance until 2000. In the following chapters we shall take empirical examples from the 1920s to the 2012 Olympics, sampling the distinct ways that urban degradation has become manifest and regeneration programmes have been implemented, under these different administrations. In this endeavour we will focus on specific cases, whilst taking London as a city that exemplifies and influences wider global trends.

Since the financial crisis of 2008, and the end of the era of the New Labour government (1997–2010), in which achieving an 'urban renaissance' was a central policy objective, regeneration has been exposed more sharply to scrutiny. There is a growing scepticism about the broad range of processes

– including gentrification and property development – subsumed under this label. Even if critical of top-down regeneration defined by hegemonic neoliberal values, we should not adopt a nostalgic position, opposed to change, or one that romanticises urban decay. It would be odd to be anti-regeneration where it is seen as the ambition to distribute the health and wealth benefits associated with living in a city more equitably, improving living conditions, the public realm and quality of life.[12]

In geography and urban studies a wide base of scholars have critiqued the way that under neoliberal urbanisation, regeneration often claims it will bring benefits to 'deprived' communities, but fails to deliver these or to engage local people in the process, instead causing direct or indirect displacement.[13] From this work we gain insights into how at national and local scales market-led strategies of urban redevelopment have been promoted, producing varied forms of gentrification, often state-led, benefiting commercial interests, and dispersing existing communities who are excluded from decision-making and any advantages or economic growth that ultimately result.[14]

It is notable, however, that although such scholars have worked with and studied grassroots organisations in contested regeneration sites, theoretical work has not, on the whole, been successfully transposed to contemporary regeneration policy and professional practice. Furthermore, if there is a mounting base of evidence to support the detrimental affects of regeneration on the communities that are supposed to benefit from it, there is not an equivalent set of long-term studies to support current strategies, and there are few follow-up evaluations. As the planning economist Michael Edwards, the author of one such evaluation, has pointed out, even the Greater London Authority – the London-wide strategic governing authority that supports the London Mayor and London Assembly – have recently noted this lack of a research base.[15]

Edwards refers to 'regeneration' as a 'slippery word'.[16] In this way, the term itself can be thought of as a displacement. In this movement the worst consequences of certain forms of neoliberal urbanisation are concealed behind a façade of social improvement. Such contradictions are evident when we consider that although regeneration is frequently justified in terms of fostering 'mixed use', 'diverse', 'creative' and 'biodiverse' neighbourhoods, it often appears to remove – in spontaneous, informal, community- and citizen-led manifestations – precisely the qualities and activities it claims to engender; attempting instead to engineer their presence more formally as part of a project of economic 'rationalisation'. Similarly, even within a regeneration drive that purportedly attempts to reverse decline and eliminate degradation, these are often heightened, commodified or exacerbated in the process.

Critical studies of regeneration have also appeared in architectural debates. The journalist and cultural critic, Owen Hatherley, for example, has labelled the 'urban renaissance' as 'good ideas badly thought out and (mostly) appallingly applied'.[17] In his work, Hatherley attempts to reclaim a utopian position from a re-examination of the ruins of architectural modernism that have often been the focus of recent regeneration campaigns. Concentrating on the New Labour era, he surveys a wide range of cities and acerbically critiques the 'pseudomodern' architecture produced through public–private partnerships such as the 'Private Finance Initiative' (PFI) – a core strategy to draw private capital into the funding of public services and infrastructure. In framing *A Guide to the New Ruins of Great Britain* (2010) Hatherley notes that 'regeneration' is an under-explored word. In architecture, he suggests that it conveys a 'vaguely religious air' appropriate to the superficial formalism of the buildings he considers, such as Daniel Libeskind's London Metropolitan University building in north London.[18] In our discussions of recent art and architecture, rather than this bland 'pseudo modernism' we instead focus on the parallel aesthetics of urban degradation that have featured in London's 'renaissance'.

In a recent account of architecture and regeneration that is less clearly politically positioned than Hatherley's, the interior and spatial designer, David Littlefield, rightly calls for us to understand the complexities of regeneration beyond the 'merely architectural' – that is, formal and aesthetic – taking into account the social, historical, cultural, political, psychological, emotional and economic dimensions of urban place.[19] The chapters that follow contribute to present-day debates about what 'regeneration', as a concept and set of processes, means, through taking an interdisciplinary approach, looking across the various dimensions Littlefield identifies. In attempting to situate regeneration historically, Littlefield turns to a canon of set pieces of urban change, from the mid-seventeenth century to the present. Rather than attempt a comprehensive survey, our approach shall be to focus on the histories of clusters of present-day regeneration sites, providing a sense of the cultural and historical production of these places over time.

Aside from architectural commentators and academics, it is important to note that in present-day London, many of the strongest critiques of regeneration, as well as the most thorough historical research on those areas subjected to it, have come from community members and activist groups who have built impressive – and freely accessible – archives on specific neighbourhoods and sites.[20] In these contexts, configurations of residents and community members, artists and others have responded to aggressive forms of redevelopment by devoting their time, skills and creativity to producing imaginative and critical analyses in texts, images, web-based archives, timelines, posters, walks, exhibitions, community events, and many other activities. Their work often necessarily involves debunking the myths and interpreting the ambiguous statements circulated by developers and local authorities, and countering them with alternative proposals.

One urban historian who has drawn attention to the conflicted narratives around urban decline is Robert Beauregard, who has noted in relation to the USA that:

> Few urban historians have embraced urban decline as an object of study … Historians whose work has direct relevance for urban decline generally have a narrower agenda: the ghetto, economic collapse, public housing or redevelopment. Scholars have generally neglected the place of decline in the popular imagination and thus its role in shaping the decisions made by countless households and institutions.[21]

Though we should be cautious about the transposition of theories of decline from one geographical context to another, this statement by Beauregard rings true for London and the UK.[22] We shall also examine 'discourses' of decline in this book, taking this concept at its most inclusive, so that it embraces diverse forms of discursive practice. We shall reach beyond the linguistic focus of Beauregard's work, and much of the existing textual discourse analysis on the stigmatisation of particular places, to consider a wide range of cultural artefacts.[23] In an expanded form, the notion of 'discourse' is useful as it bridges different kinds of representational practice and media, exploring how power operates through a range of aesthetic strategies and cultural forms that play a role in the material production and experience of urban space.

Though there has been a growing interest in culture-led regeneration and 'creative cities', critical discussions of the cultural dimensions of urban regeneration – its place in the 'popular imagination' – have tended to be confined to specific fields, such as architecture, art, city branding and so on. In contrast, in this book we shall explore the imaginaries of urban regeneration and degradation – those representations that have an active role in shaping the experience, understanding and material conditions of contested places – across a wide range of sources, including journalism, photojournalism, cinema, site-specific and performance art, theatre, architectural design, advertising and television. In dealing with such eclectic media, similar questions reverberate around the cultural politics of London's regeneration, the ethics of representing poverty and degradation, and the relationships between projections of urban change as produced by built environment professionals and by others.

Rather than think of these conflicted discourses in terms of different understandings of 'place image' – which has a visual emphasis, suggests rather fixed and singular associations, and externalises understandings of place – it is perhaps more helpful to understand them as place imaginaries.[24] The concepts of the 'imaginary' and 'imaginaries' have been used in psychoanalytic and neo-Marxian theoretical traditions. For example, in the work of Jacques Lacan, the 'Imaginary Order' is where the subject, in the pre-verbal mirror stage, constructs an internalised image of the whole self.[25] In this realm, relationships between the external world and the subject's psyche, between private and social arenas, are negotiated. It is where 'the subject' is constructed as a representation itself. This image continues to play an important role in the construction of the ego in relation to objects once the child has entered the Symbolic Order. The Imaginary, in Lacan's sense, is in part illusory, leading to the misconception of oneself as whole, rather than fragmented; but it is necessary in the establishment of meaningful relationships with the external, material world.

Related to this Lacanian conception, the notions of the 'imaginary' and 'imaginaries' are also prominent in the work of neo-Marxian theorist, Cornelius Castoriadis, in comprehending social configurations and structures of social and political change in the modern West.[26] For Castoriadis, the imaginary, in its common meaning, is 'separate from the real, whether it claims to take the latter's place (a lie) or makes no such claim (a novel)'.[27] As invention, the imaginary has 'deep and obscure relations' with the symbolic (language, in the broadest sense), through which it must necessarily be represented in order 'to pass from the virtual'.[28] In his own work, these notions appear in various forms, including the 'social imaginary'; and the 'tightening grip of the capitalist imaginary', which is in tension with the emancipatory 'creative imaginary', the tool of autonomous individuals in achieving change and resistance to capitalist domination.[29] Castoriadis demonstrates the potential of the concept, both to critique distorting myths about the world and propose alternatives, taking advantage of cracks that appear during times, and in places, of crisis. Adapted to an urban context the notion of 'place imaginaries' can usefully articulate the ways that contested sites are constructed, recognised or distorted from multiple and conflicted perspectives, through forms of representation that are not passive but have agency and are affective within urban change as they engage with particular empirical features and material conditions.

If broader critical approaches to the understanding of regeneration as culturally produced across different media have been lacking in contemporary scholarship, so too have critical historical perspectives. Contested understandings of history are central to the conflicts that surround urban restructuring. In these contexts, the past is drawn into fraught relationships with the present, and with the anticipated futures of specific sites. Here, distant and recent history may be constructed and narrated in complex ways, often being distorted, buried or neutralised as anodyne heritage. With this in mind, we shall frame the dominant discourses that have propelled the recent restructuring of London within a longer-term historical framework. The intention is to draw attention to the short-termism, and a neglect or distortion of lessons from the past in recent policy and practice. The purpose is also to connect the restructuring of late-modern London with the modern city, because intractable challenges in the present are structured through earlier forms of urbanisation. Many of today's regeneration sites have been subject to repeated programmes of improvement, and the tropes through which places are stigmatised often recur in different forms from one period to another.

We begin in the 1920s, when London was governed by the LCC, and prior to the establishment of the Welfare State and town planning system. The first chapters take examples from the post-war reconstruction of the 1940s, and the expansion out of the Welfare State in the middle decades of the twentieth century. We then consider the de-industrialisation of the city, and the forms of decline associated with certain examples of modernist architecture and planning in the 1970s and 1980s. From the mid-1970s onwards, we trace the rise of neoliberal approaches to urban transformation and management, concluding our story with the Olympic-led restructuring of the city in the years leading up to the 2012 Games.

The formation of new attitudes towards dirt and waste matter, at an individual and collective level, comprised an important ingredient of the modern industrial city, and played a central role in defining understandings of place, processes of urbanisation and the social relations through which they were constituted. Our story therefore includes historical accounts of public-health-driven slum clearances and housing reform in the 1920s, 1930s and 1940s. However, in various guises, dirt and degradation have also played a major role in the discourses of urban decline and renewal since de-industrialisation, and less attention has been paid to this topic. We focus particularly, therefore, on the late-modern city, and consider narratives of cleansing and contamination even as they feature in the latest Olympic-led restructuring in the east of the city, debates about the legacies of which are ongoing at the time of writing.

The last quarter of the twentieth century, as architectural theorist, Joe Kerr, has noted, was a period of particularly intense development for London, catalysed after 1979 by a period of laissez-faire Conservatism, a declining role for the state, and a strategy of privatisation intended to counteract the preceding years of underinvestment and weak management of the public realm.[30] By the time of the Labour Party Conference in 1976, neoliberal economic strategies had begun to take hold amongst the right in the Labour government, as well as in the Conservative Party. By the mid-1980s, and alongside the deregulation of the financial markets in 1986, having come to power in 1979, Margaret Thatcher's government accelerated key strategies such as the privatisation of utilities. Since then, successive UK governments have committed themselves to neoliberal urbanism in various forms.

Writing in 2008 and reflecting on his book *Soft City*, published in 1974, the travel writer and novelist, Jonathan Raban, lamented the loss of 'a London far seedier than it is now'.[31] For Raban, diversity has been suffocated by escalating rents, 'driven from the central city to its remote peripheries – a trend that is reflected in metropolitan areas around the world'.[32] The various plans to reshape the areas that are the focus of this book in the late twentieth century fit within this wider ongoing pattern of economic 'rationalisation', described by Raban in relation to once marginal – and affordable and cosmopolitan – districts in west London, now 'expensively reconstructed' into bland homogeneity. Raban's observations raise the important point that regeneration has concentrated on those more affordable parts of London that are also most socially mixed, and hence it reflects our values and attitudes towards diversity.

Our case studies – Somers Town, King's Cross, the Elephant and Castle, Hackney Wick, Walworth and Shoreditch – have provided a particular focus for, and challenge to, the agents of regeneration as a form of economic 'rationalisation'. They have been the focus for grand projects, but within each loose cluster of examples we shall also consider smaller-scale initiatives. Antagonistic to London's image as a 'global' city through their demonstration of its contradictions, and through their slow transformation, these places – even while still inhabited – provided space to project and develop visions of the future city. They have been subject to numerous campaigns to record and represent their environments and communities, shaped by the interests and resources of particular groups – whether academics, activists, archaeologists, architects, developers, planners, politicians or the media – and put to work within the discourses of renewal. The motives behind these endeavours are as varied as the agencies behind them, but four general categories can be noted: first, the legitimisation or contestation of redevelopment plans; second, anxieties of potential loss associated with imminent and irreversible change; third, the perception that the problems or failures of the past must be documented to avoid future repetition; and, finally, representations produced by professionals for specific effects within the redevelopment process.

Looking across these different categories, the geographical spread of our examples avoids the juxtaposition of east and west London, established in Victorian accounts, and which has remained typical in commentaries on the capital.[33] The emphasis on an east–west dynamic features strongly in commentaries on London's post-industrial architecture, art and urbanism.[34] This reflects the fact that the city's most radical physical, economic and social restructuring took place in the docklands on the fringes of the City of London to the east. However, over-emphasis on these areas precludes a more nuanced understanding of the shifts – perhaps slower or more fragmentary – that took place elsewhere. By the late twentieth century, and at the beginning of the twenty-first, the places with which we are concerned prominently displayed the 'ruins' of earlier and now obsolete phases of technological development and urbanisation.

Theories of degradation and the polarised city

As the object of our study, produced through aggregate phenomena, urban degradation calls for a hybrid analytic framework through which to explore relationships between materiality, subjectivity and society. With this in mind, post-Freudian psychoanalytic and neo-Marxian theories inform the book's preoccupations and interpretations. For some post-structuralist theorists, urban squalor features as central to the definition, representation and experience of late-modern cities. Writing at the beginning of the 1990s, feminist psychoanalytic theorist, Julia Kristeva, envisioned:

> a sprawling metropolis with glass and steel buildings that reach to the sky, reflect it, reflect each other, and reflect you – a city filled with people steeped in their

own image who rush about with overdone makeup on and who are cloaked in gold, pearls and fine leather, while in the next street over, heaps of filth abound and drugs accompany the sleep or the fury of the social outcasts.[35]

This striking image of the polarised city chimes with *Remaking London*'s epigraph: psychoanalytic theorist Dominique Laporte's conception of the city as 'a jewel fed by lowly operations' in *History of Shit*.[36] Laporte is talking about the relationship between the ordinary and the spectacular in the modern city, but Kristeva's account is typical of representations of the late-modern metropolis as a 'dual city' of extremes. There is an impending sense of crisis embodied in the 'heaps of filth' and 'social outcasts' evoked as the harsh but inevitable accompaniment to gleaming corporate towers.

While this urban scene is not taken from Kristeva's highly influential theory of abjection, we can imagine a connection here, where at the city scale there is a continuous attempt to negotiate the abject – 'what disturbs identity, system, order' – and actively exclude it.[37] Kristeva develops her theory of abjection in reference to George Bataille's essay 'Abjection et les formes misérables' [Abjection and forms of wretchedness], and Mary Douglas' account of 'dirt' in social anthropology.[38] For Douglas, in response to dirt, we are all involved in a perpetual spatial process of arranging and rearranging the environment, 'making the world conform to an idea'.[39] Abjection, however, is a more violent expulsion of what is deemed to be threatening or repulsive.[40] In the formation of subjectivity, the abject causes strong and apparently 'natural' reactions: it is a 'revolt of the person against an external menace from which one wants to keep oneself at a distance', but it gives the sense of being internal, menacing from the inside.[41] These can range from physiological disgust responses to a rotting object to the moral repulsion prompted by news of a horrific crime.[42]

Abjection refers to spatialised processes through which the subject, or society, attempts to impose or maintain a state of purity. Importantly, the concept accounts for a level of ambivalence on the part of the subject – the abject may attract as well as repel. Through the notion of 'spaces of abjection', Kristeva's concept has been put to use to examine order, disorder and hygienism in architecture, and to highlight the relationships between marginalised people and the places with which they are associated.[43] The idea of abjection is also a powerful notion with which to underpin our thinking about the various displacements performed in the name of urban regeneration and the degraded conditions it purports to counter.[44]

The scene of polarisation evoked by Kristeva can be situated within a prominent trope of the anxious city in theorisations of late-modern urbanism and aesthetics.[45] Kristeva argues that the experience of abjection constitutes 'a massive and sudden emergence of uncanniness'.[46] While there was a discussion of the abject as an expressive mode in Anglo-American art of the 1990s, in discussions of urban and architectural theory the uncanny has featured more often.[47] In Freud's theory, the uncanny accounts for certain 'qualities of feeling' evoked through literary techniques that produce simultaneously a sense of familiarity and alienation.[48] Taking this forward in relation to the late-modern city, the architectural theorist, Anthony Vidler, comments that the uncanny 'erupts in empty parking lots around abandoned or run-down shopping malls, in the screened *trompe l'oeil* of simulated space, in, that is, the wasted margins and surface appearances of postindustrial culture'.[49] It is in sites of urban transformation that such dislocations of time and space, and material contrasts, are at their most apparent.

Urban decline also features in the work of the cultural critic, Fredric Jameson. For him, the cultural experience of late capitalism is one where in 'the extraordinary surfaces of the photorealist cityscape ... the automobile wrecks gleam with some new hallucinatory splendor'.[50] These exhilarating surfaces are 'all the more paradoxical in that their essential content – the city itself – has deteriorated or disintegrated'. Jameson thus highlights the aesthetic commodification of 'urban squalor' accompanying the degraded and fractured 'city itself'. Yet urban studies researchers have not yet adequately researched this disjuncture, and over two decades after the publication of Jameson's book there is a need to expand his discussion of the imaginaries of urban squalor.

The work of scholars who have adopted a neo-Marxian theoretical position in the investigation of the production of urban nature and waste provides another key context for the empirical investigations in *Remaking London*. For example, these commentators have emphasised the social relationships underpinning the production and transformation of certain forms of nature in the city, as well as problematic 'subnatures' to use the architectural historian and theorist David Gissen's term for phenomena such as polluted air or pests.[51] Such concerns are evident in Marx's own conception of the relationships between dirt, cleanliness and civilisation. For him, isolated from the Promethean technologies that effect the civilising transformation of nature, the worker is forced to live in and on dirt, conceived as 'putrefied nature', the by-product of industrialisation.[52]

Neo-Marxian analyses of degradation are rooted firmly in the political, economic and historical dynamics behind the production of particular urban spaces.[53] For Maria Kaïka and Erik Swyngedouw:

> No matter how sanitized and clean, both in symbolic and literary terms, our cities have become, the 'urban trash' in the form of networks, dirt, sewerage, pipes, homeless people etc. keeps lurking underneath the city, in the corners, at the outskirts, bursting out on occasion in the form of rats, disease, homelessness, garbage piles, polluted water, floods, bursting pipes.[54]

The suggestion that these scholars make is that, in the context of the late-modern city, such juxtapositions have become more intense and more visible. Pollutants are themselves seen to have a historically, culturally and geographically specific 'nature', while one can also make meaningful connections across the discourses around, for example, nineteenth-century industrial and organic wastes, and twenty-first-century bacteriological and environmental concerns.

With these theoretical reference points in mind, we begin our exploration of urban degradation and regeneration with an examination of the St Pancras House Improvement Society's slum clearance and house-building programme in Somers Town in the 1920s and 1930s. In particular, the emphasis shall be on the Society's innovative use of media stunts to draw attention to the degraded material conditions in which people lived, and to their vision for change. As a creative response to housing need, and to legislative and financial structures imposed by the state, this vision was implemented through an experimental collaboration between the church, a university settlement, built environment professionals, philanthropists and the community. The specific focus of the chapter is on the central role of pest infestations as a serious public health problem experienced by slum residents, as a motivation for the reformers' work, and as a metaphor deployed in the discourses of renewal.

We then turn to the Elephant and Castle in south-east London with a consideration of photojournalist Bert Hardy and writer A. L. (Bert) Lloyd's account of the neighbourhood as a slum area set for imminent reconstruction in the late 1940s. The discussion here centres on the photographic and written conventions underlying the depiction of 'the Elephant' as a place of ruin and environmental degradation, caught in the process of modernisation, and of its socially and economically marginalised communities.

Changing scale, in Chapter 3 we examine two buildings central to the mid-twentieth-century reconstruction of the Elephant and Castle, and to its subsequent 'image problem': Alexander Fleming House, the offices of the Department for Health and Social Security, a 'sick building', later converted to luxury flats; and the Elephant and Castle Shopping Centre. These cases clarify and historicise the conventions of representation underlying the depiction of the Elephant as a place of environmental degradation and poverty, stigmatised through a discourse of 'ugliness'.

The Aylesbury Estate, one of the most iconic, large-scale stigmatised housing schemes in Europe, and part of the Labour government's expansion of the Welfare State under Harold Wilson, has been symbolically central to the discourses of late-twentieth-century urban blight in London and to New Labour's neoliberal urban renaissance agenda. In Chapter 4, we shall therefore devote attention to understanding the intersecting discourses around this estate in the arenas of architecture, national and local media, urban politics and policy, sociology and popular culture. A specific aim here, will be to re-evaluate arguments about environmental determinism and contextualise the theory of 'defensible space', imported from the United States, in relation to the specific history of this estate. We shall see how the Aylesbury, and its sister estate the Heygate, have been depicted through a generalised iconography of the dysfunctional 'sink estate'.

We next examine the post-industrial decline of King's Cross, a long-contentious zone in north inner London, recently subject to massive change associated with the opening of the Channel Tunnel Rail Link. The focus here, in particular, is on the late 1980s, the imaginary decline that developed around the time of the 1987 King's Cross fire, and the regeneration proposals of the late 1980s and early 1990s. Engaging a wide range of official and cultural representations in relation to key events, we shall explore the depiction of the area as a dysfunctional, ex-industrial 'wasteland' and as a red-light district. We then examine a site-specific urban art and architectural project in millennial King's Cross, realised with state funding. This project elaborated aspects of the reputation of King's Cross as a degraded and disorderly inner-city territory, but also emphasised its place as a locus of informal creativity.

In the penultimate chapter we turn to the case of the 'Dirty House' (2001–2), designed by architect, David Adjaye, for the British artists, Tim Noble and Sue Webster, as an example that illuminates contemporary aesthetic interests in urban decay across architecture, art and urbanism. A high-specification luxury house, part of the art-led gentrification of Hoxton, Adjaye's building commodifies the area's association with urban decay. Here, the aim shall be to clarify the confusing ideas about urban 'grit', 'dirtiness' and 'recycling' that have been evoked in relation to Adjaye's building.

In the final chapter we bring the history of London's reinvention up to date by turning to the London 2012 Olympic Games. Through examining the work of Hackney-based photographer, Stephen Gill, we shall consider relationships between different forms of physical and symbolic displacement and sanitisation, centred on the washing of contaminated soil. Gill's work comprises an archive of the Olympic Park before its redevelopment. It prompts reflection on the narratives and physical processes that accompanied this instance of mega-event led regeneration.

1

SLUM SPECTACLE

> In Dickens' day, Somers Town had become shabby-genteel;
> today it is merely shabby.
>
> *Estates Gazette* (1930)[1]

The housing stock in Somers Town changed so completely over the course of the twentieth century that it is difficult to imagine the experience of living in this neighbourhood for workers and their families in the 1920s and 1930s. Streets now occupied by medium-rise modernist blocks of flats were at that time characterised by rows of overcrowded terraces hastily constructed during the rapid expansion of the capital in the 1820s. For the most part, these fell well short of the standards of housing for wealthier Londoners on the opposite, southern, side of the New (now Euston) Road. One hundred years later, these buildings were extremely dilapidated. Conditions had become particularly dire as a result of ineffective state housing policies, the inactivity of the local municipal authorities and neglectful landlords. The community had to cope without proper sanitation, in dwellings that suffered from rot, and were severely infested with various kinds of pests, including rats, fleas and cockroaches, as well as the minute but severely disruptive common bedbug, *Cimex lectularius*.

It was in this context that in 1924 the St Pancras House Improvement Society (SPHIS) was established. It is still active in north London, though now in a different form and renamed 'Origin Housing'.[2] The founding committee of the Society comprised a group of energetic and committed social workers from various existing welfare organisations, chaired by the charismatic and locally-popular Father Basil Jellicoe (1899–1935), who had been sent to Somers Town in 1921 to lead a Magdalen College Mission settlement.[3] The Society's members were united by a non-denominational Christian welfare ethic, mobilising their work as reformers within a religious framework whereby the slums, poverty, overcrowding and infestations were conceived as the 'devil's work'.[4] Strongly influenced by the Garden Cities and Town Planning Association, they resolved to establish a house improvement and rehousing programme, centred initially on Somers Town.[5]

After conducting a damning survey of the existing housing stock in 1925, the Society set out to tackle the evident problems and improve the area's reputation.[6] In so doing, they intended to demonstrate that slum clearance and rehousing were financially and practically viable, with the rents for new properties remaining at a consistent level with the old.[7] They operated as a public utility society – a category specified within the *Industrial and Provident Societies Act* (1893), and later the *Housing Act* (1932), as a philanthropic provider of housing for the working classes. In effect, many such societies functioned without any philanthropic motive.[8] The St Pancras Society was unusual in that it addressed the housing needs of those who lived in extreme poverty, and did so with a commitment to rehousing people with minimal displacement and fragmentation of their communities. Housing grants were available via the state, but the Committee members soon attracted the investment of a range of influential and affluent shareholders, including the Prince of Wales.[9] Architectural historian, Elizabeth Darling, places the Society as one of a number of voluntary housing sector organisations formed in the inter-war period that addressed housing issues for the working-classes, particularly concentrating on those slum dwellers who were neglected by state housing policies that ignored the poorest social stratas.[10]

Uncanny nature

Infestations were a problem that had a particular prominence in journalistic accounts of Somers Town, known colloquially as 'little hell'. One journalist described the area in 1930 as a place of:

> vermin-ridden dens ... the worst hovels in London ... where mothers are afraid to put their children to bed for fear of rats and other vermin of all descriptions.[11]

By the mid-1920s, when the Society was forming, what we would now call 'pest control' was a highly specialised and organised industry offering an array of skills, expertise, new technologies and products. For example, in 1926, 'expert in sanitary building construction', Ernest Blake, published a manual for the protection of buildings against vermin, as part of a series of 'practical manuals for practical men' aimed at tradesmen in the construction industry and building crafts. In its introduction he observes:

> The word vermin is a very comprehensive term, and includes quite a number of different kinds of animals and insects. Some of these are the authors of a great deal of damage to house property, and as they consume large quantities of foodstuffs they are universally detested, while others are objected to, more on the score of their repulsive appearance, and the unsavoury conditions which they are usually associated ... The presence of vermin in a building indicates, either that there is a regular supply of food of some kind or other to which they have access, or else, that the condition of the place is so insanitary, that various species of insects are encouraged to breed and thrive in the dirt and filth that ought to be kept down.[12]

Acknowledging the wide scope of the category 'vermin', Blake emphasises the parasitic relationship of these animals to humans and their waste. He also highlights the strong association assumed between vermin, 'dirt and filth', and 'insanitary' or neglected environments. The manual focuses on vermin that can be found in enclosed areas and inhabited structures: including brown and black rats, the common house mouse, the cockroach, ants and houseflies. The material costs of vermin to property owners are also a central concern. These include damage to the structures of buildings, and the wider economic losses that might accrue from, for example, destruction of stock in a warehouse; or the spread of disease. Reflecting on the manual today, the suggestion that pest infestations and control are bound inextricably to underlying structures of property ownership, building conditions and responsibility for maintenance remains crucial.[13]

Of all the pests in 1920s Somers Town, the common bedbug, *Cimex lectularius,* caused the most anxiety because of the extent and effects of infestations. Called 'wall bugs' in some countries, bedbugs were (and are) a particular threat to the home where, intimately occupying a building's material core, fixtures and fittings, they 'hide in cracks and crevices in beds, wooden furniture, floors, and walls'.[14] The degraded slums of Somers Town and their furnishings were riddled with these insects. In the overcrowded and decaying brick and timber buildings, the tenants had to develop tactics to cope with the bugs, such as sealing their clothes in paper bags and hanging them from the ceiling when they arrived home, a strategy the Society documented photographically (see Figures 1.1 and 1.2).[15]

Figure 1.1: 'The Devil's Architecture.
A typical crumbling and vermin-ridden staircase'.

Bedbugs were already a feature of life in medieval London, but their detection, extermination and management emerged as an increasingly complex industry in the modern metropolis.[16] Armed with gases and chemical solutions, in the late nineteenth century and early twentieth, modernising reformers sought to control these insects as part of a wider civilising process focused on public health and housing.[17] In the 1920s and 1930s, bedbugs occupied a prominent place in the discourses of reformers and commentators focused on the problem of slum housing, both because of the extent of infestations, and because of their symbolic power to convey, in a more general sense, societal ills, and the abject poverty and suffering in which people lived.

How should we understand pests as a form of unwanted urban nature? In recent research bridging urban geography and architecture, scholars such as Matthew Gandy, David Gissen, Maria Kaïka and Erik Swyngedouw have conceived of the city 'as a process of transformed nature', and have examined the networks, conduits and infrastructures that facilitate processes of nature transformation and 'nature production' (see pages 14–15).[18] Focusing particularly on forms of nature – such as water – that are commodified and fetishised

Figure 1.2: *'Mrs Fry and her baby in her old house in Gee Street', c. 1920s.*

because of their use-value, and the further cultural, aesthetic and symbolic values they offer within the context of the modern and late-modern metropolis, these authors demonstrate collectively that 'the production of urban nature is a microcosm of wider tensions in urban society'.[19] This is a helpful framework through which to think about how pests feature in the discourses associated with housing reform in Somers Town, where their presence was highlighted to indicate the impoverished and degraded conditions in which people lived.

For Swyngedouw and Kaïka, in tension with an increasingly physically and symbolically sanitised city environment, unwanted and disorderly manifestations of nature – ranging from rats to polluted water – are an inevitable part of urban life under capitalism.[20] Concurring, Gissen refers to such problematic manifestations of nature as 'subnature'.[21] These analyses prompt us to consider the relationships of particular species to flows of capital, investment and disinvestment; to other kinds of dirt, waste and urban nature; and to the wider cultural, environmental and political processes that produce particular urban locales. Ultimately, the history of fluctuating pest populations highlights the city as an environment with a nature of its own (rather than a territory defined against nature); and nature itself as a social and cultural product. As unwanted, 'bad' nature, associated with dirt, insanitary conditions and contamination, these species threaten in particular to destabilise the security of domestic environments. In such contexts they constitute an uncanny intrusion of nature, lurking in the hidden services and structures of houses, and adversely affecting the perception of the home as a secure place.

George Orwell's anthropomorphic depiction of bedbugs as soldiers on the march in *Down and Out in London and Paris*, published in 1933, well illustrates this idea of infestation as a domestic disruption and highlights the prominence of bedbugs in the popular imagination at this time. Mobilising the military and sacrificial metaphors commonly deployed by modernising hygiene reformers, he writes:

The walls were as thin as matchwood, and to hide the cracks they had been covered with layer after layer of pink paper, which had come loose and housed innumerable bugs. Near the ceiling long lines of bugs marched all day like columns of soldiers, and at night came down ravenously hungry, so that one had to get up every few hours and kill them in hecatombs. Sometimes when the bugs got too bad one used to burn sulphur and drive them into the next room; whereupon the lodger next door would retort by having his room sulphured, and drive the bugs back. It was a dirty place, but homelike.[22]

Orwell emphasises the intimately close relationship between neglected, dilapidated and overcrowded buildings and bedbug infestations. This episode suggests the insects to be integral to the decaying fabric of a poorly built and run-down boarding house occupied by low-income workers. The accretion of wallpapers indexes the landlord's long-term negligence. Orwell is just one author in a wider literary heritage of using bedbugs to represent the suffering of the abject poor.[23] The passage also emphasises the difficulty of eliminating the bugs permanently – made nearly impossible through a cyclical process of infestation-disinfestation-reinfestation, in a building comprised of individual lodgings occupied by tenants with no sense of shared ownership or structures in place to orchestrate an effective, collective defence. The bedbugs' invasion of this dirty-but-homely space is presented in a comedic tone, forming part of the 'spectacle of the slum', to borrow the literature scholar Keith Gandal's term.[24] Orwell's comment that 'it was a dirty place, but homelike' is particularly interesting. Disputing a simple equation of domestic cleanliness and comfort, we can also detect in this phrase a form of middle-class 'nostalgia for the mud'.[25]

Founding members of the Society's committee – architect Ian Hamilton, and chartered surveyors Irene Barclay and Evelyn Perry – provided an intentionally alarming evocation of the bedbugs as an uncanny intrusion in an article resonant with Orwell's description: [26]

> Ghosts and hobgoblins are not legendary creatures of the past nor figments of a disordered imagination. They exist in Somers Town. Here nearly every house is a haunted house. After dark there is no place more eerie, no torture more prolonged and blood-curdling than that enacted here year after year, no atrocity more revolting than the nightly human sacrifice. For there are vampires. Not creatures of classical mythology, but solid hair-raising scientific facts. I have seen them. I have smelt them.[27]

This piece was first published and later appeared in a widely circulated manual, *Housing: A Citizen's Guide to the Problem* (1931). Such colourful and provocative first-person accounts were an important tool for the Society as its members went about raising awareness of the problems of bedbugs and slum life in general, attempting to attract funding for their work.[28] The analogy with haunted houses was a key trope in early-twentieth-century discourses about domestic hygiene.[29] This was a time of general anxiety about the state and health of the nation, with increasing, but patchy, attempts to improve the lives of the poor through early welfare legislation.[30]

In his account of modernist aesthetics of hygiene and cleanliness, the architectural historian, Adrian Forty, examines how the reform of cleaning practices was implemented through emotional, as well as rational and scientific, arguments, to the benefit of the wealthier classes. In the early twentieth century, Forty identifies the emergence of an 'imagery of exaggerated hygiene', which was incorporated into the design of household objects and interiors, and actively influenced behaviour. He details how the designs of specific objects were shaped by particular class- and gender-based social constructions of dirt and cleanliness. The hygiene aesthetic in 1930s architecture and furniture design, Forty observes, had emerged from the reform movements of late-nineteenth- and early-twentieth-century Europe and the United States.[31] The use of architecture and design in hygiene reform were not simply middle-class benevolence, but rather a means of social control, and an attempt to ensure the health and longevity of a productive proletariat.

In the case of Somers Town, the reformers were either living in the area (Jellicoe) or were there every day (Barclay and Perry), and they worked closely with the community, gaining an intimate awareness of the bedbug problem. To potential donors – for whom the slums were more distant – they described the bugs as a source of both horror and fascination, the focus of a 'war to the death, its object the extermination of this interesting species'.[32] Residents were similarly presented as a source of quasi-sociological fascination. Barclay caricatured them as 'cheerful cockneys', noting how they ranged from 'the wonderfully clean to the wonderfully dirty'.[33] However condescending that might sound to readers today, Barclay and the others involved in this work were at least using their elite status and professional abilities to address social need with imagination and impressive energy, and contemporary accounts suggest that their work was much appreciated by the residents – especially that of Father Jellicoe, whose untimely death shocked the community. In contrast to local authorities during this period, they were committed to rehousing people on the sites of their former slums, with their friends and families – even those they perceived as 'problem' tenants.[34]

Through a personal evocation of the slums she visited during the 1925 survey, Barclay later described the bedbug problem with added relish:

> For the brickwork was sodden and bulging, the chimneys were full of holes, the plaster crumbling, the staircases unsound. Then there was *Cimex lectularius*, or the common bedbug. This insect, we discovered, is a prolific breeder: the female lays 150 eggs at a time, and they hatch out in ten days. They feed on

blood, and attack the soft bodies of children unmercifully. They thrive on stuffy warmth, and hide in woodwork and plaster, emerging at night to gorge on their prey. Many live in iron bedsteads, conveniently for the source of their nourishment. They smell disgusting. Directly these old buildings were touched, clusters and bunches of these vile insects were uncovered. I remember seeing a cross taken down from a wall, and its exact outline remained for a few seconds in living bugs.[35]

Barclay's description suggests that the insects both thrive in particular materials and degraded architectural conditions, and affect the sensory experience and immaterial architectural qualities of the slums as well.[36] Both Orwell's and Barclay's evocations of bedbugs, hidden in the dilapidated architectural fabric, suggest that, for reformers, their presence indicated the landlords' neglect, and caused anxiety through signifying a troubling loss of human control over the environment, over nature–city relations: a premature impulse to ruination.[37]

The bedbugs were acknowledged as a real problem, but also took on a symbolic function as a metaphor for the impossibility of cleanliness in the slums, and the impotence of the state in improving housing conditions. The challenge of eliminating these 'vampiric' pests – rendered by both authors in flesh-crawling detail – was stated to be 'the most difficult problem', leading to the assumption that the buildings were irreversibly infested.[38] The result was that the reconditioning of the existing properties was considered too problematic, and the insects became a principal motive in the decision to rebuild rather than renovate which, as an 'Improvement Society', the committee had first set out to do.[39]

Ceremonial pest control

As well as direct action to improve the physical environment through reconditioning properties, demolishing slums and building new housing, the Society conducted environmental surveys and research. However, in large part, as Darling argues, it operated as a 'propaganda machine', often using 'flamboyant' methods, aiming to raise awareness of housing issues, provoke debate and lobby for improved state provision.[40] Events were staged by the society at each milestone in the process of construction, and the techniques of film, photographic and written documentation and dissemination they employed were experimental and extremely powerful.

The activities associated with the slum clearances that led to the construction of St Christopher's Flats – one wing of the Society's Sydney Estate – attest to its imaginative approach to publicity, and its members understanding of the value of symbolic purification. On a lot purchased in 1802, the particular houses undergoing demolition to make way for the Sydney Estate were developed by John Johnson, a highly successful scavenger, builder and paviour, who played a central role in the development of Somers Town, as detailed by building and labour historian Linda Clarke.[41] The approach of Johnson and his collaborators to building was profit-led, rapid and newly regularised, which resulted ultimately in monotonous, overcrowded and low-quality architectural environments.[42]

Since its earliest development, a large proportion of the workers living in the neighbourhood were themselves directly involved with the building industry. The houses, completed in the 1820s, were 'highly standardised', with a lack of differentiation between the four storeys, suggesting their use for single-class tenements.[43] The development was uniform and dense, implying, according to Clarke, a 'greater concentration and quicker turnover of building capital' and 'a more regularized use of building labour and skills than in the earlier phase of the town'.[44] Clarke notes that, when combined with the neglect of self-interested landlords, this style of development reinforced the structures of poverty and exacerbated public health problems. The houses deteriorated quickly, and many of them failed to last the length of their 99-year leases, ultimately being demolished as infested slums.

In 1929, in the course of the demolitions to make way for St Christopher's Flats, monstrously oversized and elaborately detailed cardboard and straw models of a cockroach, rat, flea and bedbug were made, impaled on wooden stands and positioned at the summit of a pile of slum rubble from the surrounding half-demolished buildings (see Figure 1.3).[45] It is clear from the surviving press photographs that considerable time and craftsmanship went into the making of these anatomically accurate but super-sized creatures, which were presumably modelled by the Society's volunteers themselves, most probably with the local children with whom they often worked.[46] The models – or 'effigies' as the Society's members referred to them – were then ceremoniously torched by a high-profile public figure: retired military leader General Sir Ian Hamilton.[47]

The impact of this symbolic community bonfire was maximised by the setting: a site between the Society's newly completed flats and the half-ruined slum housing undergoing demolition. The event, the setting and the effigies

Figure 1.3: *Somers Town – cockroach, rat, flea and bedbug set alight, 1929 –
site of St Christopher's Flats, Werrington Street.*

poignantly articulated 'the transition from the old to the new' through a physical, performative and visually impressive act.[48] The ceremonial bonfire had been advertised in national newspapers such as *The Times* and *Sunday Times,* and the models, and the act of their incineration in front of a sizeable audience, were carefully documented through film, photography and written accounts by the Society's members, as well as through numerous articles, many illustrated, in the local and national press.[49]

Though the making and burning of the vermin effigies was apparently a unique event, it echoed pre-modern responses to vermin involving the ritualistic use of fire. It also found a parallel in the public dynamiting of tenement blocks, which, though less playful, had previously provided a theatrical symbolic focus for slum clearances.[50] The staging of such events, their documentation and publicity, all emphasise the skill of the Society's committee members as propagandists.[51] Reminiscent of a sacrifice or public execution, the incineration was just the first act of purification in an extended sequence of ceremonies to mark the construction of St Christopher's Flats, and to celebrate the Society's sixth birthday.[52] It was followed one month later by the blessing of the first brick by Father Nigel Scott; and later in 1931 by the inauguration by Princess Helena Victoria, and the blessing of the completed building by the Bishop of Truro.[53]

As a spectacular publicity event, the effigy burning rated in its theatricality alongside later productions such as the Society's 'Chamber of Horrors' display at the *New Homes for Old* exhibition (December 1931), which included similar oversized models of common slum pests.[54] As props intended to draw attention to slum conditions, the effigies also compared to another tool discussed by Darling: a widely displayed scale model of an overcrowded slum room, used to communicate to potential donors the claustrophobic domestic environments experienced by Somers Town residents.

The Society's films, such as *Paradox City* (1934), were equally powerful and experimental.[55] As film archivist, Ros Cranston, has observed, in its exposé of slum life in Somers Town, and its documentation of the Society's demolition and rebuilding work, this film 'demands the audience's engagement ... in what is an unusually direct style of filmmaking for the period'.[56] Juxtaposing London's wealthy West End residences and public monuments with protracted shots of the smoky chimneys of Somers Town's slums, which seem to extend infinitely, this silent film uses the montage techniques of Soviet filmmakers of the 1920s. Striking visual images are interspersed with pithy commentaries on residents' lives, to powerful effect. Other equally direct films focused on specific problems, such as bedbugs, showing close-ups of infested furniture covered in crawling bugs and of the bugs themselves.[57] The Society's magazine, *House Happenings*, also included disturbing close-up photographs of bugs and degraded domestic interiors.[58] In these photographs, as in the films, the making and burning of the vermin effigies had a didactic function, bringing aspects of slum life into sharp focus for a wider (healthier and wealthier) public.

Also, like the films, the models, as productions, and the spectacle of their incineration, had entertainment value and provided the focus for a celebratory community event marking a new beginning for Somers Town's residents. Barclay's description of the infestations she witnessed during the 1925 survey seems subdued in comparison with the first-hand account in *House Happenings* of the burning of the 'itchingly realistic' models, 'magnified to the proportions of well-fed tabbies'.[59] The author of the article describes the occasion in all its theatrical and sensory detail, adding to the drama evoked in the photographic records:

> Fiery tongues licked the planks and reared towards the pale azure of the sky, to the tune of 'Keep the Home Fires Burning'; and the house breakers positioned in the background of the photographs drove their picks into the ruins sending bricks cascading to the ground in a cloud of dust.[60]

This animated image of the demolition men foreshadows a scene in *Paradox City* where, grim-reaper-like, the Society's chairman is shot from below, looming threateningly with his pickaxe as he sets the demolition process in motion. Apocalyptic, and sensationally expressed, the imagery used in the written account demonstrates the importance of the moment in the public erasure of the existing urban environment, perceived to be impossibly infested, and the envisioning of a new (and vermin-free) neighbourhood.

The reference in *House Happenings* to the tune of Ivor Novello's popular sentimental First World War song, 'Keep the Home Fires Burning', positions the battle to reclaim the slums from the occupying forces of pests alongside the protection of the homeland by families awaiting the return of their loved ones from the battlefields.[61] While entertaining and playfully executed, the making and burning of the models was a highly charged symbolic act, intended to project the idea of progress and control over nature. The occasion marked a triumph in the re-imagining of the neighbourhood.

Cleansing nature

If the pests represented an unwanted intrusion of 'subnature', in response Hamilton, as the architect for the Society, produced designs for the new flats that projected a Garden Cities Movement-inspired redemptive, cleansing nature, expressed through open spaces, courtyard gardens, trees, planting and ponds (see Plate 1).[62] The Society aimed to completely rework the urban environment, from the purification of the air to the improvement of the material conditions of the architecture. The architect depicted the new estate from the air, to maximise the vision of a new order for the neighbourhood. The modern flats, with their pitched roofs and impressively tall chimney stacks, stand out above the surrounding narrow, terraced streets. They surround a spacious cruciform courtyard, centring on a group of trees, and are illuminated by sunlight from the left of the picture plane, their white walls contrasting with the shaded roofs of the slums. The familiar modernist architectural motif of a single tiny car parked in front of the central block at the forefront of the drawing reinforces the sense of modernisation. This image was circulated on the back cover of the Christmas 1931 edition of the Society's magazine, with a nativity scene set in the centre of the new estate.

In the drawing, a pair of trees mark out each gateway. Window boxes, though not visible in the scheme as planned, were also to become an important feature.[63] These interventions were intended to redress what the architect perceived as slum tenants' starvation of 'pure' nature: 'one or two at least there have told me that they have never seen grass growing', he was quoted as saying emotively in the *Sunday Times*.[64] His vision is made clear in *House Happenings*:

> We have got to lift up our people out of their sordid surroundings and give them in its place an environment and atmosphere of beauty which certainly comes from God ... undoubtedly man's natural surroundings are trees and flowers and works of nature. We want to bring some of these into Somers Town.[65]

Equally important in reorganising the city–nature dynamics of the neighbourhood were the design tactics employed by Hamilton to prevent future infestations by unwanted and intrusive pests, and the process of gas fumigation applied to furniture and bedding as tenants were moved into the new flats (see Figure 1.4).[66] Drawing on up-to-date expertise of the kind in

Blake's manual, Hamilton targeted these insects through the employment of specific design, material and decorative tactics, including the avoidance of wallpaper and picture rails where bugs would be able to hide, and the use of specific kinds of plaster intended to reduce the risk of infestation.[67] The Society also set up House Furnishings Ltd, to sell furniture to the tenants. Like the architecture, the furniture was designed to reduce the possibility of infestation.

The ceremonial burning of the pest effigies and the discourses around bedbugs emphasise the serious influence such species had on the experience of living in poverty in the city at this time. Significant resources were required to protect people's homes from invasions by unwanted and anxiety-inducing forms of nature. This episode also suggests that, in 1920s Somers Town, the presence of specific kinds of vermin, and the extent of infestations, reflected the long-term underlying structures of urban development and property ownership; the nature and density of occupation; and the materials, quality, character and methods of the production of the houses. That the reformers designated the slums as terminally infested also meant that they could reorder the neighbourhood more quickly and more comprehensively than if they had reconditioned the existing housing stock.

As a mix of socially concerned professionals and philanthropists occupying positions of class superiority, the Society sought to reorganise the lives of the Somers Town poor. However, as philanthropic hygiene reformers, in their attitudes and actions they were unusually direct in being critical of the underlying structures that produced the conditions they witnessed, and of the inadequacy of state intervention.[68] Through the celebratory ritual burning of the vermin effigies, and other stunts, they drew attention to the pest problem imaginatively and effectively.

Reconstructing the history of housing conditions in reference to pests raises a wide range of questions of urban development: issues of social struggle, class difference and inter-class representation are encountered in the sources that document the Society's work. In this case of urban restructuring, we see the use of architectural and urban design as forms of sanitisation, and the use of architectural settings as propaganda. While 'regeneration' was not a term that was used, the degenerative and redemptive powers of nature were central.

Urban pests provide a point of intersection between discussions of the material conditions of housing in the city, and the policies and discourses of urban development. In the history of Somers Town we encounter vermin, and specifically bedbugs, as a material problem, experienced in very tangible

Figure 1.4: *Fumigators sealing a fumigation van, c. 1930.*

ways by residents. This material condition became a pretext for the innovative actions of housing reformers, while in their accounts of slum life these manifestations of 'bad' nature were mobilised as a general metaphor for the conditions of the slums, conceived as irrevocably infested, and degraded in both physical and moral terms. As with the manipulation of other forms of nature, the control of pests constitutes one of the transformations necessary to make 'civilised' urban life possible, and is indicative of different understand-ings of what that might mean at particular moments in time. In the next chapter we turn to the Elephant and Castle to consider another response to housing crisis and environmental degradation, focusing this time on post-war reconstruction and the discourses that accompanied it.

2

LIFE IN THE RUINS

This important sector of London compares very unfavourably with the corresponding sector on the north bank. Built a hundred to a hundred and fifty years ago, the district has been singularly slow in regenerating itself. Good buildings line a few of the main roads, and a number of tenement blocks have recently been built, but on the whole the area demands drastic reconstruction. Mean streets, a tangle of overhead railways with their associated disfigurements, indiscriminate mixing of industry with housing, both of which are largely obsolescent, and an almost entire lack of open space characterise it.

John Forshaw and Patrick Abercrombie (1943)[1]

With rubble next to new trams and traffic lights, photojournalist Bert Hardy's award-winning photographs of the Elephant and Castle in 1948 poignantly evoke the sense of an area on the cusp of modernisation (see Figures 2.1 and 2.2, and Plate 2).[2] Published as a photo-essay in *Picture Post*, Hardy's powerful images were reinforced by his collaborator – the writer A. L. (Bert) Lloyd – sharp evocations of modernisation, such as 'the smell of horse-sweat and dung over the petrol fumes'.[3] Using the forms of the cityscape they depict as framing devices, the photographs impose a strong sense of visual and spatial order on a severely bombed-out neighbourhood. To take the opening shot (see Figure 2.1), Hardy had climbed to the top of the Elephant and Castle pub, allowing him to frame a view looking down over the pub's sign, itself unscathed by war damage, and well above the streets and rubble.[4] That the area is said, in some accounts, to have been named after this pub, lends the image added impact.[5] In the distance, an optimistic billboard promises 'Jobs'. The photograph depicts the city in a process of reconstruction, showing not ruins but cleared bombsites awaiting the construction of new buildings. This image occupies a central place in the series, acting as a reference to locate the

Figure 2.1: *Bert Hardy, 'The Emblem of the Cockney World'*
Elephant and Castle, 1948.

other shots of populated streets and interiors, forcing narrative coherence on a neighbourhood Hardy later said had seemed to have 'no unity'.[6]

With an intimacy achieved by the proximity afforded by newly portable camera technology, these photographs would become iconic in their depiction of working-class life in post-war London.[7] Unlike the opening view, in general the series features ground-level shots of the Elephant and Castle's residents occupying everyday spaces: street scenes, backyards, leisure spaces, slum interiors, shops, markets and other workplaces. All this at a moment just prior to the dramatic London County Council-led redevelopment of the area in the mid-1950s, which continued over the next two decades.

A disorderly territory

The sociologist, Garry Robson, has argued that south London as a whole is 'an area which remains chronically underhistoricised'; and Southwark historian, Leonard Reilly, has noted that historical reference works on this borough 'have simply ignored the modern period'.[8] Historical accounts of a pre-Second World War Elephant emphasise the area's long-held reputation as a tainted place within the disorderly geography of Southwark as a whole.

In his polemical and nostalgic memoir *The Likes of Us* (2004), Elephant and Castle resident, Michael Collins, caricatures the area as one that has 'soldiered on as the poor whore across the water, housing the smells, the produce, the noise, the prisons and leper hospitals'.[9] After the Industrial Revolution, Southwark was an area of diverse industrial activity, with the manufacture of products ranging from leather to glass, beer and gas. A 'reputation for lawless-ness' continued to develop.[10] Robson argues that, by the end of the nineteenth century,

> the 'Elephant and Castle' was understood to be sufficiently coterminous with disorder, violence and criminality to make it a primary site around which bour-geois anxieties ... could be focused.[11]

In the historical narratives of more recent regeneration initiatives the last decade of the nineteenth century up to the Second World War are argued to be the Elephant's 'heyday', but by the 1890s this working-class area was already strained physically and in terms of its infrastructure.[12] This much is suggested by a plan from 1897 to improve the layout of the intersecting roads and ease congestion, in which a representative of the LCC commented on 'a general feeling that some improvement was highly desirable and the present opportunity must not be allowed to go by'.[13] In 1900, Arthur Harrison, Borough Engineer and Surveyor of Southwark, designed a subway system which, as part of a wider road reorganisation scheme, eventually opened in 1906. The post-war Elephant and Castle subways have been a major focus for discourses about the area's dysfunctionality. That they were preceded by Harrison's scheme for the LCC highlights the longer-term challenge of creat-ing a liveable environment at this major traffic intersection. The subways were a response to the construction of the underground (Bakerloo line) railway, and the perceived dangers of the tramline intersections and omnibus traffic to railway passengers and pedestrians commuting to the City and Westminster.[14] However, these LCC investments in the built environment were ineffective and by the 1930s the Elephant was notoriously deprived and associated with slum housing.

During the Second World War the area was subjected to bombing of a severity second only to the City of London. The resultant devastation gave cause for the whole district to be 'radically replanned' in a 'complete redevelop-ment' that formed part of a wider reorganisation of the city's road network.[15] Conceived as the South Bank's 'hinterland', the district was categorised among the 'Central Areas Needing Renewal' by John Forshaw and Patrick Abercrombie in the *County of London Plan* (1943), produced for the LCC. They envisioned a 50-year programme of reconstruction for the South Bank, arguing that this should extend to the Elephant and Castle.

The passage from the plan reproduced at the opening of this chapter serves to remind us that 'regeneration' was already in use as a metaphor for urban change in 1940s London. By way of comparison, in the mid-twentieth century, in the context of New York City, regeneration was deployed as a socio-biological metaphor by urban commentator and activist, Jane Jacobs, when she wrote that: 'lively, diverse, intense cities contain the seeds of their own regeneration, with energy enough to carry over for problems and needs outside themselves'.[16] This is an interesting historical usage of the term, since Jacobs is using it in defence of communities threatened by relentless, large-scale urban redevelopment. She shares with the *County of London Plan* (1943) a sense that good cities regenerate themselves; but where they did not, Abercrombie and Forshaw advocated comprehensive redevelopment on a scale to which Jacobs was opposed.

After Stepney/Poplar, in east London, the Elephant became the second designated post-war reconstruction zone under the *Town and Country Planning Act* (1947) – legislation passed by the post-war Labour government to require permission for any development, providing the foundation of the modern town and country planning system. A report in *The Municipal Journal and Local Government Administrator* regarding the proposals for the Elephant concluded that, over the course of 15 years, 'one of the worst danger spots in the Metropolis will be eliminated'.[17] In line with Forshaw and Abercrombie's plan, the reconstruction began in earnest in 1956.

The camera's 'social eye'

Though produced independently of the LCC, rather than providing a straightforward visual chronicle of the war-wasted landscape and its working-class residents prior to redevelopment, Hardy's 1948 photographs and their accompanying texts actively support the idea that modernisation was necessary, while simultaneously celebrating the existing character and social and physical textures of the Elephant.

Born locally into a working-class family, Hardy had the authentic viewpoint of an 'insider'. His photography both claims to record for posterity something of the experiences of the everyday lives of the district's residents, while also engaging what cultural theorist Stuart Hall has termed the 'social eye' of the camera – that is, its ability to raise critical awareness of social relationships and material conditions.[18] Hardy's photographic sensibility is characterised by a desire to privilege socially marginal subjects, yet at times this is contrived through the staging of scenes for nostalgic effect. Even while they draw attention to the difficult material conditions in which people live, these photographs are at pains to suggest a narrative of dignified endurance and community spirit. At the same time they invite the viewer to elicit aesthetic pleasure in the ruined landscapes of the post-war city, and to cast a vicarious, voyeuristic gaze on abject lives.

Drawing on Susan Sontag's observation that 'to photograph is to confer importance', in the late 1970s cultural theorist Glenn Jordan interpreted Hardy's photographs of the immigrant populations of Cardiff's 1950s Tiger Bay as politically and socially concerned journalism, which aimed not only to document but also to actively improve the conditions of the poor and excluded, through conferring importance on ordinary people and challenging class- and race-based prejudices, or at least heightening their visibility.[19] This interpretation can be extended to the Elephant photo-story and its representation of the economically, socially and politically marginalised subjects depicted, such as female prostitutes and homeless men. However, evidencing exactly how Hardy's photographs might have changed perceptions or had political agency is problematic. Following the logic of Roland Barthes' semiotic approach to the analysis of photography, as Jordan does, depending on the 'reader' and the context in which the photographs are 'read', they might, of course, just as well have confirmed stereotypes as challenged them.

The magazine has been compared naively to the Mass Observation documentary, in being 'in the business of reporting what it witnessed without imposing its own agenda', a magazine without politics, but both the photographs and accompanying text refute this.[20] Some consideration of the original context of *Picture Post* is helpful. Michael Hallett argues that *Picture Post* 'appealed to the common man', unlike its predecessors – the *Illustrated London News*, for example – which targeted the upper classes.[21] Clearly the popularity of magazines such as *Picture Post* relied on the interest and patronage of a broad readership. The populist and eclectic nature of the magazine is suggested by the range of material in the issue, sandwiched as the story is between 'One Baby's Breakfast', a feature on a baby chimpanzee, and 'New Joy for the Sick', an article about a new machine designed to turn the pages of books for incapacitated hospital patients. Hardy and Lloyd's 'Life in the Elephant' was the main feature in the edition, taking prominence on the cover page, and this positioning suggests the editors' interest in highlighting the pressing social issues of the day – even if this was in part simply a commercial strategy to address a new anthropological fascination with the everyday lives of the working-classes.

Hall argues that the reformist politics of *Picture Post*, though left-leaning, were opaque, because the social problems identified in the magazine's features – the clear-lensed 'social eye' of the photographs and text – were not explored in relation to their underlying causes. He understands the emergence of *Picture Post* in relation to the development of three contemporaneous cultural phenomena: first, the 'British documentary style', exemplified by 1930s British documentary cinema; second, the Mass Observation study, established in 1937 'to record, observe and recount, in its fascinating detail, the endless variety of the ordinary lives of ordinary people'; and third, the advent of literary *rapportage*.[22] He continues:

> The documentary style was, at one level, a form of writing, photographing, filming, recording. But at another level, it was an emergent form of social consciousness: it registered, in the formation of a social rhetoric, the emergent structure of feeling in the immediate pre-war and war periods. Here we encounter that fateful nexus where there is a striking rendezvous between the subject-matter and content of historical experience, the revolutionary development of the means of reproduction, and – in response – the evolving forms and styles of collective social perception.[23]

This idea that, in the documentary style, technology and means of representation converged with the 'structure of feeling' of post-war society suggests that documentary not only reflected but also played an active role in forming, or transforming, experience.

Hardy's work is often placed in a tradition of humanist photography, concerned with ordinary people and everyday life.[24] Perhaps even more than in earlier 'slum photography', such as Jacob Riis' photographs of overcrowded tenement buildings in the Lower East Side of late-nineteenth-century New York, the fact of their poetic and narrative character, as much as their value as ethnographic evidence, make these photographs difficult to read for their original political aspirations, which in any case may be destabilised by the context and form of their reception.[25]

Keith Gandal's study of slum photography and fiction in the books of 'muckraker' photojournalist Riis, and slum writer Stephen Crane in 1890s New York City, provides an important reference in any discussion of the photographic and literary spectacle of urban degradation and poverty. Gandal conceives of Riis and Crane's work as discursive practices, which both reflected and challenged contemporary ethics towards, and understandings of, the poor, the experience of poverty and the urban environment. Gandal sees their work as a development from the earliest slum photography, represented by John Thomson's *Street Life in London* (1877).[26] From the 1890s, he argues, new opportunities for closer proximity to slum subjects resulted in the emergence of 'new ethnographic, aesthetic and psychological styles of describing the poor'.[27] He sees this attention to slum life as a particularly masculinist phenomenon, accompanied by an 'ethos of adventure'.[28]

Gandal's study reveals Riis' and Crane's forms of social realism to be highly complex and multi-layered; simultaneously a part of a system of spectacle within the culture of consumer capitalism, and a product and instrument of a disciplinary 'culture of surveillance'.[29] Riis' photographs stereotype the poor and make slums look picturesque, but at the same time, knowingly or not, they make a direct challenge to the viewer, implying a relationship between degraded environments and poverty; and hence they have been claimed as effective instruments in propelling social reforms, slum clearances and building regulations.[30]

Arguments for the effective agency of photographs in urban change are in tension with Sontag's idea that, politically speaking, 'photographing is essentially an act of non-intervention'.[31] In later work on war photography, however, Sontag returns to the question of photographic agency in relation to depictions of suffering and ruination, arguing that they are 'a means of making "real" (or "more real") matters that the privileged and the merely safe might prefer to ignore'.[32] These photographs and Hardy's other images of impoverished city dwellers, such as those of the Glasgow Gorbals (1948), seem to have been intended to provoke a reaction of moral outrage, providing visual evidence to support slum clearance and redevelopment campaigns. At the same time they offered to entertain *Picture Post* subscribers with an exoticised representation of an alien world. On one level, such photographs of working-class Cockney life were a parallel to the depiction of foreign territories and people in publications such as *National Geographic Magazine*.[33]

Occupied ruins and the 'right to look'

Hardy's photographs feature bomb-damaged buildings through composi-
tional techniques that recall Romantic representations of classical ruins. Here,
however, the ruins are occupied and animated by the figures of local people.
Only the most photogenic aspects of the slums and run-down urban environment are emphasised. Hardy's work was not news- or event-driven, instead
producing a more sentimental, anecdotal form of social documentary. In this,
conditions of smog and architectural dilapidation are used to pictorial effect.

The subjects of Hardy's photographs are portrayed either as comfortable
being pictured in their ruined environment, or unaware of the photographer's presence, as with the boys playing in the rubble in 'A Ghost Strayed
from old Greece' (see Plate 2). The boys are apparently rebuilding a wall,
themselves an integral feature of a ruined but regenerating landscape: model
future citizens already contributing to London's reconstruction. Through
the frame of damaged buildings, we see the classical portico of a church,
apparently unblemished. Taken from the site of what is now the contentious
Elephant and Castle Shopping Centre, completed in 1965 (see Chapter 3,
pages 57–75), the deception of the photograph is that, behind the classical
façade, the Metropolitan Tabernacle Methodist church had been almost
entirely destroyed. The play on time – the image of classical civilisation, the
frozen moment of regeneration and the evocation of a future reconstructed
city – recall George Simmel's understanding of the ruin as a place of resolu-
tion between the past and the present.[34]

The narrative of the circumstances behind the 1948 shoot, published later
on, emphasises Hardy's working-class identity – he 'battled his way up from
boy assistant in the dark-room of a chemist's shop'[35] – legitimating his right
to look at, and ability to represent empathetically, the intimate scenes and
subjects of slum interiors, and street and market scenes. As well as class empathy he also had an affiliation with and personal knowledge of the area. He
was born nearby and his family lived locally.[36] Hardy's working-class status
is accentuated in accounts of this specific series, but also more generally in
commentaries on his photographic sensibility in dealing with poverty, warfare
and other emotive subjects.

With regard to Hardy's working processes, and the inception of 'Life in
the Elephant', his autobiography records that he and Lloyd were alone while
shooting the story, that the idea for it originated with them, and that they
worked on it intermittently, in between other jobs.[37] However, the meaning of

the final photo-story was very much determined through editorial presentation and captioning (see Figure 2.2). 'All photographs', writes Sontag, 'wait to be explained or falsified by their captions'.[38] In 'Life in the Elephant' the captions do not claim to be neutral; instead they explicitly reinforce the visual story, as in the photograph in Plate 2. In another example, next to an image of a baby being bathed, and producing a narrative that directly reinforces the need for slum clearance and redevelopment, a caption reads: 'when she grows up her bath will still be a basin. Unless she moves. Or the Elephant changes' (Figure 2.2).[39]

Troublingly, although the subjects of Hardy's published photographs were all white, the contact sheets include portraits of a young black woman and of children of different races playing together, suggesting editorial intervention to communicate the idea of a resilient white British 'Cockney' community in the process of post-war reconstruction.[40] Furthermore, close inspection of the contact sheets demonstrates that a number of the images have been montaged together from more than one photograph, in order to better fit the layout.

The text by Lloyd that accompanied Hardy's photographs was typical of *Picture Post* and the other large-circulation weekly photographic magazines that arrived in Europe and North America in the 1930s, in further dramatising and developing the photo-story. While in contemporary newspapers the image was the accompaniment, in *Picture Post* the text was intended to enhance the visual rhetoric.[41] As with the earlier Gorbals story, 'Life in the Elephant' saw Hardy and Lloyd working carefully together in developing dialectical images through photographs and texts. The photographs of ruins and smog are accompanied by emphatic descriptions of a claustrophobic, run-down, inner-city environment:

> a festering of mean little streets, whose flat-faced houses line up by the grimy hundred, and whose alleys look as if they were made for hiding in when the rent-man comes.[42]

In both the written and photographic representation, the area is romanticised and animated in anthropomorphic terms – embodied in the anatomy of its working-class inhabitants: 'its voice has the rasp of trams, trains and trucks; its eyes have the blaze of street stalls'.[43] Lloyd's richly textured descriptions are Dickensian in their emphasis on an all-pervading dirt, evoking the degraded materiality of the urban fabric, and the suffocating smoke and soot-filled 'grimy air', in this period just prior to the introduction of the *Clean Air Act* (1956).[44]

The Waiting Room Where Even Elephant Folk Are Subdued
*Some come with a sore chest from a damp house. Some come with a boy sick from a salmon tin.
All wait for the overworked doctor in his bombed and shored-up surgery.*

in New Kent Road, and you realise that dirt and boredom are not the essential things about the neighbourhood. It has more than its share of the paradox of those monotonous and hilarious, cruel and tender forces that operate together in life. And everywhere it is haunted by old ghosts of kindness, grossness and wit. The people who breathe the air of the Elephant are not hopeless and futile, like many slum-dwellers. They are, instead, an admirable people, lively, resourceful, and prepared to kick, who get what they can by fair means (and sometimes, if it comes to the worst, by foul) and who won't be put upon by anyone. Elephant folk are keenly concerned about what they call 'conditions,' and in the General Elections they returned Labour with a three-to-one majority in all the three divisions that meet in the area (some of the toughest streets in the locality fall into the Southwark North constituency, represented by George Isaacs, the Minister of Labour). On the Southwark Borough Council there are sixty councillors, ten aldermen. One of the seventy, an alderman, is Conservative.

The district has a formidable history. In Roman times it was the greatest traffic terminal in Britain, and the apex of the road system serving the Channel ports, the Wealden iron-mines, and the coastal provinces of the South. Some of Harold's army must have marched hopefully through it, on the way to Hastings (and trailed back tired, after it was

The Gloomy Yard That Fails to Damp the Spirit
*A losing battle with the grimy air. Two bob where four should be. And nowhere to keep the baby's
pram. Yet still the local housewife is a battler, whose tone has eloquence and force.*

14

Figure 2.2: *Albert L. Lloyd, 'Life in the Elephant', with photographs by Bert Hardy,
Picture Post, 42, January 1949, double page spread showing layout
and image-text relationships*

In Thousands of Similar Basements Live Tens of Thousands of Similar Folk: Yet Each Is Different

There are countless rooms like it at the Elephant, innumerable folk in the same image. Yet every one is special. The hunger, the love, the dreams and indignations, are shared by all, yet particular to each. One contemplates a new job, another a new boy-friend. Somebody plans to bath a baby. Somebody plans to burgle a baker's. Somebody wonders if her husband's untrue. Somebody wonders how much he'll make tonight on his chestnut can.

all over). The pilgrim-transport trade was centred there too, and the local hackneymen working the Canterbury and Dover roads formed the first traffic combine. To this day—as a legacy from the Middle Ages—much of the property round the Elephant is owned by the Dean and Chapter of Canterbury. In nearby St. George's Fields, Gerard picked wild flowers for his *Herbal;* and where the Elephant and Castle pub is now, the old Newington Theatre stood—the third theatre built in London, where Shakespeare is said to have played *Hamlet* and *The Taming of the Shrew.* When Rowlandson knew and drew the place, the new Thames bridges leading straight to the Elephant were already built, and the pub stood at a hurly-burly crossroads, as one of the main posting houses for coaches bound for Kent, Surrey, and points south.

One who must have known the Elephant and Castle pub when it was a new house, is the original of the *Beggar's Opera* character, Mat of the Mint, who, dreaming under the rattle of the trams and trucks, must prick up his ghostly ears of an early morning to the clatter of ponies' hoofs on the way in to the sales at the Elephant and Castle Horse

Repository. If he could rise up above the labyrinthine subways, and perch on the railings of a traffic island, how Mat would grin to sniff the smell of horse-sweat and dung over the petrol fumes, and to see two gypsy-copers—diddy-kais, they call them locally—disappearing into the Elephant pub, lugging a foal with them, to finish a deal over a pint of brown in the public bar.

The Elephant by day has something out of the *Beggar's Opera,* something out of Dickens, something out of a revolutionary pamphlet, and most that is just out of normal decent toilsome and unremarkable life. But the Elephant by night is a different place. Pleasure is found in the pubs that are on almost every corner, or in the big Trocadero Cinema, or out at the Manor Place Baths, where for five shillings the fans can watch local boxers like Claude Dennington and little George Daly thumping away for their supper. Ever since the old South London Palace was closed, those who fancy a music-hall have had to travel to the Empress, Brixton, or the New Cross Empire. But around eight o'clock of a pay-night, half of the Elephant seems to be on parade, along the pavements, outside the eel-stalls, in the pubs and the
Continued overleaf

Prospect for Elephant Baby
When she grows up her bath will still be a basin.
Unless she moves. Or the Elephant changes.   15

In *The Country and the City* (1973), the cultural critic, Raymond Williams, interested in the disjunction between 'working' or 'lived' and 'consumed' landscapes, discusses Dickens' perception 'that there is at once a connection and a confusion between the shapes and appearances of buildings and the real shapes and appearances of the people who live in them', seeing the city 'as at once a social fact and a human landscape'.[45] This is a characteristic shared by Lloyd's writing. There is also an underlying anti-urban sentiment, which references a persistent English literary tradition, also discussed by Williams, of presenting London in monstrous terms.[46] Descriptions of the post-war environment of the Elephant as a 'concrete jungle' have become commonplace, but Lloyd's text reveals that an image of the district as a man-made 'jungle' predates the 1950s redevelopment.[47] Indeed, the theme of a peculiarly tainted, urbanised nature is a recurrent motif, alongside other folkloric themes of the area's identity: gangs and criminality, the labyrinthine physical environment, an association with industry, and so on.[48] These tropes are accompanied by historical and literary references that valorise the area in reference to its importance as a Roman transport interchange, and its association with authors such as Shakespeare, and indeed, Dickens.

Embellishing Hardy's photographs, Lloyd's writing conveys a phenomenological dimension that extends beyond the possibilities of photographic representation. While it contains vivid descriptions of the environment and its inhabitants, the overall structure of the text is fragmented, a spatial reflection of the physically fractured environment. It jumps in an ungainly way from wildly speculative romanticism to prosaic demographic information. Like Hardy's photographs, while exaggerating and reinforcing certain myths and motifs, the text casts a positive humanist light on the place and its 'natives': when you witness the area coming to life at night, Lloyd writes, 'you realise that dirt and boredom are not the essential things about the neighbourhood' – a backhanded compliment.[49]

In the only monograph dedicated to his *oeuvre*, Hardy describes how, arriving in the Elephant, he and Lloyd felt themselves to be outsiders, detached from and unable to engage with the environment and its residents: 'We saw nothing; no unity of any kind to make our story.'[50] Their big break arrived when they spotted 'a very young couple, terribly in love, oblivious of the squalor', who Hardy, after asking their permission, photographed.[51] In the monograph, Hardy then recalls being asked by 'an old dear' to take her picture, and is invited into her yard. From then on she becomes his guide. A more detailed account of this story, later published in Hardy's autobiography, identifies the 'old dear' as Maisie, a prostitute, living in the Elephant and working the streets of Piccadilly.

Two of several photographs of Maisie were included in the autobiography (see Figure 2.3), and one of these featured in recent exhibitions of the photographs, though she did not appear in the original photo-essay.[52] In comparison to the dry monograph version, the autobiographical account elaborates Hardy's encounters with Maisie in depth. The photographs of her are remarkably intimate. She is in bed, smoking; or stripped to the waist, being washed by a friend.[53] Hardy's portrayal of Maisie, her petty-criminal antics and her violent clients is colourful, verging on slapstick. In this it contrasts with the more sober, socially concerned, autobiographical account of the process of making the Glasgow Gorbals photo-story.

However, the earlier (monograph) version suggests Hardy's reluctance to see himself in the role of tourist or voyeur, and his conception that a photographer–subject relationship formed on such a basis would be inauthentic. Jean-Claude Gautrand argues that 'co-operation, implicit at the very least, would prove to be one of the primary characteristics of humanist photography'.[54] As an invited outsider, the photographer claims a moral legitimacy denied to the detached observer, and has a heightened presence in the photograph. However, Hardy's elaborated autobiographical version of

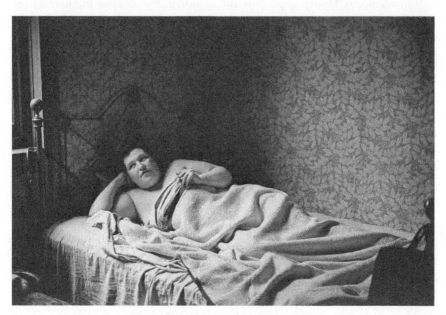

Figure 2.3: Bert Hardy, 'Maisie', 1948.

the photographic process for 'Life in the Elephant' suggests a complicated 'contract'. He is quick to point out that he offered to pay Maisie; and remarks also that another prostitute and friend of Maisie's, 'totally unconcerned' at being photographed, 'watched me blankly', passive to the intrusive photographic gaze.[55]

Hardy's anecdotes – where he is invited by residents of the Elephant to take photographs of them – and the photographs themselves also make claims to authenticity in their representation of everyday life. The photographer's intervention is suggested to be minimal, 'capturing' people going about their ordinary business. In this, the viewer is invited to act as a voyeur. Photojournalists such as Hardy were the agents of a new and more intimate exposition of urban lives in deprived areas, previously not visually accessible to the majority. Lightweight cameras, first developed in the 1920s, could be exposed quickly multiple times before the film had to be reloaded, providing new potential to represent the subject 'naturally'.[56] The greatly respected *Picture Post* name would have been a big advantage to Hardy in persuading people to let him take their photograph, and the magazine was admired for recording 'real life'; in contrast, for example, with the 'toffee-nosed' *Illustrated London News*.[57]

However, even though the modern and portable photographic technology available to Hardy gave him the opportunity to take pictures faster than ever before, the camera and photographer were still an intrusive presence, and, in their concealment of this fact, the 'honesty' of the images must be questioned. Though the photos appear to be spontaneous, their formal composition often points towards Hardy carefully selecting and stage-directing 'Life in the Elephant'. But the photos would have us believe that he was absent from the scene, giving the viewer the idea that they are witnessing something more 'real' than a photograph – a first-hand, unmediated, experience. This is what Jordan describes as Hardy's skill of presenting a 'window onto reality'.[58] As photojournalist and Elephant resident, Mark Chilvers, observes:

> it's theatrical, and he's sort of creating a theatrical scene – he's not photographing reality in a true *reportage* sense of [Henri] Cartier-Bresson – the decisive moment – trying to be more a fly on the wall and not influencing the subject, but just photographing what you see. Bert Hardy wasn't quite so strict with that principle.[59]

We should challenge the idea that there is any true reality that can be photographed, as Chilvers suggests. In Hardy's case, although publications on his work do not refer to it, it is known that he staged some of his photographs, using family and friends as models.[60] This was an accepted practice, and unproblematic from the point of view of *Picture Post*'s editors, who may have known but did not care; or its readers, who were likely, as present-day viewers might be, to accept the photographs as straightforward documents.[61] An examination of the surviving negatives suggests that most of the photos were taken quickly, with only a few exposures.[62] There are those, however, that seem more posed, such as the image of Maisie smoking in bed.

Hardy's return

Though he later became known for his contribution to war photography, Hardy's images of life in poor urban neighbourhoods have remained popular, and have been at the forefront of a renewed interest in his work. The photographs from 'Life in the Elephant' have been commercially successful far beyond their use in *Picture Post*, circulating in print, and later digitally, as individual images, the copyright and distribution of which now lies with Getty Images.[63]

In 2005, Southwark Council – the local authority that now holds administrative responsibility for the Elephant and Castle – bought a set of Hardy's prints to exhibit and keep in their archive. At the same time, they commissioned professional photojournalist and local resident, Mark Chilvers, to direct a parallel digital photographic project, financed by the UK's Heritage Lottery fund, documenting the district in collaboration with young residents, who also took photographs of it (see Figure 2.4).[64] Chilvers is a commercial photographer. For this project, however, it was his status as a local resident that was emphasised when the photographs were disseminated.[65] Exhibiting both sets of photographs side by side, Southwark's councillors mobilised both Hardy and Chilvers' photographic sequences within the discourses around the area's ongoing regeneration. The £1.5 billion scheme covers 170 acres of land, much of it owned by Southwark Council.[66] Led by Southwark and developers Lend Lease, it envisages 'a new quarter for central London' to replace what it describes as the current 'missing quarter'.[67] Presumably, the young, affluent middle-class professionals to whom the development was being marketed,

Figure 2.4: *Philip Michael, Elephant and Castle shopping centre as seen from the London College of Communication.*

and the capital they would bring to the area, were the elements deemed to be missing from an already diverse and densely populated area.

Much of the existing local post-war built environment, itself the result of a vision of total reconstruction (as we shall explore in Chapter 3), is now planned for 'comprehensive regeneration and renewal'. The scheme is focused on creating a new civic centre and landmark buildings, through the demolition of much of the 1960s building stock, including municipal housing owned and managed by Southwark. New housing in the area will be a mix of private, social rented and shared ownership – owned by 'registered social landlords'.[68] The scheme is driven primarily by an economic prerogative, intended to stimulate growth through private-sector investment. Within the narratives of this new phase of regeneration, the developers and Southwark Council typically emphasise only the most anodyne of cultural and historical references: a nostalgia for the area's lost pre-war social character, or a focus on local heroes, or on distant histories drawn from ancient archaeology.[69]

Chilvers responded directly to Hardy's series of photographs, creating with his co-photographers a comparable photo-essay (compare Figures 2.1 and 2.4). Exhibited side by side, the old and new series prompted observation of both changes and what was unchanged in the physical and social composition of the district. If, in Hardy's photographs, the overriding narrative is one of reconstruction and modernisation, in the 2005 series the emphasis is on documenting the material degradation of the post-war environment: a backdrop of neglected semi-ruins – structures set to disappear as the master plan proceeds. Residents are depicted by their fellow photographer-residents in the context of a decaying, stained and weathered urban fabric, against the detritus of rubbish and litter. Peeling paint and graffiti are highlighted in forensic detail. The sense is of a place run into the ground.

One photograph from the 2005 series records a particularly disturbing image: a homeless man propped uncomfortably against the flaking wall of the Elephant's squalid pedestrian subway, sitting on cardboard placed over the stained concrete, framed claustrophobically by rough concrete surfaces at the intersection of two tunnels.[70] The man's single crutch lies next to him, adjacent to a beer can. The subject stares – blankly, with resignation rather than co-operation – in the direction of the camera. The image encapsulates a stereotypical environmental determinism common in debates about the area, summed up by the historian, Roy Porter, when he describes it as centred on 'a warren of bleak walkways and tunnels, tailor-made for drunks, dossers and drug addicts'.[71] Reinforcing this caricature, and contrasting the usual sanitised visual representations that accompany urban regeneration public relations campaigns, it is necessary to remind oneself that the local authority responsible for the area commissioned and actively disseminated this image, which, even while it may support the rhetoric of necessary change, seems also to suggest their own failure, or the challenges they face.

The co-authorship of the 2005 project by local young people, alongside Chilvers' status as a resident, provided additional authority for the photographs as a direct form of documentation. Unlike Hardy's images, the 2005 series does not have a text narrative to support it, but the portraits are accompanied by recordings of interviews with the subjects, giving them a more direct (though still edited) voice.[72] Of the photographers, we do not know how they will be affected by the regeneration; perhaps many of them have been, or will be, displaced. The process would, on the surface, show Southwark in a good light, empowering the workshop participants with new photographic skills.[73] Yet the images serve another function, reinforcing Southwark and the developers' narrative that the 'revolutionary ideas' of the 1960s have failed and 'made life more difficult' for local people because of the intrinsic qualities of the built environment – a problematic assertion, given the more complicated picture we shall go on to examine in Chapter 3.[74] Viewed now, one effect of Hardy's photographs might be to provide a nostalgic diversion from the reality of the contemporary ruins depicted in Chilvers' and his co-photographers' images, and from the developers' de-contextualised computer renderings of possible futures.

By commissioning Chilvers to work with local young people to construct a self-documenting visual archive in response to Hardy's photo-essay, with its themes of social deprivation and endurance, environmental ruin and reconstruction, and then exhibiting both sequences side-by-side, Southwark Council have shown an awareness of the potential of photographic rhetoric as a political tool in the redevelopment process. Hardy's lightweight cameras provided new opportunities for proximity, and in Chilvers' case this intimacy deepens further through digital photography – with the ability to take many photographs quietly, without intrusion – and even handing the camera to the subjects themselves.

Next to Chilvers' images of controversially dilapidated buildings and structures, occupied by local residents and facing imminent demolition, Hardy's 'windows' on to life in the working-class Elephant take on a revived immediacy, while paradoxically appearing more contrived, with the photographs' aesthetic function dominating any earlier political intention. The 2005 series follows Hardy's lead in the choice of locations and its focus on abject social groups. However, Hardy's pictorial approach has been replaced with a cruder, more amateurish manner, and with a sharp focus on the degraded urban fabric. The photographic archive produced in 2005, and the exhibition 'Life in the Elephant 1948 and 2005', memorialises the blighted landscape of an area set, once again, for comprehensive economic and social transformation. In this sense it can be viewed as a kind of 'scene of the crime' photography, witness to years of neglect, while paradoxically being used to mobilise support for the next phase of redevelopment.

3

REGENERATION AD NAUSEAM

In seeing negative objects we lose our footing in existence. We glimpse
our lack of life, the death of what we need to live. Traditionally this
is the vanitas, the reminder of mortality. In terms of building it
appears as those spaces which can be thought of as a vacuum, negative
constructions in which we experience a kind of horror.

Mark Cousins (1995)[1]

Speaking as the Labour government's Culture Secretary at a design conference
in 2001, Tessa Jowell used the Elephant and Castle as an exemplar of the 'ugly'
buildings and public spaces that had come to characterise British public architecture.[2] In its second term, New Labour, she suggested, would herald a new era
of design quality. Caricatures of urban dysfunction and dystopia were essential
to Jowell's – and New Labour's – projections of a new and better future.

As we have seen, ugliness has a longer history as a prominent trope in the
portrayal of the Elephant's post-war environment. Yet, towards the end of
the twentieth century and the beginning of the twenty-first, this classification was used increasingly, and became a major feature of the regeneration
discourse, and of debates about specific landmark buildings. A 2001 *Sunday
Times* feature on regeneration proposals from the late 1990s was headlined
'London's ugliest landmark', referring to the area around the Elephant as a
whole.[3] Another piece in *The Times* from 2000, headlined, typically, 'Ugly
Elephant', described the district as 'one of the capital's ugliest carbuncles'.[4]
Polemic expressions of ridicule, disgust and distaste have become increasingly extreme. Restaurant critic, Giles Coren, for example, referred to the
area as 'a stabby shite hole of staggering grimness' in 2009.[5] The perception
of ugliness has also been used to justify suggestions that the area should be
completely 'erased'.[6] In the media, the Elephant and Castle's ugliness has
been communicated through an iconography of anomaly, disfigurement and

Figure 3.1: Optimistic view of the redevelopment of the Elephant and Castle in 1962 with sunburst.

monstrosity, rooted in the kind of historical representations we considered in the last chapter, and elaborated through descriptions of the area's dirtiness, deprivation and material degradation. Ideas about ugliness have also been bound up with references to its so-called 'brutalist' and 'brutal' modernist architecture. Ironically enough, the Strata tower – the poorly named new landmark regeneration tower that dominates the Elephant's skyline (see cover illustration) – has already won the 'carbuncle cup' (2010), an award for 'the worst new building of the year'.[7]

In this chapter we shall examine the histories of two buildings that were pivotal within the Elephant's 1960s redevelopment (see Figure 3.1), and which subsequently became central to its blight: Hungarian-born architect

Ernö Goldfinger's Alexander Fleming House (see Figure 3.2 and Plate 3); and the Elephant and Castle Shopping Centre designed by the architects Boissevain & Osmond in partnership with the developer, William Willett.

The architectural historian and translator, Haruko Watanabe, has drawn on psychoanalytic architectural theorist Mark Cousins' three essays on 'the ugly', written in the mid-1990s, to examine the 'perceived failure' of the post-war redevelopment of the Elephant, and Alexander Fleming House in particular.[8] Watanabe explored the negative public image of the exterior of Alexander Fleming House up to the mid-1990s. Here we shall develop this productive line of inquiry, extending it to the wider politicisation of the ugliness ascribed to the building, and the ideas of dysfunction that encircled it, both before and after its conversion in 1996 to a luxury gated apartment complex.

Figure 3.2: *Ernö Goldfinger, Alexander Fleming House, Elephant and Castle, c. 1967.*

In his three essays on 'the ugly', Cousins extended Mary Douglas' work on dirt to consider ugliness and monstrosity in architecture. He argued that:

> in so far as dirt is matter out of place it must have passed a boundary, limit or threshold into a space where it should not be. The dirt is an ugly deduction from 'good' space, not simply by virtue of occupying the space, but by threatening to contaminate all the good space around it. In this light, 'dirt', the ugly object, has a spatial power quite lacking in the beautiful object.[9]

In contrast to Douglas' spatial but more static understanding of the category of dirt in a rigidly structured world, in Cousins' extrapolation, the dirty or ugly object is not just 'matter out of place' but, being animate or potentially animate, embodies the power to spread. Furthermore, in this theory, ugliness can be a 'moment' in the unfolding of beauty – a positive moment within a process of creative production.[10] The first of these arguments is useful in envisaging the dynamic relationships between blighted districts, conceived as degraded and potentially contaminating, and the purer antitheses they threaten. The second argument points to the place of dirt (and ugliness) in art and architectural aesthetics, as part of a creative act of production, and as constructed through relations between the artist, object, viewer and setting. These ideas will be useful for us to hold in mind when considering the histories of these two buildings central to the Elephant's post-war reconstruction, and to its late-twentieth-century reputation as an ugly and blighted place.

The architecture and planning of the LCC's post-war reconstruction of the Elephant were conceived through a set of design principles typical of mid-century modernism in Britain. There was particular emphasis, for example, on order: on the zoning of functions, the separation of vehicles and pedestrians, and the clear expression of structures, with materials being used for their intrinsic properties. In an image of this protracted reconstruction effort in progress, the sun bursts through the clouds, encapsulating the sense of optimism which the LCC wanted people to embrace (see Figure 3.1). The application of diagrammatic labels to a panoramic photographic image of the site expresses the exertion of professional expertise in this re-ordering of city space. These arrows and labels serve to fix and stabalise the construction site and point towards completion and a positive future.

Why did this same environment become stigmatised so quickly? The subsequent debates about the dysfunctionality and material degradation of the buildings and environments created in this period must be contextualised within wider discourses in the UK about what is indiscriminately labelled as 'brutalist' architecture. Debates about brutalism and modernist architectural 'carbuncles' raged in the 1980s and 1990s, fuelled by Prince Charles' 'monstrous carbuncle' speech of 1984 about a projected extension to the National Gallery.[11]

'Brutalist' is a term that was related initially to materials, rather than form, but in public debates about modernist architecture it has been detached from its origins – a reference to the *Breton brut* rough-cast concrete of Le Corbusier's *Unité d'habitation* (completed 1952) in Marseille. It has also been detached from its connotation of the anti-aesthetics, anti-formalism, and low-status materials used 'as found', associated with the New Brutalists – the name given by the critic Reyner Banham to the work of Alison and Peter Smithson and their collaborators, who were influenced by *art brut*.[12] 'Brutalist' has become a largely derogatory label, applied to buildings in which concrete is prominent, and implying wider failures for British post-war modernism.

Often categorised stylistically by commentators as 'brutalist' or 'New Brutalist', the Elephant's architecture and environment have also frequently been described through a related family of adjectives, deployed in a derogatory sense, such as 'brutal', 'brutish', 'monstrous' and so on.[13] These terms communicate hostility but also masculinity, implicitly suggesting post-war reconstruction as a violent and dehumanising process of obliteration imposed by (male) modernist architects and planners. Related to this, as Adrian Forty has argued, from the 1970s, concrete – predominant in the Elephant's post-war environment – developed an increasingly severe 'image problem'.[14]

In health, and in sickness: Alexander Fleming House

Designed by Goldfinger, an architect central to the post-war planning of London as a whole, and particularly to the master-planning of the Elephant, the office block Alexander Fleming House (now Metro Central Heights) was constructed between 1959 and 1963 (see Figure 3.2 and Plate 3). On its opening, in 1963, it was leased to the government's Department of Health and Social Services (DHSS) as their headquarters. It occupied one of a number of office sites (known as 'site 2') formed by the LCC's 1950s' reconfiguration of the road system.[15] Sandwiched between Newington Causeway and the New Kent Road, as built the scheme comprised three main blocks linked by bridges, two of seven storeys and one of 18, with an enclosed pedestrian courtyard. The complex was designed to relate to the neighbouring cinema, later demolished.[16] It received positive comments in the mainstream press and within the architectural profession, and won a Civic Trust award in 1964.[17] The DHSS were reportedly happy with the building and viewed it as an appropriate representation of the department's image and values.

However, by the 1970s, Alexander Fleming House was already proving unpopular with its civil servant tenants, by the 1980s it had an extremely negative media image, and by the late 1980s, it had come to be considered as 'one of London's most hated buildings'; 'a concrete monstrosity'.[18] By then the building was in a poor state of internal and external repair. The tenants complained in particular of leaks and extremes of temperature.[19] Office workers were said to have suffered 'flu-like symptoms' because of erratic temperature fluctuations and the poor quality of the air conditioning.[20] In this period, the building gained a reputation as an exemplar of 'sick building syndrome', all the more ironic given its function in housing the DHSS.[21]

In 1988, the year that Goldfinger's neighbouring Odeon Cinema was demolished, Environment Minister Virginia Bottomley – who in her former role as Secretary of State for Health had worked in Alexander Fleming House, and who was the Conservative government minister with primary responsibility for determining what should be valued as architectural heritage – refused its application for listing. The official reason she gave was that:

Few think that Alexander Fleming House has proved a satisfactory building, either to look at or to work in. We are listing only the most outstanding modern buildings where there is a broad consensus about their quality.[22]

However, in the building's mythology, Bottomley is reputed to have given another, more telling, explanation: 'We don't want to list that – it's concrete, it's Communist!'[23] This apocryphal statement suggests the contradictory ideological associations of the building, of its predominant material and of the aesthetic principles that governed its design. In spite of its being built as a private office speculation, the architect's Constructivist concrete forms apparently denoted Communist allegiances. This remark associated the building's – and by implication, modern architecture's – failures with 'communist' politics, the 'revolutionary ideas' referred to in today's regeneration discourses, rather than with a neglect of the maintenance of public assets and irresponsible management of public funds.

In any case, the DHSS remained in the building until 1991, at which point the Department of Health moved to Hannibal House, above the shopping centre; and the Department for Social Security moved to new premises in Richmond House, north of the river. After 1991, the building lay empty, though controversially it continued to be leased by the government until 1997, for an annual rent that in 1994 totalled £800,000.[24] On inspecting the building after its civil servant occupants had moved out, its owners, Imry Merchant Developers, 'declared it a health hazard' and claimed that '[i]t looked as though a bunch of animals had just come out of it'.[25] Bryan Martin, Director of Imry, complained to a local newspaper about 'mountains of rubbish and extensive vandalism [which] have left the building uninhabitable and a fire risk'.[26] The public debate around the building now extended to its degraded interiors, hidden behind the modulations of its glass and concrete façades. This discussion continued into the mid-1990s, when Labour MP and

Shadow Health Secretary, David Blunkett, wrote to Bottomley, raising parliamentary questions about the building, and complaining that the government's renting of the empty and 'unlettable' offices represented a 'scandalous waste' of taxpayers' money.[27]

In response to negative media attention in the early 1990s, Imry were prompted to announce a number of different planning applications.[28] In 1991, following a structural survey, the owners submitted a proposal to demolish the building and erect new offices for the Department of Health. This was approved subject to legal agreement, in April 1991, but did not ultimately go ahead.[29] The new building comprised a postmodern office block of coloured aluminium and polished granite, with pitched roofs, and eclectic stylistic and historical references. This inevitably fuelled debates about the mode of Goldfinger's modernism, with the new design being described as 'vulgar' by the champions of Alexander Fleming House, celebrated for its rational aesthetic and structural 'purity'.[30] As with other Goldfinger buildings, by this point there was a clear disparity between the building's bad public image and the celebration of the academic rigours of its Constructivist design within the architectural profession.[31]

In the 1990s, responding to accusations that the building was an eyesore, its defenders emphasised the inevitable effects of 'thirty years of minimal maintenance in a polluted environment'; and suggested that all it really needed was a good clean.[32] In a piece subtitled 'Architects say it's highbrow, but to the public it's a nightmare', the architectural journalist, Jonathan Glancey, summarised the arguments on both sides.[33] Advancing the heroic vocabulary commonly employed to describe Goldfinger's work, he pondered the causes of the building's unpopularity and proposed demolition. He blamed the 'brutish', 'rough and weather-stained nature of its bush hammered concrete'; but also suggested that the formal mathematical qualities of the architect's uncompromisingly academic design and its 'foreignness' were root causes. A sense of the exotic was a positive feature of early coverage of the enclosed Italianate 'piazza' of Goldfinger's office scheme;[34] however, this quality of 'foreignness' to context later became symptomatic of a general feeling of unease about the break from a cultural and historical context that the post-war redevelopment represented.[35] In terms of its relationship to the immediate context of the Elephant, whether the building was blighting the area, or the area blighting the building, also became a moot point.[36]

Goldfinger's supporters pursued a defence of Alexander Fleming House that is interesting, given Cousins' description of ugliness as a moment in the unfolding of beauty, based on its architectural aesthetics. The architect's Constructivist and Beaux-Arts-influenced structural rationalism, rigorously articulated geometry and façades, and exposed concrete forms, they argued, resulted in a sublime object: 'art of fearsome beauty'.[37] Related to this, in architectural history and theory, brutalism has been described as a 'self-consciously ugly' style of architecture; and the effect of the New Brutalist approach (see pages 132–133) as 'inelegance and even ugliness'.[38] Goldfinger did not state an explicit desire to create a work of ugliness. Yet, in writing about his work at the Elephant in 1962, he suggested that the architect's role was to 'fulfil certain well-defined requirements' which, if done well, has the potential to produce 'thrilling architecture' with 'subconscious impact': in other words, to produce effect.[39] He would probably have been appreciative of the building's later reception as a work of 'art of fearsome beauty', and its structures as 'both beautiful and terrifying' in the sense of sublime.[40] For the building's admirers, it was a purposefully confrontational building, appreciation of which constituted a sublime experience, the unfolding of a thrill. As a counterpoint it was labelled 'ugly' by the media, based on the prejudices of visual taste, at the same time as the area's modernist built environment as a whole was derided within a new regeneration discourse that advocated a laissez-faire approach.

A lifestyle apart: Metro Central Heights

In 1996, Southwark Council granted planning permission for the conversion of Goldfinger's offices to private residential use. The gated apartment complex was designed by Fairhurst, the architects who had also been involved in earlier failed re-cladding proposals, put forward by the owners, Imry, and developers St George Developments (see Figure 3.3). It comprised 60 studio, 139 one-bedroom, 193 two-bedroom and 30 three-bedroom flats, as well as the re-landscaping of the 'piazza'; a new gym and swimming pool; concierge facilities; and separate retail and restaurant units facing the Elephant's northernmost roundabout. The exterior conversion involved – controversially from the perspective of the heritage lobbyists[41] – painting the concrete white and inserting blue spandrel panels, thus altering the pattern of modulation of Goldfinger's façades. Providing an obvious 'facelift' was crucial to the building's re-branding, given the negative attention paid to its concrete exterior.

Figure 3.3: *Metro Central Heights, 2009.*

The scheme was cited by Southwark Council as proof of the area's regeneration.[42] In a press release repeated verbatim by the local newspapers, they hailed the planned development as proof of the borough's wider regeneration through private investment: 'a further massive vote of confidence in Southwark from the business community'.

In their marketing brochure, estate agents Knight Frank International referred to the development as 'a fashionable new urban village in the heart of the inner city', and a 'vibrant home for style-conscious Londoners'.[43] The name Metro Central – which later became Metro Central Heights for its added sense of exclusivity – emphasised the centrality of the Elephant to the 'heart' of inner London. It communicated a sense of metropolitan sophistication, and referenced the glamorous gated communities of North American cities – residences located in 'gritty' inner-city locations, yet providing a sense of physical and psychological security for a professional class of urban dwellers. The building's re-branding performed what in Cousins' psychoanalytic terms would constitute a 'narcissistic turning away from ugliness': an act of masking and separation from the stigmatised area, and from the building's controversies, which, from the developers' perspective, was remarkably effective. The result of this redevelopment was the creation of a gated 'ghetto of affluence', to use the urban geographer Dave Harvey's term, marketed on grounds of exclusivity, security and proximity to the city's centres of wealth.[44]

Tube and road maps re-positioned the Elephant, 'a new heart of London' as part of the West End and City of London zone of cultural and financial prosperity. On another page of the brochure, a photograph shows a lift attendant in a natty braided uniform, white gloves and hat, while the detail of a CCTV camera is displayed next to a collage of apartment interiors. A living room is occupied by a smartly dressed white, middle-aged couple sitting stiffly on designer chairs, the white walls adorned with plainly-framed abstract prints, and simple modern furniture and upholstery. Given the building's previous office use, and its 'sick building' reputation, these images of the interior were as important to the re-branding as the exterior cladding and painting. Strangely, considering the building's height, and the extensive use of glazing, none of the interior shots show any windows or views – they either present window-less rooms or details, or the curtains are drawn. Presumably this strategy was intended to emphasise the self-sufficiency and security of the complex, imply-ing that it was hermetically sealed, detached from its context.

In 1997, an inquiry was launched by Southwark's Trading Standards Unit into claims made about the location in the brochure. The *Evening Standard* derided the 'cool dudes and hip chicks, wearing designer shades, drink-ing coffee and mineral water and eating croissants', while at the same time reinforcing a stereotypical view of the Elephant as 'plagued by crime, unem-ployment and poverty'.[45]

In spite of such ridicule, from the developers' perspective the refurbishment was highly successful in economic terms, with the flats being sold very quickly. A 'thirty-something' professional, who was one of the first to purchase a flat, sums up his sentiments about the building and the area at the time, and on moving out ten years later:

> The Elephant was a dump when I moved there in November 1997 and, despite much talk of regeneration, especially of the shopping centre, was still a dump when I left, a decade later. I think Metro was one of few major projects while I was there. However, it was urban, central and very convenient, suited to the young crowd that lived there. The building was converted to a very low spec, with the cheapest fittings imaginable and was marketed as a young urbanite's starter home. It was nevertheless a special place, with windows reaching to the top of the nine foot ceiling, and in most cases, stunning views of London.[46]

The market for young professionals attracted to a centrally-located gated community was very different from Goldfinger's trendy Trellick Tower in West London, where around 18 per cent of the former council flats are privately owned, purchased by those pulled towards the 'authentic urbanity' of living in a mainly working-class brutalist tower.[47]

Misfit mall: the Elephant and Castle shopping centre

More recent public debates in which the Elephant has been maligned as an ugly place have centred most prominently on the shopping centre (see Figure 3.4). Completed in 1965, this building resulted from an LCC open competition, announced in 1959, and entered by a number of brutalist architects.[48] It was won by the partnership of developer William Willett Ltd and architects Boissevain & Osmond. The design was hailed by the LCC jurors as 'the best solution, being quite outstanding in its original conception of an arcaded multi-level shopping centre' (see Plates 4a and 4b).[49] It consisted of a 235,000 square-foot rectangular podium containing three storeys with over a hundred shops, as well as a 'banqueting hall', restaurant, two public houses and a bowling alley, all sitting on a storage basement and car parking area, with a separately articulated 90,000 square-foot 11-storey office block – Hannibal House – above. The shopping volume was set in a sunken 'piazza' with a beer garden attached to one of the pubs. The centre was one of the first in the UK and was hailed as the largest self-contained shopping centre in Europe.[50]

Figure 3.4: Elephant and Castle shopping centre, photograph taken from outside Metropolitan Tabernacle, c. 1965.

However, on the opening day under half of the shops were occupied; and by 1966 just 65 per cent of the units had been leased.[51] In commentating on the phenomenon of the mall in the context of North America, Harvey argues that: 'the construction of safe, secure, well-ordered, easily accessible, and above all pleasant, soothing and non-conflictual environments was the key to commercial success. The shopping mall was conceived of as a fantasy world in which the commodity reigned supreme'.[52] As designed, the Elephant and Castle shopping centre conformed to these principles, representing a modernist protoype of later malls – a classic type of postmodern urbanism, sanitised and highly regulated spaces of consumption that project an image of public space.[53]

A public relations brochure, produced for the Willett Group and printed in colour to market the centre to the press and potential tenants, is revealing of the developers' and architects' intentions (see Figure 3.5 and Plates 4a and 4b).[54] The main image used is an artist's impression by A. J. Middleton of the centre as conceived in 1962. It shows a busy, mechanistically efficient environment animated by pedestrians and flowing traffic. The area containing the shopping

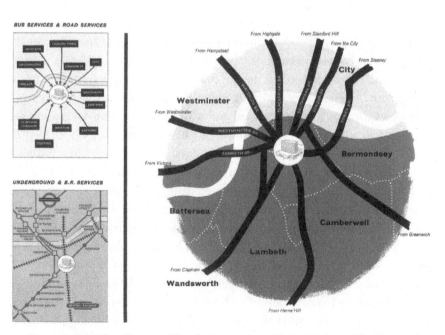

Figure 3.5: *Willett Group public relations and marketing brochure, Elephant and Castle shopping centre, transport links, 1962.*

mall is wedged neatly between the rust-coloured railway tracks and the new road and roundabout system. People and vehicles are separated, and the 'moat' around the building's base – which much later came to be occupied by market stalls – provides a buffer zone for pedestrians to sit and relax, brought down to 'human scale' with street furniture and planting, and connected to the mall by a bridge and a ramp. The rational planning of the whole complex is suggested through its representation from above. The picture is composed of two triangular sections. In the foreground are the Michael Faraday Memorial (also shown in Figure 3.1 atop the London Transport electricity substation) and the spacious new roads and roundabouts. The concrete and glass surfaces of the new buildings appear luminous, and the drawing emphasises orderly modernist geometries.[55] In contrast with the bright foreground, the shady and disorganised 'old' city lies beyond, its buildings densely packed, amorphous and fragmented. In the brochure, and as published in newspaper reports, this image accompanied a text emphasising the scale and wholesale nature of the transformation taking place: the 'vast redevelopment involves the almost complete clearance of 31 acres'.[56]

An architect's drawing of the interior shows a bright environment with light streaming in from the retractable glazed 'sunshine roof' above, peopled by smartly and brightly dressed shoppers who mill around, admiring the spectacle of the shops and the architecture in equal measure (Plate 4b). Snugly wrapped in a fur coat, a mother stands with her daughter in the right-hand foreground looking down on the main concourse from a gallery; a place to see and be seen. The mall is dotted with sculptures, water features, palm trees and café tables topped with cheerful red and white parasols, thus reinforcing the fantasy of an attractive, bright, clean, exotic new environment.

The brochure stresses the centre's excellent location and transport connections (Figure 3.5), access features, and the comfort and safety of its pedestrian-only interior. Providing a precedent for the marketing of Metro Central Heights, a series of maps graphically reposition the Elephant at the centre of London, and these are accompanied by a narrative highlighting the area's historical function as a 'natural focus of highways, drove roads and field paths connecting the Thames crossing with the Southern Counties'.[57]

The centre's promoters also emphasised the North American influence in the design and conception of the 'one-stop' shopping centre. Architect, Paul Boissevain, had visited the United States prior to designing the building.[58] This influence is explicitly apparent in the brochure. Some sections of the building's façades are animated with illuminated advertisements, in the manner of Piccadilly Circus, resonating with the LCC's stated aim of recreating the Elephant as a space of consumption and spectacle: a 'Piccadilly of the South'.[59]

Another marketing brochure produced in 1967, two years after the opening, is elaborate in its celebration of the development's success. A quote from the then Mayor of Southwark claims that the building has put the borough on the map, and – rather optimistically – that 'visitors from all over the world now put the Shopping Centre high on the list of places to visit alongside the Houses of Parliament and the Tower of London'.[60] This publication should clearly be read as an attempt to counter the perception that the centre was failing to live up to its promise, in financial terms, or in the sense of its potential as social space for the area as a whole.[61]

As with other features of the Elephant's environment, discourses around the ugliness and degraded materiality of the shopping centre soon developed, in parallel with reports of social disorder. As the geographer, David Sibley, has argued in studies of media representations of stigmatised communities, the abjection of 'disorderly' people and places often goes hand in hand.[62] It is interesting to note, therefore, the number of historical events related to the shopping centre that have been reported with emphasis on disorderly disruptions. On the opening of the centre, Minister of Labour Ray Gunter was interrupted in delivering his speech: first by Communist Party candidate Joe Bent, who wanted to highlight the poor housing conditions nearby; and then by 'Hooligans dressed in jeans' – youths and children – who damaged equipment, sprayed shoppers with a fire hose and threw missiles at onlookers.[63] The sociologist, Garry Robson, has also commented on the Elephant's association with the original use of the term 'hooligan', and with rioting Teddy Boys in the 1950s.[64]

Distress aesthetics

The fact that the centre has only ever been partially occupied has had an increasingly negative effect on the perception of it. In addition, demolition discourses have long contributed to its blight, intensifying in the late 1990s. Traders have pointed out that, while the protracted threat of demolition has hung over them, customer numbers have fallen, rents have continued to rise, and they have continued to pay service charges on the building despite a lack of maintenance.[65] In the first decade of the twenty-first century, the building operated as an exemplar of architectural ugliness. In a *Time Out* readers' poll in 2005, the shopping centre was voted 'London's ugliest structure'.[66] In 2007, from a choice of pre-selected 'eyesores', the same magazine's readers voted it as the landmark Londoners 'would most like to see burned down'.[67] The developers responsible for the regeneration have drawn on and reinforced this reputation for unsightliness. Project director, Chris Horn, for example, responded to *Time Out*'s 2005 poll by remarking that 'to be frank it is a monstrosity ... Even though it's red now it will always be a pink blot in people's minds'.[68]

Horn's comment referred to an act of emergency 'facelift' regeneration in the early 1990s, in which the original 'murky green' of the building's impenetrable façade was over-painted in 'lipstick pink'.[69] This was an attempt to rebrand the centre by its then new owners, the property company UK Land. It was both a literal and a metaphorical act, brightening up the Elephant's image and countering the area's reputation as a drab place. It was also at this point that a stretched fabric pavilion was added to the 'drawbridge' entrance, and a number of other superficial changes were implemented with the aim of rebranding it as 'safe, clean, pleasant, and lively ... humming with life, colour and customers'.[70] However, as Horn's comments suggest, the pink paint only added to the centre's image problems, attracting ridicule.[71] The journalist reporting Horn's words took the imagery even further, describing the building as a 'sprawling fortress':

> Monolithic, windowless and with watermarks staining its lurid red paintwork, retail heaven it isn't. Drawing closer and peering down into the moat at the foot of the complex you can see a ramshackle arrangement of stalls awkwardly hunched in the lee of the hulking building, doing nothing to enhance the general ambience ... Inside though, there is a defeated air. Unflinching strip lighting illuminates ugly metal framed shop fronts and tired marble flooring. Corridors finish in dead ends while the outside market area is cramped and tatty. A worn Boots shop sign looks 20 years out of date while shops and restaurants exist in a miasma of credit transfer outlets, cheap furniture and luggage stores, discount shoes and bling jewellery.[72]

In this statement, the building's ugliness is multifarious, located at once in its scale, the lack of light and air suggested by windowless façades, its weathered surfaces and brash, tasteless colour, the awkwardness of its 'hunched' and 'hulking' volumes, and the spatial disorder resulting from its informal colonisation by aesthetically disfiguring market stalls. The material architectural environment is fatigued and degraded. The harsh lighting reveals a place that is too real, seen in all its ugly strip-lit detail. Even the air is polluted by an atmosphere of 'defeat' – in a nineteenth-century reference to the bad air in slum districts – a 'miasma' of poverty and bad taste. It is so far behind the times that it has a nostalgic value as a haven of kitsch. There is some representation in McAuslan's article of the positive views of 'local residents who use the centre regularly [and] regard it with affection' and who 'feel that the shopping centre is unfairly maligned and just run down', but these are embedded within a series of images that reinforce the notion of the building as an ugly place.[73] The description suggests an association between degraded aesthetics and materials, poverty and the 'defeated air', but the nature of these relationships remain opaque.

In a further twist in the imaginaries encircling the shopping centre, in 2002 it provided the setting for a series of high-profile television advertisements for Levi's 'Worn Out' jeans produced by advertising agency Bartle Bogle Hegarty. As reported in the *Guardian*, the agency:

> chose the south east London site, famous for its decaying red shopping centre and high-rise sink estates, after research showed consumers were tired of advertisers using glitzy locations to promote their products ... The grungy location was considered perfect to promote Levi's Worn Out jeans, a range of distressed denims designed to look as if they have been worn for years.[74]

The advertisers' choice of the Elephant was determined by the association of the area's worn-down material environment with a sense of authenticity – with the 'real life' of the working metropolis, 'a place where the work gets done'.[75] Of course, only a minority of the advertisers' international audience would recognise the exact location. However, this example of commodification demonstrates how, in its degraded state, images of the Elephant's built environment have recently fed a wider cultural appreciation of distress aesthetics.

The shopping centre's original tenants' lease strictly regulated the organisation, design and fittings for individual shop units.[76] The accretions of successive improvement schemes may have taken the centre away from the modernist geometries of its original design, and the strict spatial division and regulation of its functions, yet its increasingly informal spatial organisation can be seen to have benefited both traders and customers. In the important minority of commentaries that attribute positive qualities to the building, it has been pointed out that it is actually a good example of a building adapting to community needs over time, accommodating a market flexibly alongside the shops inside, and in the perimeter moat.[77] More important, it has provided affordable space for shopkeepers and market traders in a good, and busy, location. This is a genuinely mixed-use environment catering for a diverse community, which has regenerated itself even in difficult circumstances – but not in the way envisioned as part of the official regeneration. As a result, traders have been treated badly, and have suffered from continuous uncertainty for many years about the centre's future. Supporting the view that the developers have brutally run the centre and its traders down as part of their 'regeneration' strategy, Baron Herman Ouseley, former chairman of the Commission for Racial Equality, has been one of those who has criticised Southwark for driving out small businesses run by its own black and minority ethnic communities.[78]

In this context, we should remember that many urban theorists have argued convincingly for the positive values of informality within cities, and for less controlled and predictable approaches to urban management. This is a position advocated repeatedly by the sociologist, Richard Sennett, who argued in *The Uses of Disorder* (1971) that the ideal of modern planning, in which all uses of space are predetermined, and growth is predictable, represents a 'naïve view of what the "good city" is'.[79] For Sennett, striving towards the orderly ideals of the rationalist city 'has crippled the very act of planning', denying urban complexity, inhibiting innovation and positive forms of sociability.

The histories of the two buildings we have considered in this chapter exemplify the paradoxical nature of the Elephant and Castle's post-war environment. As designed, they advanced a quest for aesthetic, material, functional and structural purity typical of high modernist architecture, and appropriate to the reconfiguration of the area as set out by the LCC and according to the modernising agenda of the Abercrombie and Forshaw plan. However, in their realisation, both buildings fell short of their functional requirements and were designated as disorderly on multiple levels. Each case demonstrates that discussions about aesthetics, surfaces and materials – and debates that focus on ugliness or dirtiness, beauty or purity – displace or conceal more profound questions regarding the organisation of metropolitan life. Underlying the discourses about the ugliness and dysfunctionality of these buildings in the 1980s and 1990s, there is a strong sense that, stuck in a recent-yet-already-obsolete past, they were unsettling because they revealed the antithesis of London's desired global city image.

In the case of Alexander Fleming House, the late 1990s redevelopment was envisioned as a 'privatopia', to use Harvey's term, which severed itself from Goldfinger's original aesthetic approach, from the building's stigmatised materiality and controversial history, and from the social, historical and cultural context of the area.[80] Transforming the building far in advance of any substantial wider regeneration of the area, Metro Central Heights came to represent a new incongruity, between the social and physical urban landscapes of the Elephant's past and its projected future.

When it opened, the privately financed shopping centre, with its escalators and retractable glass roof, represented a space of commodity spectacle: clean, bright, modern, and intended to attract economic investment into the area. However, in spite of intensive marketing, including attempts to emphasise the Elephant's central location within the geography of London, it was commercially unsuccessful, in the manner intended, as a result of misjudged demand. In subsequent years, and despite cosmetic regeneration efforts, the centre has become emblematic of the failures of the post-war redevelopment, and widely rejected as an eyesore. However, simultaneously, it has remained popular with local businesses and residents, providing space at reasonable rents for local shopkeepers and market traders.

4

SINK ESTATE SPECTACLE

There is another Modernism well worth rescuing from the dustbin of
history and the blandishments of heritage ... [T]he Left Modernisms
of the 20th century continue to be useful: a potential index of ideas,
successful or failed, tried, untried or broken on the wheel of the market
or the state. Even in their ruinous condition, they can still offer a sense
of possibility which decades of being told that 'There is No Alternative'
has almost beaten out of us.

Owen Hatherley (2008)[1]

Southwark has an enormous variety of fantastic locations. There are
lovely parks, Victorian streets as well as Britain's largest housing estates.

Southwark Council Film Office (2008)[2]

Since the start of its construction in the late 1960s, the Aylesbury Estate in
south-east London has been one of the highest-profile and most contentious
urban settings in Europe (see Figure 4.1 and Plate 5). Ever since it was built,
using industrialised methods and prefabricated components, and even during
the fanfare of the opening ceremony, a powerful and multi-faceted imaginary of decline has encircled the architecture of this system-built estate and
distorted our understanding of it. This has been shaped by – and has itself
actively influenced – housing and regeneration policy, and changing attitudes
towards public housing, post-war modernism and welfare provision. The
construction methods used embodied Prime Minister Harold Wilson's Labour
government's belief in system building – using large sections manufactured off
site and assembled on site – as a solution to dire housing need, and as a mechanism for the expansion of the Welfare State. At that time, local authorities were
incentivised to provide housing not only for society's most vulnerable, but also
for ordinary working people.

Figure 4.1: *The Aylesbury Estate, Aylesbury Road Redevelopment Area, Opening Ceremony brochure, 1970.*

Looking back, the Aylesbury Estate is a microcosm through which we can trace the diminishing value UK governments have attached to the state provision of housing – and modernist tower and slab blocks in particular – since their peak in the mid-1970s. Its history reflects successive waves of privatisation, from Margaret Thatcher's 'right-to-buy' policy initiated in 1980, to New Labour's Public–Private Partnership approach of the late 1990s and 2000s, and the current Conservative-led Coalition's renewed gusto for shedding government responsibility for housing.[3]

To critically examine and challenge discourses about the Aylesbury's decline, we shall explore the estate's architectural history, before focusing on a selection of representations in architectural debates, the media and popular culture. To date, analyses of the Aylesbury have remained in the silos of particular disciplines, and have neglected the question of how the estate's representation, its

architecture, and the material, political and economic contexts of its production and reproduction intersect.

In addressing this we first examine the historical context of the design and
production of the estate. Second, through the lens of a film he made on the
Aylesbury in 1974, we revisit the theory of 'defensible space' proposed by the
Canadian architect, Oscar Newman, and subsequently extended in the UK by
the geographer, Alice Coleman.[4] Through government and police-led initiatives, such as 'secured by design', and the *Sustainable and Secure Buildings Act*
(2004), in the UK defensible space continues to have considerable influence
on the design and management of housing for both rich and poor, as well
as public space in general.[5] Third, we consider how the estate was used by
New Labour when launching its urban regeneration programme, and how it
featured in journalists' accounts of this. In 1997, it was chosen as the backdrop

for Tony Blair's first speech as prime minister: a scene of urban collapse and a canvas for projecting a different future. Finally, we turn to recent representations of the estate as a modern ruin – or 'modernity in ruins' – in popular culture. Partly in contradiction to the authorities' drive to regenerate the estate, and partly reinforcing it, the Aylesbury has in recent times often been imagined through a mode of sink estate spectacle in mainstream television and film portrayals, as well as in fine art.[6]

Ambition and infamy

Located just south of the Elephant and Castle, the Aylesbury was designed by the newly formed architects' office of the London Borough of Southwark, led initially by the patrician figure of Frank Hayes, and later by Hans Peter Trenton. The site was within the Aylesbury Road Redevelopment Area. The designs for the estate were approved in 1966, and it was built by John Laing Construction between 1967 and 1977 to a budget of £10,996,178.[7] The Labour government required the larger local authorities to adopt industrialised system building as a main mode of production. This was seen as being advantageous in terms of speed of construction, efficiency, quality control and a decreased need for building tradesmen at a time of labour shortages in construction.

The newly formed London Borough of Southwark, with a strong Labour majority, embraced industrialised methods enthusiastically as a fast and economical solution to housing shortages.[8] However, the scale of the Aylesbury, and the fact that its sister estate, the Heygate (constructed 1970–4), was built at all, are remarkable because anti-modernist sentiment intensified on both the left and right during this decade, with an increasing distrust of grand projects, centralised planning, industrialised building and *tabula rasa* urban redevelopment.

In Bridget Cherry and Nikolaus Pevsner's classic series of guides to the buildings of England, the Aylesbury is described as 'the most ambitious post-war plan of any London borough', emphasising the utopian vision that underpinned its design, scale and social objectives.[9] However, the guide also notes that the Aylesbury and the Heygate became 'some of the most notorious products of industrialised architecture ever built'.[10] This phrase has become canonical, often recycled in journalists' accounts, even while the original ambition has been largely forgotten.[11]

Both estates are constructed mainly using a Danish prefabricated concrete large panel system (LPS) known as 12M Jespersen – pre-cast reinforced concrete components, assembled *in situ* – procured by the government. The initial belief in such a system as a new and efficient model of architectural production, with positive results for society, is captured in the energy and positivity of one of the original sketches of the Heygate, where a family arrive in a modern new car with the number plate 'JESP 12M', to be welcomed to the lushly planted estate by waving friends (see Plate 6).

The Aylesbury comprises a 60-acre complex of buildings arranged geometrically, with an emphasis on long, linear blocks, in order to accommodate the cranes and heavy goods vehicles necessary during construction. At its opening it included 2,400 dwellings in blocks of varied heights, between four and 14 storeys. The low-rise blocks ran east to west, and the higher-rise north to south. Conceived as a single redevelopment area, and intended as a 'self-sufficient' environment, as well as homes built to Parker Morris standards, the scheme included generous provision of space for social use and amenities: shops, laundries, a health centre and a day nursery, club rooms, a district boiler house to provide heating and hot water, a young peoples' centre, a boys' hostel, a children's home, flats for elderly people, communal gardens, open spaces, and play and relaxation areas.

The Aylesbury was planned as a way of efficiently rehousing the thousands on Southwark's waiting list, while achieving an 'effective structure and order' for an area thought to be spatially fragmented, and separated from more prosperous southern Southwark by the barrier of the Old Kent Road.[12] The sites of the Heygate and Aylesbury were reputedly chosen by Hayes, John O'Brian from Southwark's Estates office, and the planner, Ian Lacey, as they were chauffeured around the area in the borough's limousine one rainy afternoon with the plans on their laps.[13] At the time, both Labour and the Conservatives were boasting competitively about the number of houses they would build during a Parliament.

In the Heygate's case, the existing housing stock comprised late-Victorian Italianate tenement blocks, interspersed with Second World War bomb sites. In the Aylesbury's case it comprised similar six- or seven-storey tenements and terraced streets from the same era, as well as some industrial buildings, such as an 'R. White's' lemonade factory, and backyard industrial workshops and tanneries.[14] The architects involved recall a mix, including some buildings that would almost certainly be refurbished today, and others that were extremely degraded and infested. Refurbishment, however, was hardly ever considered as an option at the time, because of the Wilson government's modernising agenda. Local authorities were instead encouraged to bid for loans to construct new housing, on a 60-year repayment model, and using the 'cost yardstick' – a standardised formula set out by the government to determine the relationship of cost to dwellings, laying out the maximum allowable cost for housing, and recognising a greater cost per square metre for high-density urban housing than for lower-density dwellings. The cost yardstick was intended to produce good value for money for public sector housing. If local authority architects conformed to it they were given preferential loan rates, but it was a crude system in which longer-term value for certain elements, such as lifts, was overlooked. Existing blocks were purchased by compulsory purchase order – the provision in UK law for land to be obtained without the consent of the owner for developments deemed to be in the public interest. They were then 'decanted' of their inhabitants, who were dispersed around the borough, so that demolition could begin. Even with system building, the construction process took long enough to prevent communities and their social networks from being re-established once the new housing was complete.

The characteristics of the designs of both the Aylesbury, and the 1,194-unit Heygate, were in many ways typical of Corbusian and Athens Charter-inspired modernist mass housing in post-war Europe: exposed concrete; 'honest' expression of structure; the repetition of geometric forms; and the elevation of slab blocks on piloti. The architects were inspired by Le Corbusier's *Unité d'Habitation* in Marseille, with its roughcast concrete, decorative relief sculptures and elegant communal roof garden, and this spirit is communicated well in the original drawings (see Figure 4.2).[15] However, in the Aylesbury's case, the contractors took the design lead once the building work was under way, and detailing and materials were dictated by cost and efficiency above all else.

The younger architects in the office were newly qualified graduates of the Architectural Association, all enthusiastic about working for a local authority on public buildings.[16] They had been impressed by the previous work of Camberwell, one of the three boroughs that had amalgamated to form Southwark's borough architects' office. In the Southwark office, Hayes continued an internal competition system he had put in place in Bermondsey, so that members of the team would put forward schemes in competition with one another, and the ones selected by Hayes would go forward for development. In the case of the Aylesbury, he, and later Hans Trenton, reportedly took a 'hands-off' approach, with Trenton rarely visiting, if at all, during the construction period.[17] The more experienced (and less ideologically

82

VIEW INTO GREEN SPACE FROM LOCAL DECK

PIG A

JUNCTION BETWEEN TALL BLOCKS

Figure 4.2: The Aylesbury Estate, architect's drawing, Aylesbury Redevelopment
brochure, c. 1966.

committed) members of the team, and the group leaders – who were work-ing on multiple schemes simultaneously – had less influence as the designs progressed at an extraordinarily high speed.[18] After the designs had been signed off by Trenton, much of the technical design work and production informa-tion was taken on by the building company, Laing, who had a contract to use the Jespersen system, with some members of the architectural team being seconded to Laing's offices.

The younger team members had also visited the Park Hill Estate in Sheffield, designed by the architects Jack Lynn and Ivor Smith, of which there were echoes in the Aylesbury Estate designs.[19] At the Aylesbury, pedestrians and vehicular traffic were separated, so that people traversed the estate on 'pedways' (the walkways), interconnected by ramps, lifts and stairs. At first-floor level, these 'local decks' allowed movement within the site and included play spaces; and at the second-floor level, wider 'route decks' had space for shops and other services, and pedestrian through movement. It was intended that the whole development could be crossed at this height. Yet the separation of vehicular and pedestrian movement resulted in convoluted access to the flats. Traffic and garages occupied the ground level. The scheme also included the longest housing block in Europe, comprising 16 'snake blocks' connected by bridges and corridors. A pamphlet produced as part of the opening ceremony stated that the intention was to 'obtain variety' through the changing heights and colours of the different blocks.[20]

The opening ceremony in October 1970 was well publicised, and Trenton appeared at that. It was also attended by the Labour government's Minister for Housing and Local Government, Anthony Greenwood. Politicians used the occasion to rhetorical effect, with Conservative MP, Ian Andrews, walking out 'in disgust', declaring the estate a 'concrete jungle and just not fit for people to live in'.[21] Andrews' language and polemical tone are typical of those used by the estate's detractors since its completion. Yet professionals involved in rehousing programmes from this period emphasise that people were in general enthusiastic about moving into new, modern flats at this time, and the Aylesbury does not seem to be an exception.[22]

In spite of this, using adjectives echoing those applied to the nearby Elephant and Castle in the pre- and post-war periods (see Chapter 3), and which would be repeated frequently in relation to the estate, the earliest archi-tectural reviews found it to be 'drab' and 'monotonous', and the scale 'massive and dehumanizing'.[23] Certainly, there were problems that arose from the scale and the nature of LPS as a construction method, and from a number of design decisions. In retrospect, members of the borough architects' office refer, for example, to problems of noise transmission caused by the integration of the pedways into the fabric of the blocks, resulting in a need for resurfacing with a sound-insulating material not long after completion.[24] The same architects also admit that the ground level of the estate suffered from the focus on car movement and multi-storey car facilities – a consequence of the anticipation, at the time, of 100 per cent car ownership – rather than pedestrian movement and residents' facilities. The pedway system meant that, in many blocks, dwellings did not appear until the third floor. In general, the ground level was unsatisfactory because *in situ* poured concrete was used, and this met the panel system above awkwardly. The use of the LPS system itself resulted in flat façades that lacked modulation, which is significant when we consider that the estate has been consistently criticised for being monotonous.

In part, the low quality of the public areas on the estate can be attributed to the cost yardstick financing structure, which encouraged a greater concentration of design effort on the interiors of individual dwellings. One of the architects recalls that 'the name of the game at that stage was to try to under-provide in those [public] areas so that you gained a kind of surplus which could then be distributed to the individual dwellings'; and another comments: 'if you asked us, "Would you live in one of the flats?" I would think, "Yeah, I wouldn't have a problem". The surrounding environment I would be more doubtful about.'[25]

Even before the estate was finished, LPS had become unpopular, particularly after the partial collapse of the Ronan Point tower in Newham, east London, in 1968.[26] The Heygate Estate has often been disparaged in similar terms to the Aylesbury, though it is notable that the architects and builders of the Heygate learned lessons from the Aylesbury. For example, they handled the communal spaces and pedways more skilfully. Visiting the Heygate in 2011, its architect, Timothy Tinker, suggested that it could easily be upgraded. As we might expect, he contends that neglect of maintenance was a bigger problem than any fundamental design flaws.[27] In both the Heygate and the Aylesbury, Tinker notes, 'the planning brief was extremely ambitious ... in how it was going to change the world. Applying that and having to cope with a system building scheme is actually quite difficult. With hindsight, I would say impossible'.[28] Despite being architecturally of a higher standard, the Heygate is also on land that is more central and better connected, and has a higher market value today. The decision to demolish it was taken in 2004. Since then, it has sat nearly empty, in spite of the housing shortage in the UK. In the meantime the communal spaces have been taken over by gardeners, artists, activists and students, as a lush and serene informal community space. Southwark Council have encouraged some official 'meantime' uses, while prohibiting certain of the remaining residents' own projects, such as a pop-up cinema.[29] Compulsory Purchase Orders are currently being served on the last few occupants, who have campaigned vociferously against the estate's demolition and replacement with 'affordable' and shared ownership housing association housing. The main criticism is that though the scheme to replace the estate will see the overall number of housing units increase, at 80 per cent of market rent even the 'affordable' properties will not genuinely be so. Furthermore, in February 2013 a leaked Council document sparked controversy by suggesting that the borough would only break even through the financial transaction set up with the developer, Lend Lease.

In critiques of the Heygate and Aylesbury the original financing, procurement and management structures have not been taken properly into account. In the Aylesbury's case, during the design and construction process, the Ministry of Housing, and Southwark's Quantity Surveyors, pressured the architects to cut back on costs, lowering the overall quality of the landscaping and 'seriously downgrading' the materials used.[30] Key elements such as the lifts were cheap and low quality. In some cases, the use of less expensive and less appropriate surfaces, such as weatherboard surrounds in communal areas rather than glazed tiles, meant a greater susceptibility to wear and tear, and vandalism. By 1975, Southwark was looking at a repair bill of £2.6 million for costs which, according to the architects, could have been avoided.[31] Maintenance was also a problem from the start, with Southwark struggling to manage all of the new housing it had built, due to a lack of financial planning and investment.

Defensible space

It was in this context of debates about vandalism and early decline as a result of compromises in the design and construction process that, in 1974, as a researcher and critic of prefabricated North American housing projects, Newman was invited by the BBC's *Horizon* programme to visit the Aylesbury and make a documentary (see Figure 4.3).[32] Two years previously, he had published the first edition of *Defensible Space* (1972), a foundational text for today's 'secured by design' and 'design against crime' initiatives.[33] In an unusually direct example of the application of architectural theory, Newman was filmed walking around the estate, critiquing the design for its lack of 'defensible space' – by which he meant a sense of individual ownership and responsibility over a clearly defined territory. The documentary was widely watched and reported in both the mainstream and professional press. *Building Design* claimed that the estate had been 'scarred forever by Oscar Neuman's [*sic*] trial by TV';[34] while *The Architect* referred to Newman's 'hysterical patrol around the estate', which at the time was not associated with high crime.[35]

Forty years on, in the context of an increasingly intense focus on the use of design against crime, it is important to remember the origins of Newman's book.[36] The underpinning research had been financed by the US Department of Justice, following the *Safe Streets Act* (1968). Defensible space theory was predicated on, and emphasised, the idea that US cities were declining into 'widespread chaos', crime and violence.[37] In the context of high crime rates in New York, Newman's approach was intended to counter the 'insecurity that plagues the city', by analysing 'the forms of our residential areas and how they contribute to our victimization by criminals'.[38]

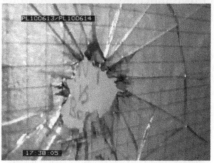

Figure 4.3: *Stills from John Mansfield (dir.),* Horizon: The Writing on the Wall, 1974.

Newman suggested that the stigma associated with public housing projects, such as Pruitt–Igoe in St Louis, Missouri, and the high levels of crime and vandalism they evidenced, resulted primarily from the lack of clearly defined boundaries, poor design, and the interaction of these factors with locations ill-suited to public housing. The result? Residents lacked a sense of self-identity, and of responsibility to others. Positioning himself as an expert in both social science and architecture, Newman saw the designer's role as one of 'neutralising' problems through design modification.[39] He acknowledged the spatial concentration of disadvantaged groups as one factor in determining high crime. However, he prioritised features of layout and design as the main causes of crime and fear of crime, and pointed the finger, in particular, at the high-rise as culprit. In response, defensible space is offered as a 'corrective prevention' model, through three parallel lines of argument.[40] According to Newman, the key to reducing crime is the definition of a sense of 'territoriality'; second, surveillance must be improved in order to exert control and enable the easy identification of unwanted people – intruders, criminals, 'bands of teenagers and addicts';[41] and third, the design of housing projects must reduce the sense of their difference – stigma – from higher-income housing, and they should be integrated into safe areas.

In his understanding of the key concepts of stigma, territoriality and community, Newman referenced work in social and behavioural psychology and anthropology, and stated the influence of sociological writings on cities by Jane Jacobs, and the Chicago School sociologist of the ghetto, Lee Rainwater.[42] However, in contrast with Jacobs, for whom encounters with strangers are essential to city life and its informal control through 'natural surveillance', for Newman, strangers are nearly always conceived negatively, as potential intruders.[43] Clearly established territories enable housing residents to distinguish those who do not belong or are engaging in 'aberrant behaviour'. His analysis is that lower-income groups are held back from improvement, bound by a sense of defeat; and that the solution is to use design to instil a 'refined sense of property and ownership' – something that provides middle-class people with self-confidence and pride.[44] This emphasis on individual ownership, at the heart of Newman's thinking, was fundamentally in tension with the values embodied in communal public housing.

Newman's view of the Aylesbury is a foregone conclusion. He 'diagnoses' the estate as a disorderly environment where 'modern architecture actually encourages people to commit crime'. Early in the *Horizon* documentary we are shown dramatic shots of Pruitt–Igoe from a helicopter. The film then cuts to the streets of New York City as seen through the windscreen of a speeding police car. The narrator details statistical evidence of high levels of murder and rape in comparison with London, and concludes: 'where everything you see is anonymous, dull and concrete, it is not perhaps surprising that inhuman tragedies occur'. We see a shot of an empty corridor and a blank concrete wall. Playing on a fear of strangers, we are asked: 'imagine your home is on this corridor. Who might be waiting for you in the shadows?' A few minutes later the director plays a sleight of hand – we think we are in the ghettos of North America when the narrator announces: 'this isn't New York. This is England'.

The filmmakers authenticate their case through tenants' testimonies. Mimicking Newman's theoretical jargon, one resident complains that the 'pattern of living develops isolation'; and another observes a 'stigma attached to saying you live there'. Others pick up on his emphasis on dangerous strangers, saying that they prefer to be in the street rather than the estate's walkways because of 'nooks and crannies' and men 'hanging around' on stairways. Attributes of the design and concerns about demographics are interwoven: children lack play places; there is an imbalance of young and old tenants; and privacy and acoustic insulation are insufficient. The estate is 'like a prison', a 'concrete jungle', 'depressing'. The narrator concedes that 'many are grateful for their new homes', but compared to the ten individuals who express complaints, just one elderly lady, a former slum resident, is positive, declaring that having a bath and running water are ''eaven'.[45]

Throughout the film, Newman's voiceover adopts a heavily ironic tone. He describes a 'delightful area' as the camera shows us a dark, north-facing walkway; and comments on the 'wonderful garages' underneath the slab-blocks that lie empty, for fear of vandalism. Concluding, he reflects:

One wonders, what happens to the children who grow up here? Do they ever really develop any sense of pride? Any sense of self? Any understanding of responsibility in an environment that is so open and undefined? … There is no evidence, as yet, that this type of environment produces criminals. We know that it facilitates the commission of crime for the simple reason that it's so easy to get away with … one wonders, will these children grow up to become the criminals that we seem to have so much of in America, in such abundance.

As Newman makes explicit here, the 'defensible space' approach is underpinned by a speculative environmental and behavioural determinism that, in the case of the Aylesbury, was being articulated even before the estate had been fully completed. A contemporaneous newspaper review supportive of Newman's views referred to a 'strong smell of stigma' and 'philanthropic paternalism expressed in pre-cast concrete': phrases that indicate the ideological rejection of large-scale public housing underlying the defensible space approach.[46]

In studies of the stigmatisation of modernist public housing, Newman's work continued to have a huge impact in the UK into the 1980s, particularly through Coleman's anti-modernist *Utopia on Trial*, modelled on *Defensible Space*, and also featuring the Aylesbury.[47] Coleman's attitude was clear when she complained:

> The core of northern Southwark is a much vaunted experiment in comprehen-
> sive redevelopment on a grandiose scale, which has become the most notorious
> ultra-Utopia in London and, according to some, in the whole of Europe.[48]

Her emphasis was on 'anti-social elements', over Newman's focus on crime. She charted indicators of environmental degradation, linking them to 'devi-ant' behaviour – writing, for example, that '[design and layout] have been mapped in detail and rigorously tested to see which of them are associated with various lapses in civilised behaviour: litter-dropping, graffiti-scrawling, vandalism, pollution by excrement, and family breakdown leading to children being placed in care'.[49] Following Newman, the vocabulary and metaphors used are socio-biological: 'forms of social malaise ... plague residents of problem estates', who 'could cope perfectly well with life in more traditional houses'; and 'problem estates can breed their own anti-social elements'.[50] Living in flats leads to 'mental disorder'.[51] This problematic lexicon of mental illness, disease and pests has been consistently unhelpful, also featuring in media and political discourses about such estates.[52] As discussed in Chapter 1, it is rhetoric that has its roots in nineteenth-century discussions of the urban poor as being vermin-like and contagious.[53]

Defensible theory?

Contemporary reviews of *Defensible Space* were largely positive, both in the USA and the UK. However, just prior to Newman's visit to the Aylesbury, architect and pioneer of space syntax, Bill Hillier, wrote a scathing review criticising the book's use of statistical data, and its underpinnings in 'discredited' behavioural theories of territory from social science.[54] Hillier's critique is wide-ranging.

He rejects the statistical basis of the claim to a direct link between design factors – specifically, building height – and crime. Unconvinced by Newman's conclusion that design had a direct influence on crime levels, he proposed instead a 'social selection hypothesis', arguing that 'height and size [of residential blocks] are already correlated with crime through social selection prior to the introduction of physical variables'.[55] Though he acknowledges that the book displays a 'strongly felt concern for the disaster that appears to have overtaken architecture in the past few years', his conclusion is: 'What remains of Newman's book after the "scientific" content – statistics, hypotheses and theories – has been debunked is a mishmash of anecdotes, speculations, attempts to verbalise intuitively felt patterns.'[56] Theoretically, he also contests the universalising tendency of 'territoriality' theory as a basis for understanding the social occupation of space; and, in spite of Newman's stated desire to write in non-technical language, his use of 'social-psychological jargon' in creating 'a fog of scientistic rubbish'.[57]

In the same year, architectural critic and advocate of New Brutalism, Reyner Banham, also challenged the architectural aspects of *Defensible Space*, while criminologist Anthony Bottoms questioned its arguments about crime.[58] Bottoms' critique again focuses on the use and interpretation of statistical data (and queries Hillier's reinterpretation). An important point in his analysis is that Newman does not address the 'early histories' of the estates: how their reputations were originally established, or where their populations had originated from and been housed previously.[59] Bottoms also asserts that 'there is a consistent tendency in the book to reify 'the criminal' as one who ever and always is a perpetual lawbreaker'.[60] That is, the social stereotypes Newman establishes are assigned static identities. This universalising tendency applies to his conception of the middle classes, the poor, teenagers, drug addicts and criminals alike.[61]

Newman and, later, Coleman were criticised for the determinism of their analyses. Coleman's answer was that her study was:

based on probabilities, not determinism. A badly designed block does not force children to become litter louts or vandals, but if the design makes it difficult for parents to supervise them and keep them away from bad company, it increases their probability of behaving anti-socially.[62]

This misses the point. It is the presumption of 'bad company' that is determinist, suggesting that special design strategies were needed to cope with the kinds of people housed on estates. In Coleman's, as in Newman's research, crime was a 'natural' factor that design had to attempt to eradicate.[63]

Debating environmental and social determinism in the 1970s, David Harvey concluded that:

> the pros and cons of these approaches are not relevant: the evidence is too slender, and the hypotheses too ambiguous. It is perhaps more reasonable to regard the city as a complex dynamic system in which spatial form and social process are in continuous interaction.[64]

This is the crux of the problem. The defensible space approach over-simplifies the relationships between environment and behaviour, and, in its myopic focus on crime, looks selectively at 'social process'. Newman understands that 'the root causes of inner city and ghetto crime lie deep in the social structure'.[65] Yet his prioritisation of design as both the cause and the solution of crime is diversionary. He neglects root causes and overlooks other possible socio-economic explanations. He does not consider, for example, specific housing policies, residents' economic and educational disadvantages, compromises in the design process, the management and servicing of buildings and facilities, or the role of the media – or indeed academic accounts – in influencing the estate's reputation.

Apart from issues of density, nor does Newman consider why the projects he studies were designed in the way that they were, making the whole book appear ahistorical. What were previous housing conditions like for the tenants of the projects he examines? How might the design and condition of the preceding slums have mapped to criminality, using his theory? Instead, historical questions are neglected, including the histories of specific neighbourhoods and sites, the history of modernism, and the history of housing in the USA or the UK. At the same time, notions of 'territoriality' and 'defensible space' are legitimised through a longer-term architectural genealogy – a bizarre evolutionary tree of 'natural' architectural forms including Neolithic residential compounds in Turkey and mud houses in Sudan.

After the flurry of heated debates about environmental determinism in the 1970s, fatigue seems to have taken hold, or new preoccupations took precedence. In the meantime, a general consensus about 'defensible space' as a productive way of thinking about buildings and cities emerged, with Newman and Coleman's research continuing to feature strongly as foundational texts.[66] Coleman's research was subsequently picked up and financed by the Thatcher government, who commissioned her to 'redesign seven misery estates'.[67] Her arguments provided a convenient 'independent' scientific justification for the government's drastic scaling back of public housing provision. But has the ongoing success of studies such as Newman's and Coleman's been justified?

As mentioned earlier, Newman also compares the Aylesbury Estate to Pruitt–Igoe, a project described as a 'sore' and a 'stigma' in the film, and which features prominently in *Defensible Space*. Perhaps one of the strongest critiques of defensible space in its interpretation of modernist mass housing came in the form of architectural historian Katharine Bristol's essay 'The Pruitt–Igoe myth' in the early 1990s. Bristol critiqued the representation of Pruitt–Igoe as an emblem of the failed modernist project – as asserted by Charles Jencks in his advocacy of architectural postmodernism, as well as by Newman in *Defensible Space*.[68] She also argued that Newman's overemphasis on design diverted attention away from more important socio-economic factors, and that it neglected historical context. For example, she observes that his evaluation of Pruitt–Igoe ignores the evidence of Rainwater's 1960s study, which suggested that the 'violence and vandalism that occurred at the project were an understandable response by its residents to poverty and racial discrimination'.[69] Newman does in fact quote Rainwater's study, but with quite different conclusions. In arguing that the institutional image of housing projects serves to stigmatise the poor and put them 'in their place', he quotes Rainwater's discussion of Pruitt–Igoe:

> the consequences for conceptions of the moral order of one's world, of one's self, and of others, are very great. Although lower class people may not adhere in action to many middle class values about neatness, cleanliness, order and proper decorum, it is apparent that they are often aware of their deviance, wishing that their world could be a nicer place, physically and socially. The presence of non-human threats conveys in devastating terms a sense that they live in an immoral and uncontrolled world. The physical evidence of trash, poor plumbing and the stink that goes with it, rats and other vermin, deepens their feeling of being moral outcasts. Their physical world is telling them that they are inferior and bad just as effectively perhaps as do their human interactions.[70]

This quotation is used by Newman to suggest that, 'unable to camouflage their identities and adopt the attitudes of private apartment dwellers', public housing residents will react against their institutional surroundings with neglect, refusing to participate in upkeep or decoration. It is taken to reinforce a direct relationship between the degraded environments of housing projects and their inhabitants' behaviour. However, for Rainwater, vandalism and neglect are fundamentally a reaction not to the degraded or institutional environment, but to poverty and racism. His research highlighted the dangers that public housing removed, which had been present in slum life; and that the majority of residents' complaints were about the behaviour of others rather than the design and maintenance of the project.[71] Furthermore, unlike Newman, Rainwater argues that design changes will be ineffective without raising income levels: a much more convincing argument.

Bristol also makes clear that Newman and Jencks' interpretations of Pruitt–Igoe have to be contextualised within contemporary debates about the next phase for architecture after modernism. These writers are united by a desire to establish a new direction for architecture, and place the architect as central in providing housing solutions for the poor. In this endeavour, Pruitt–Igoe – and the Aylesbury Estate – and their demolition take on particular symbolic resonance in a narrative that reinforces a sense of the failure of modern architecture and architects, while ignoring the role of the state and wider historical and socio-economic factors. As one of the architects notes: 'it wasn't so much a failure of modernism, it was an inability to apply some really good notions of modernism in this particular circumstance because of the other things … the decision to go for [an] industrialised building system, the size of the scheme, the speed'.[72]

Apart from Bristol, there have been surprisingly few strong critiques of defensible space, but Anna Minton's recent book, *Ground Control: Fear and Happiness in the Twenty-First Century City* (2009), provides a welcome exception to the consensus in the UK and the USA around this apparently common-sense, 'can do' approach to designing crime away. Rather than safer homes and public places, she argues, 'defensible space' confuses actual crime and fear of crime, diminishes trust in others, and 'produces isolated, often empty enclaves which promote fear rather than the safety and reassurance which automatically come in busy places, where people are free to wander around and come and go'.[73]

Walking around the Aylesbury and Heygate estates today one need not look far to find evidence of defensible space interventions – some which seem practical and benign, but others more aggressive, a physical counterpart to the hostile language used in media discourses about the estate, reinforcing rather than alleviating problems. Rather than 'design', these tend to involve blocking flows and partitioning spaces, as well as improving lighting and adding CCTV.

Some measures have been implemented by the authorities, such as the removal of connecting bridges between blocks in the 2000s. Moves like this have been argued to address crime directly by limiting escape routes, though this is not well evidenced. At ground level, garage spaces have been fenced off, making the buildings less permeable. Residents have also appended obvious security features to their own flats, putting grilles on windows and balconies, for example. Around features such as playgrounds, fence systems have become layered, at different heights, and in different colours and materials, leaving unusable moat spaces in which litter collects. Worried about high crime levels, and fuelled by media reports of its prevalence, residents have clearly been attracted to defensible space thinking, as when in 1994 tenants successfully pressured the council to employ private security guards to patrol the estate.[74] However, the question we have to ask is why the state had avoided its own responsibility for policing the estate to the extent that this was felt to be necessary.

What is clear is that the defensible space approach has worked against the original intentions of the architecture, heightening a sense of potential danger, promoting individualism over communal living and the partitioning of collective space. This is a shift that has seen residents argue, for example, for the compartmentalisation of communal gardens – a type of shared space that works well in the wealthiest parts of the city.

As Minton points out, crime statistics are hard to read and are often misinterpreted by the media. Until recently, most of the available data was broken down by borough, and the Aylesbury overlapped different administrative wards with varying levels of recorded crime and anti-social behaviour.[75] Set up in 1999, The Aylesbury Estate New Deal for Communities went on to produce five years of crime statistics for the estate (2000–2005), comparing these with the borough average.[76] These show that crime rates were consistently lower on the estate than for the borough as a whole.

In the media spotlight

In her survey of 20 'problem estates' across Europe, social policy theorist Anne Power writes:

> Once on the track of dramatic decay or lurid crime stories, serious disorder or breakdown, journalists would herd into the estates and pick up the most extreme versions of events they could find. The link between threatened social breakdown and the estates was constantly made.

The press were fascinated by problem estates because they contained every kind of human, social and physical problem. They could chastise politicians and ridicule professionals. They could blame rejected groups or they could blame society and show the victims to be cruelly exploited or mistreated. Sensational headlines pointed to cities on the brink of collapse. The media focus had an overpowering effect on politicians, as they were questioned on their record.[77]

In this account, media attention has both positive and negative consequences. The Aylesbury had a high-profile media presence around the time of its opening in the 1970s, while in the 1980s it was one of those studied by Coleman, but had less of a presence in national media debates.[78] The 1980s were, in general, a time of disinvestment in public housing, meaning that maintenance suffered. Since the mid-1990s attention has been particularly intense and has centred on a number of key events, including the defensible space interventions referred to above. Reinforcing the power of media representation in shaping the reputation of the estate and its residents, in 2005 journalists homed in on a sensationalist statistic, suggesting that one criminal offence occurred on the estate every four hours.[79] Even appearing in the rare articles purporting to challenge the estate's negative image, such reports have repeatedly naturalised the interpretation of the Aylesbury as a crime-ridden dystopia.[80]

Contradicting this dominant media narrative of the estate's hopeless blight, in 2002 residents again attracted wide publicity when 73 per cent of them, on a 76 per cent turnout, rejected 'starchitect' Will Alsop's master plan for redevelopment, and the proposal to transfer the estate's ownership from the municipality, Southwark, to a registered social landlord, Horizon Housing Group. Coverage was again intense, three years later, when Liberal Democrat-led Southwark took the decision to demolish and rebuild the estate, citing the prohibitive cost of refurbishment.[81] Southwark argued that, after the tenants' vote, unforeseen costs had been calculated – in particular, structural refurbishment for the LPS blocks, replacement of gas cookers, repairs to the heating system that had broken down in the winter of 2004/5 – resulting in a total that was unfeasible, given available funds. Although some have challenged the scope of the repairs needed, it was decided – in line with New Labour's original intentions when allocating the NDC funds, and in line with the London Plan – to replace the existing buildings with higher-density mixed tenure developments comprising, in total, around 2,200 social housing units provided by registered social landlords, and approximately 2,700 homes for sale or shared ownership.[82]

The lion's share of media attention, however, has been sparked by a series of visits by politicians, and a visit by Prince William in 1999 – part of the tenth annual Eton College geography class field trip to the estate as an example of urban blight. Neil Kinnock also toured the Aylesbury as Labour leader of the opposition, foreshadowing high-profile visits by Tony Blair as prime minister in 1997 and 2005. Michael Howard also visited as Conservative leader of the opposition in 2005.

In taking the decision to deliver his first prime ministerial speech from the Aylesbury, Blair recognised its power to encapsulate ruined Britain at the end of an era of Conservative government, and to place in those ruins a vision of future 'regeneration'. The estate's environment served as a poignant backdrop to the nascent rhetoric of New Labour: 'I have chosen this housing estate ... for a very simple reason. For 18 years, the poorest people in our country have been forgotten by government ... There will be no forgotten people in the Britain I want to build.'[83] Blair commented on a 'desperate need for urban regeneration', and located this within a generalised imaginary of post-war council estates: 'There are estates where the biggest employer is the drugs industry, where all that is left of the high hopes of the post-war planners is derelict concrete.'[84]

The photoshoot also gave Blair the opportunity to surround himself with young residents while he described, in nineteenth-century terms, an alienated 'underclass', a 'workless class'. The estate and its residents were being used to embody what Power refers to as a 'post-industrial world of incipient ghettos and breakdown'.[85] The geographer, Loretta Lees, has commented on the importance of the council estate as an ideological 'signifier of a spatially concentrated, dysfunctional underclass', and critiqued the way in which the 'regeneration' of the Aylesbury, presented as a set of choices for residents, actually proceeded through a consensus politics that shut down options and neutralised voices of dissent.[86]

Blair toured the Aylesbury accompanied by a uniformed policeman (see Figure 4.4), recalling Victorian philanthropists' slum excursions in which, as Judith Walkowitz has noted in the context of the East End of London, 'to buttress their own "eye of power" ... [they] were frequently accompanied by the state representative of order, a trusty policeman'.[87] In retrospect, one tabloid journalist remarked that Blair's tour was 'reminiscent of the visit of Edward, Prince of Wales, to the Welsh slums in the 30s, when the future king said the immortal words: "Something must be done"'.[88] As a publicity spectacle, the event does indeed appear to be an exaggerated version of the propaganda events associated with the 1930s slum clearance campaigns discussed in Chapter 1.[89] The visit lasted 90 minutes, during which time the prime minister visited a training centre and did a walkabout while being photographed by the press. Journalists made much of reports that the stair-wells – those menacing, liminal spaces referred to in Newman's documentary – had reportedly been perfumed for his visit.[90]

Blair's 1997 speech inevitably intensified media attention. Journalists referred to the estate and the area as 'rundown', 'no-go', 'one of the rough-est in the country', 'the estate from hell' and a 'mighty sprawl'.[91] Generic images of its degraded external fabric and seemingly uncared-for communal areas have been used as illustrations for television news stories on deprivation ever since.[92] The Aylesbury remained a focus for journalists, as a barometer of Blair's and New Labour's efficacy, for the whole period they held power. On visiting, Blair had originally promised to return, but did not do so until 2005: a cause of much criticism. The estate gradually came to be portrayed as a symbol of the failures of Blair and New Labour, as well as the failures of modern architecture and planning.[93]

Figure 4.4: Prime Minister Tony Blair with Police Constable Kevin Holland, Aylesbury Estate, photographed by Stefan Rousseau, 1997.

The label 'sink estate' was used increasingly to refer to the Aylesbury and similarly stigmatised estates and their residents from the late 1990s. During a speech given at a refurbished estate in 1998, Blair referred to 'so-called sink estates', thus distancing himself from the term while reinforcing its associations.[94] More recently, in the tabloid media, it has been used to refer to the Aylesbury's residents themselves: 'a deprived south London sink community plagued by crime'.[95] Along with the conception of an 'underclass', the idea of sink estates connects with the late-nineteenth-century concept of 'residuum' to refer to the poorest of the urban poor, as well as to the actual subsidence of slum housing.[96]

In their study of modernist hygiene aesthetics, and specifically of the sink in Le Corbusier's *Villa Savoye* (1929), architectural historians, Nadir Lahiji and Daniel Friedman, provide a useful definition of 'sink':

'Sink' in the verb form means to go down in stages, to fall gradually or drop to a lower level or condition. A 'sinking feeling' suggests the weight of great disappointment, discouragement, or depression, as though from a loss of prestige or position. 'To sink' means to pass slowly into sleep, despair, lethargy, weakness, or fatigue; or to become dangerously ill, to approach death, to fail or fall. In its transitive construction 'to sink' means to cause to descend beneath a surface or to force into the ground; to reduce in quantity or worth; to debase the nature of something, to degrade it, ruin it, defeat it, or plunge it into destruction. First and second meanings of 'sink' in its noun form alternate from one dictionary to the next, between 'sewer or cesspool' and 'any various basins or receptacles connected with a drain pipe and water supply'; most dictionaries offer a third definition, in which 'sink' refers to a place regarded as wicked, corrupt, or morally filthy.[97]

The use of 'sink' to describe an estate or an economically deprived area is a relatively recent etymological development. In 1972, both the *Daily Mail* and the *Guardian* newspapers referred to 'sink' schools. Slightly later, in 1976, *New Society* defined the term 'sink estate' as: 'the roughest and shabbiest on the books, disproportionately tenanted by families with problems, and despised both by those who live there and the town at large'.[98] In 1979, the term was used in a report on how to manage 'difficult tenants', and it was used without explanation, suggesting that the meaning was widely known by then. It is used in Parliament in 1983.[99] It seems to have been used with increasing frequency in the professional press and academic work in the 1980s and early

1990s, including in Coleman's work, but it is nearly always problematised through the use of inverted commas.

Sink estate spectacle

Geographer Guy Baeten has argued: 'Downtown dirt and danger is a source of bourgeois contempt but, in its neatly polished and commodified version, quickly turns into a source of bourgeois desires.'[100] Citing the examples of music and fashion, Baeten argues that the 'street cultures' of deprived urban areas are often exported in commodified forms for the more affluent. Related to this, art historian, Julian Stallabrass, and art and architecture theorist, Jane Rendell, have commented on the use of the British council estate in late-twentieth-century fine art.[101] However, increasingly in the 1990s and 2000s, sink estate spectacle has become a major trope in mainstream popular culture, having an adverse impact on the understanding and reception of modernist mass housing. Like defensible space, such discourses distract from the specific contexts and histories of particular estates, taking them into a representational realm of abstract generalisation.

In 2008, on their website, Southwark Council's film office marketed the borough's housing estates as potential film locations alongside other landmarks and heritage sites. Across the river, the London Borough of Hackney has made a spectacle of the demolition of a number of stigmatised modernist estates.[102] Southwark has rather capitalised on estates as gritty film locations, and the Aylesbury and Heygate have been used by numerous film, TV and music production companies. These range from their repeated use as a down-at-heel council estates in popular police TV drama *The Bill*; to news features on housing benefits and employment.[103] Often, the sense of degradation has been enhanced, as in 2007, when a company filming an advertisement for a special edition Fiat 500 Viral 'Street Art' car added graffiti and murals to the walls of the slab-blocks in post-production.[104] With cheap and plentiful space available, and in the context of what Stallabrass, refers to in reference to 'Brit Art' of the 1990s as a contemporary 'cultural celebration of urban debasement', it is not surprising that these estates have become so popular as film locations.[105]

In 2006, the Heygate provided the setting for the video that accompanied French house music DJ David Guetta's single, *Love Don't Let Me Go*.[106] Here, the architecture acts as a playground for breakdancing and 'parkour', commonly known as 'free running'. In the video, dancers jump between buildings, over concrete walls, down stairwells and across fences. The estate is distanced from its function as occupied housing, its architectural features simply object for the runners to negotiate with their bodies. In this context we might usefully recall the architectural historian, Iain Borden's, description of early skateboarders' use of found spaces in the city: a practice of 'adopting and exploiting a given physical terrain in order to present skaters with new and distinctive uses other than the original function of that terrain'.[107] It seems as if the estate has been abandoned, transformed into a futuristic wasteland. The dancers advance through a gritty urban obstacle course in which the major sources of criticism of the estate – its hostile scale and materials – are the very conditions that are celebrated.

The founders of parkour, which originated in the suburbs of Paris, compare the participants' movements to those required in an emergency: a controlled and rapid flight along the most direct path possible, as if escaping from, or chasing, someone.[108] In Guetta's video, the estate is an environment of controlled danger, a sublime concrete playscape, where the mental and physical agility of the (male) runners can be tested, eventually winning over the (female) dancers. Here, the estate can be likened to contemporary industrial ruins, understood as environments of 'adventurous play'.[109] By virtue of being off-limits, the 'ghetto' estate is an attractive space of fantasy, representing adventure and freedom.[110] Through association with criminality and violence, and through its rundown appearance, the setting is imbued with a combined sense of danger and excitement. However, unlike industrial ruins, at the time it was made these buildings retained their original function, and were still occupied as social housing.

Another key contemporary representation of the Aylesbury takes the form of an 'ident' (identity) logo film sequence commissioned for Channel 4 for use between its TV programmes.[111] This film forms part of a series commissioned and directed by Channel 4's creative director, Brett Foraker, and advertising company MPC. The idea of these films was to update the 1980s Channel 4 logo, in which coloured blocks flew into position to form the numeral '4'. The series used a number of locations around the world, chosen because they were considered 'visually interesting … either quirky or iconic or both'.[112] One features skyscrapers in Manhattan; another a field of electricity pylons; and another a London street market. In each case the scenes were shot in 'hand held style' and the dislocated sections of the '4' were inserted in post-production through computer generation.[113]

In the Aylesbury Estate ident, the camera moves through a section of the estate, emerging into the light from a dark confined corridor space, past a discarded shopping trolley, and out on to a rubbish-strewn landing. Grubby-looking washing (put there by the filmmakers) hangs across the shadowy balconies, flapping against a grey sky in a brisk wind. The concrete is sodden, drab, graffitied and embellished randomly with a mess of satellite dishes. As the camera turns the corner, pigeons emerge from crevices, and a waste bin comes into view. As if part of the estate's architecture, the '4' of the logo emerges from pre-fabricated rectangular blocks suspended in mid-air; and then its geometric elements float apart again. In this depiction, the Aylesbury appears as a desolate concrete dystopia. It provides a visual confirmation of tabloid journalists' descriptions of a 'ghost town' estate.[114] Though the filmmakers suggest that the Aylesbury was chosen purely because it was 'visually striking', they went to a lot of effort to enhance the impression of degradation.

As a frame for Channel 4's programming, the idents do not communicate a consistent or easily legible identity, except that, through iconic, and visually and spatially impressive, settings they suggest aesthetic and cultural sophistication; and the computer-generated imagery of the logo in each case demonstrates technical virtuosity.[115] As a counterpoint to other idents featuring hi-tech commercial architecture, the run-down Aylesbury communicates a sense of 'ghetto chic': the ultimate edgy urban environment, enjoyed from a safe and mediated distance. It is not entirely clear how Channel 4 wished their viewers to interpret these images of the estate. Viewer responses were reportedly split between those who praised the film, those who complained that it was 'depressing' and were unhappy about having to see the dirty laundry and pigeons featuring in it, and those who thought it was offensive to use recognisable images of a still-occupied and blighted estate.[116]

In response to complaints, Southwark have now introduced regulations for filming, and the residents of the Aylesbury Estate have mobilised themselves to ban the filming they once encouraged in order to attract funding for community activities. In this context, Jean Bartlett, chair of the residents' and tenants' association, comments that she cringes every time she sees the Channel 4 logo.[117]

Endorsed by the local authority that owns and manages the estates and is responsible for their regeneration, the gritty realist depictions of the Aylesbury and Heygate distance us from the contexts that have shaped their production, and the experiences and struggles of their residents.[118] Within this recent sink estate spectacle, certain consistent motifs that have been present since their completion (and even prior to this) have been exaggerated. When we examine the uses of the estates in architectural and political discourses we see that these representations of decline are far from neutral; rather, they result from specific ideological positions on the provision of housing, treatment of the poor and architectural modernism. They also conceal, rather than clarify, the important factors underlying the estates' material decline.

For Newman, and the makers of *Horizon*, the estate embodied a repugnant paternalism, and a dystopian vision of future social breakdown and violent crime. For Tony Blair and New Labour, the architecture and residents acted as an emblem of post-industrial social deterioration under the Conservative government, while justifying an entrepreneurial approach to urban regeneration. For Guetta and Channel 4, the estates' architecture has become a futuristic wasteland, an animated ruin in which the textures of urban degradation and the hostile concrete forms of slab-blocks are a pleasure ground and spectacle. Misrepresenting reality, negative imaginaries of decline have also caused paralysis about how to improve these environments, and have contributed to an unhelpful polarisation of debate.

There is something to be said for reclaiming post-war housing, even in ruins, as a symbol of collective social ambition, as the architectural critic, Owen Hatherley, has recently suggested (see quote at head of this chapter, p. 77).[119] In the Aylesbury's case, many of the problems can be attributed to original cutbacks and compromises, complex costing models, inexperience in the use of system building, over-ambitious scale, poor communication between the architects and housing offices, and a lack of sustained investment and maintenance. The Heygate, by contrast, is of a higher quality and more coherent as a scheme. At a time of acute shortage of affordable housing, with changes to housing benefit that will force those on low incomes towards the periphery of the city, we have to question Southwark's motives in condemning the Heygate to demolition, and then leaving it near-empty for many years.

At the time of writing, the Aylesbury's seemingly perpetual regeneration is once again paused because of public spending cuts, announced in 2010, that leave Southwark Council seeking a development partner. Reflection on the longer-term history of the estate emphasises the powerful distorting effects that negative imaginaries of decline have had on public debates about its future. Perhaps what really underlies the drive to tear down these buildings now is not the desire to eliminate poverty but the wish to eliminate its visibility, as the lowest income groups, excluded from so-called 'affordable' housing, rent privately from a new generation of slum landlords on the margins of the city. In many ways, conditions on this estate have fallen short of the political and architectural ideals that drove the original design. However, instead of providing remedies, successive governments and policy changes have hindered rather than helped the situation. The latest Private Finance Initiative (PFI) approach has been discredited by experts on both the left and the right.[120] Perhaps it is now time for more radical alternatives, and a more democratic and incremental approach, responsive to residents and the existing built environment, and less vulnerable to short-term ideological and economic shifts.

5

CRISIS AND CREATIVITY

You can't come across a site that is more ridden with all the problems
of the inner city than King's Cross. It's a deprived area. It's a wasteland,
close to the heart of the city. All those sidings, and a big question mark.
Dereliction. An opportunity, an incredible opportunity, but a difficult one.

Norman Foster (1992)[1]

The last thing we want is for King's Cross to become an antiseptic,
Disneyfied 'anywhere'. The urban grittiness of the area should be
retained … You have to give room for a sense of place to develop. Saying
2 + 2 + 2 = 6 just doesn't work. The right feel will develop over time and
the right place for niche venues will then be realised.

Robert Evans, Argent Group (2008)[2]

Since its urbanisation in the 1830s, and in its previous incarnation as 'Battle
Bridge', debates about King's Cross have been imbued with a feeling of both
decline and potential.[3] It has often been portrayed as a dissonant locale, partly
through an association with the 'low'-grade activities and workers it has
accommodated; partly through its nature as a busy rail terminus and intersection; and partly through the massive social and physical ruptures in its fabric
brought about through industry, and with the development and operations of
the canals, gasworks and railways. Those disruptions recently resonated within
the large-scale works associated with the new Channel Tunnel Rail Link at St
Pancras, and the redevelopment of 'King's Cross Central' – a triangular area
of 27 hectares of railway lands north of King's Cross and St Pancras stations.
As with the Aylesbury and Heygate Estates (see Chapter 4), this process of
reconfiguration has featured a prominent and multi-faceted discourse of
blight, elaborated through the statements of built environment professionals,
politicians, the media and in popular culture. Here, we shall first consider

the historical background to the de-industrialisation of King's Cross, and the narratives of blight and regeneration that circulated in the late 1980s around the time of the 1987 King's Cross underground station fire. We shall build on existing academic accounts by engaging with various visual sources and other cultural artefacts from that period. Next, we shall focus on the intensification of efforts to 'clean up' King's Cross in the 1990s and 2000s, concluding with an analysis of the Almeida at King's Cross, a temporary theatre project partly-funded through central government regeneration funds.

In his survey of London history, Robert Gray notes the effects of the mid-nineteenth-century railway development on the area:

> North of King's Cross, St Pancras and Euston [stations] ... the railways created the wasteland which separates the respectable districts of Regent's Park and Islington, while even Bloomsbury, to the south of these termini, declined in reputation as a result of their presence.[4]

In this account, even during its most functional era, the land north of King's Cross and St Pancras stations became understood as a 'wasteland' as a result of the railway boom. The economic historian, Gareth Stedman-Jones, also details the intense demolitions associated with railway construction in the 1860s and 1870s in inner London.[5] Such wholesale clearances had inevitable social effects, not least the worsening of overcrowding in neighbouring housing. The railways that cut through the city from King's Cross in the mid-nineteenth century also contributed to the east/west social divide in the city as a whole.[6]

If the mid-nineteenth century was a defining moment, so too was the mid-twentieth, as the status of the 'wasteland' and infrastructural spaces in King's Cross, so vital to the Victorian and early-twentieth-century city, changed between the 1950s and the 1970s in response to the decline of the industries they supported. An aerial photograph of the railway lands, taken from a light aircraft by Aerofilms surveyors in September 1963, captures King's Cross as a working landscape (see Figure 5.1). It is covered in a dense web of railway tracks, roads and canals, punctuated by goods sheds, rolling stock, water towers, coal drops, signal points and other industrial structures. The image makes sense of what must have been a dauntingly complex environment on the ground. Yet by the time it was taken, industrial decline was already under way, spurred by factors such as the shift from canal to road transport, and the *Clean Air Act* (1956), which reduced demand for the coal-based freight industries.[7] On a closer inspection, it is apparent that this aerial view has captured a landscape in the throes of a transition, between the obsolete age of steam, and the newer technologies run on diesel and electricity. The building known as the 'Top Shed' – the most northerly shed, for the older steam engines – lies empty, while the newer diesel trains occupy the larger, modern sheds. Here is London caught in the process of restructuring, with a sense of King's Cross as a place particularly vulnerable to transformations brought about through technological shifts.

Opened as engine stables in 1850, and closed as a steam shed in 1963 – at around the time that the aerial photograph was taken – the life of the Top Shed spanned a century of industry. Evoking the noisy, unpleasantly hot and polluted atmosphere of the railway lands on its closure, the shed master commented that, in spite of nostalgia for the steam age:

the end was inevitable. People generally were not prepared to accept the dirt, grime and smoke associated with steam traction and there were many menial

Figure 5.1: *King's Cross from the air, 1963, photographed by Simmons Aerofilms from a light aircraft.*

unpleasant tasks which had to be carried out in primitive conditions at depots which few men really wanted to do.[8]

This aversion to grime and smoke should be understood against the backdrop of the deadly London smogs of 1952 and 1962. Londoners became acutely aware of the dangers of dirty working conditions, and were reluctant to suffer them much longer.[9]

In line with the general decline of industry in London, between the 1960s and the 1990s the landscape of the railway lands changed remarkably in economic, functional and social character. Describing London in 1977, the architectural historian, Joe Kerr, writes of 'strange pockets of silence and stillness, the spaces vacated by unwanted trades and industries ... contributing to the general atmosphere of slow decline that pervades so much of the metropolis'.[10] In King's Cross, this general decline was concentrated, just as it was in the Docklands. Markets and goods depots closed, and were either demolished, abandoned or turned over to new, low-grade uses. New council housing estates were built on the western and northern parts of the railway lands, but many of these soon fell into disrepair. By the 1980s, the area had also gained a reputation as a socially blighted place, associated with street prostitution and drug-dealing. In the mid-1980s there was already a national public debate about the need for investment, and a call for an intensive social and physical 'clean up' campaign.[11]

With a greatly expanded parliamentary majority following the general election of 1983, in her second term Margaret Thatcher had the mandate she needed to implement her government's privatisation agenda. This resulted in the gradual selling off of public utilities and infrastructure, including land owned by British Rail, which was not itself to be privatised until 1993.[12] In King's Cross, the Greater London Council (GLC) had produced a draft plan for the area north of King's Cross and St Pancras stations, but this went no further because the GLC was disestablished in 1986, leaving London with no central governing body.

In 1987, another fascinating documentary photograph of the railway lands was taken, this time as part of a series commissioned by the British Rail Property Board (BRPB), the arm of British Rail responsible for its land (see Figure 5.2).[13] The image is one of an industrial wasteland, left to ruin. Taken on an overcast day, the photograph shows the area as a derelict landscape, where crumbling industrial structures lay prone to rust and weeds. The foreground is occupied by a sodden earth track. The image centres on a brick chimney, teetering precariously to the right of the frame. Broken fragments of timber and masonry rubble, edging a path, suggest a long-term piling up of detritus: an archaeological site in the making. This and a number of similar images were displayed at a press conference during which the Board invited bids for the sale of the railway lands. Later that same year, a House of Lords Committee made a surprise announcement that King's Cross was the ideal terminus for the Channel Tunnel Rail Link (at this time the Committee favoured King's Cross, rather than neighbouring St Pancras, for this purpose).[14]

The photograph and the series it formed part of communicated the idea of an 'anxious landscape' in the terms described by the architectural and engineering historian, Antoine Picon: an unsettling, technologically saturated environment composed of degraded and abandoned buildings, obsolete industrial leftovers and disjointed infrastructure, normally found on the fringes of the 'post-industrial' city. Here, relationships between the city and nature take on paramount importance: 'these are places where nature seems to have obliterated itself or at least yielded to man-made artifacts'.[15] Such environments are disturbing because they are not landscapes understood as 'natural',

Figure 5.2: King's Cross Railwaylands, 1987, photographed by British Rail Property Board.

unspoilt and restorative. They are, rather, tainted and anxiety-inducing polluted peripheries, which require new conceptual frames and vocabularies, or the reworking of aesthetic categories used in landscape interpretation, in their analysis.

Connecting with Picon's conception of anxious landscapes and contemporary ruins, the geographer, Tim Edensor, has examined industrial ruins in the north of England and Scotland against the socio-economic and political context of de-industrialisation in the UK.[16] In this he observes that ruins are an inevitable, proliferating, part of capitalism's intensifying processes of creative destruction. Yet, rather than being problematic, Edensor asserts that such spaces constitute an alternative to over-coded urban forms, fostering creativity.[17]

For British Rail, under government pressure to operate as a commercial enterprise in the lead-up to its eventual privatisation, however, the only creative opportunity seen in the industrial ruins of King's Cross comprised economic potential. The scene of the decaying railway lands and goods yards made clear the shift of industry away from the ring of areas that until the 1950s had encircled central London. Yet it also projected the promise of a new phase of capital production at a time when commercially driven architecture and speculative office development were booming. At the press conference, the photographs of ruined structures and empty, waterlogged land framed a larger aerial view of the railway lands encircled with a thick red line – always a suspect graphic technique – demarcating the territory to be flattened as if it were a piece of jigsaw, ready simply to be lifted out and replaced.

In 1988, redevelopment proposals were put forward by the London Regeneration Consortium (LRC), a partnership between the National Freight Corporation and developers, Stanhope Rosehaugh, with Norman Foster and his practice, as the architects responsible for the master-planning of the site. Confident that the boom would continue, the scheme was dominated by office space (700,000 m²).

Working in the late 1980s and 1990s, academics, activists and community members responded to this threat of King's Cross being developed using a similar model to the 'enterprise zone' of the London Docklands. They formed the King's Cross Railway Lands Group to challenge the proposals, and later produced their own alternative vision, *Towards a Peoples' Plan* (1990). These campaigners continue their work within the ongoing King's Cross regeneration at the time of writing, and have been celebrated for their impact in encouraging a better development than would otherwise have been realised.[18]

For them, it was crucial to question the definition of the area as empty and in need of 'renewal'. For many living and working in King's Cross, its portrayal as a place of extreme blight contradicted their own views and feelings about the place.[19] To counter the negative discourses that accompanied the redevelopment proposals, they pointed out that the area was not derelict but had a large residential population, and affordable space for commercial and cultural uses, arguing that such neighbourhoods are essential.[20] Plentiful and informal space, low rents, cheap land, low property values and good accessibility had resulted in a diverse community, and a range of important small-scale, socially-oriented institutions, including charities, trade unions and civil rights organisations. The campaigners countered one perception of the area as an unproductive 'wasteland' with a more positive one, of the railway lands as a space of radical politics, leisure and creativity.[21] Yet the idea of King's Cross as a place of community and cultural activity was ignored by the developers.[22]

The case of Camley Street Nature Reserve provides a notable contrast to the official regeneration narrative emerging in late 1980s King's Cross.[23] Next to the area's iconic gasholders, this GLC-owned site had been used to store coal transported along the Regent's Canal. By the 1960s, however, these had been replaced by a municipal dump. In the mid-1980s, as more and more plants, animals and insects appeared, local residents noticed the formation of a spontaneous urban park, and nurtured it into a thriving nature reserve. Camley Street Wildlife Trust opened to the public in 1985. The site became the subject of a campaign by local people to protect it as a nature reserve in the face of redevelopment. The presence of Camley Street shows how simplistic King's Cross' reputation as a 'wasteland' was. The nature reserve would not exist except for a strong and mobilised residential population with a collective sense of imagination and responsibility in reconfiguring the industrial landscape. Their achievement brought about a creative new use for a contaminated site that was valuable for reasons other than real estate: an urban arcadia that emerged as the result of a community project on land heavily polluted by industry. Bob Catterall, editor of CITY: Analysis of Urban Theory, Culture, Policy, Action – a journal that has provided an important focus for critical commentary on the regeneration of King's Cross since its original foundation as Regenerating Cities in 1992 – has detailed the struggle that brought the reserve into being and saved it from redevelopment.[24] Interestingly, the main developers in the ongoing regeneration, Argent, now promote it as an attraction.[25]

Blight in urban culture

Contemporary with British Rail's photographs, and with the opening of the Camley Street Nature Reserve, Neil Jordan's film noir, *Mona Lisa* (1986), depicted the area as a red-light zone, and the locus of a dangerous criminal underworld (see Plate 7).[26] In the film's portrayal of the area, through a car windscreen, from the perspective of a male driver, we see smoky night scenes of a bridge behind a station, busy with streetwalkers and kerb crawlers, and identified in the dialogue as King's Cross.[27] The film returns to this space, and the haunting, murmuring figures that occupy it, several times. This is presumably meant to be Goods Way, described as 'a bleak road behind the main line station bordered by gas-holders and railway lines and frequented by prostitutes'.[28] This street behind King's Cross and St Pancras stations runs east–west across the railway lands, and forms one of the boundaries of Camley Street nature reserve. It became notorious for kerb crawling in the 1980s and 1990s following the displacement of sex workers from residential locations in King's Cross.[29]

Cultural theorist, Lola Young, has argued that 'the [film's] scenes in the mythically reconstructed King's Cross with their grotesque population, swirling mists and constant fires are clearly meant to signify some kind of hell'.[30] In the dialogue, the area is referred to as the 'meat-rack', a 'downmarket' red-light zone, contrasted with the more organised brothels of Soho, and with luxury places such as the Ritz Hotel where 'Simone', a high-class call girl, goes to meet her wealthy clients.[31]

The film uses the setting of King's Cross to raise issues of racial and sexual politics: the racist 'George', the white main protagonist, falls in love with Simone, whom Young argues to be an exotic and enigmatic representation of black femininity. In this the director draws on the iconography of King's Cross as a place of ruin and decay. There is a suggestion of a symbiotic relationship between marginalised, abject characters and the semi-ruined urban landscape. King's Cross is presented bleakly, as an oppressive place, a symbol of moral and physical degradation. In spite of their caricatural nature, in 1991 these film scenes were to be referred to in tabloid newspaper accounts of the area.[32] Later still, reports on regeneration plans referred to *Mona Lisa* as the antithesis of what the 'revamped' area would be like.[33]

Contemporary with *Mona Lisa*, the 1987 pop song 'King's Cross', by the dance music duo Pet Shop Boys, also plays on a downbeat imaginary of King's Cross low life.[34] In a later interpretation of the lyrics, songwriter Neil Tennant explained:

King's Cross is the station you come to when you come down to London looking for opportunity from the Northeast, then the most depressed part of England. And there's lots of crime around King's Cross – prostitution, drug addicts, and a lot of tramps come up to you there. I just thought that was a metaphor for Britain – people arriving at this place, waiting for an opportunity that doesn't happen, waiting for the dole queue or some documentation for the NHS. It's about hopes being dashed … it's an angry song about Thatcherism.[35]

The song, described by Tennant as an 'epic nightmare', evokes the social anxiety and the sense of political impotence among the disaffected in Thatcher's Britain.[36] This is expressed spatially and temporally through lyrics that refer to lingering, 'hanging around', 'waiting in a line' and 'walking around the block', all set to a sombre melody.

In the ambiguous narrative a detective hunts a murderer, but is unable to resolve the crime because of the multitude of 'dead and wounded':

Only last night I found myself lost
By the station called King's Cross
Dead and wounded on either side
You know it's only a matter of time

Tennant identifies this image as a reference to the AIDS crisis, media hysteria around which peaked in 1987.

Part of the attraction of King's Cross for the Pet Shop Boys must have been that, as well as its associations with prostitution and the drugs trade, at the time the song was written, like other run-down 'inner-city' areas in the ring of ex-industrial zones around London's West End, the area was a place of gay nightlife and activism.[37] It was the location of late-night gay venues including The Bell, and later Central Station; artists such as Leigh Bowery performed in former industrial warehouses; lesbian, gay, bisexual and transgender (LGBT) activists, and organisations such as the Lesbian and Gay Switchboard and the Camden Lesbian Centre, met in the area and operated from cheaply rented offices. In 1987, the first and only National Black Gay Men's Conference was held in the area – a landmark event.

For their 1989 tour, the Pet Shop Boys commissioned queer filmmaker and activist, Derek Jarman, to direct background projections for their set, including a haunting black and white sequence for 'King's Cross' filmed in the area (see Figure 5.3).[38] It echoes the elegiac atmosphere of the song, and the

Figure 5.3: Derek Jarman, stills from Pet Shop Boys' 'King's Cross', tour video, 1989.

sense of suspension and disorientation.[39] Different scenes are superimposed, distorting time and space through montage. The screen is bleached white, then dark and obscure. Traces leak from one scene to the next. We follow the unpredictable handheld camera as it judders and sways from the iconic mid-nineteenth-century gasworks, enclosed by a barbed-wire fence, through a street filled with market stalls and litter, into the crowded underground foyer, ending on a train leaving London.[40]

The dreamlike portrayal of the gasworks as a brooding presence in the railway lands prefigures Jarman's treatment of industrial forms, ruins and landscapes in the Docklands in *The Last of England* (1988).[41] The sequence is similarly impressionistic rather than having a conventional linear narrative. In contrast with the Docklands, however, King's Cross is presented as a busy, functional part of the city rather than a ruin or wasteland.

In the same year as Jarman's film was projected, Isaac Julien released his meditation on the life of US poet, Langston Hughes, *Looking for Langston* (1989).[42] This film used footage shot on location in St Pancras Chambers, around the iconic gasholders, and in St Pancras Gardens, just north of the station. Although King's Cross was not named in the film, these geographically close sites bind it together.[43] The staircase of the Midland Grand Hotel, then the most high profile of King's Cross' many abandoned railway buildings, is a key setting. Here, as in *Mona Lisa*, King's Cross is an underworld, a landscape in

IN THE NAME OF THE BABE OF BETHLEHEM

WILL

YOU

HELP US TO
RESTORE THE HOMES
WHICH HAVE BEEN
STOLEN BY THE
DEVIL?

Printed at the Pelican Press, 2 Carmelite Street, London, E.C.4

Plate 1: *Sidney Street Estate, St Pancras, View from the Air, 1931, back cover of* House Happenings, *Christmas 1931.*

Plate 2: *Bert Hardy, 'A Ghost Strayed from Old Greece',*
'Life in the Elephant', 1948, Picture Post *collection.*

Plate 3: *Ernö Goldfinger, Alexander Fleming House, Elephant and Castle,* c. *1967.*

Plate 4a: *Elephant and Castle Shopping Centre, artistic impression by A. J. Middleton, 1962.*

Plate 4b: *Willett Group public relations and marketing brochure, Elephant and Castle Shopping Centre, drawing by A. J. Middleton showing the centre as conceived, 1962.*

Plate 5: *Elevated view of the Aylesbury Estate, Walworth, photographed by Mike Seaborne, 1997.*

Looking East along a first floor walkway

Plate 6: *London Borough of Southwark, Department of Architecture and Planning, 'Looking east along a first floor walkway' (left) and 'Arriving by car' (below), concept drawings,* Heygate redevelopment, *1969.*

Arriving by car

Plate 7: Stills from Mona Lisa, *dir. Neil Jordan, 1986, showing a depiction of King's Cross.*

Plate 8: *Haworth Tomkins Architects, The Almeida at King's Cross, temporary theatre 2001 (demolished 2002), external view at night, photographed by Philip Vile, 2001.*

Plate 9: *The Dirty House, photographed by Lyndon Douglas, 2002.*

Plate 10: *Stephen Gill, extract from* Buried *series, 2006.*

which racial and sexual politics are heightened, and black gay desire can be explored. Resonating with Jarman's film, a shot of the gasworks draws on the area's seamy reputation for an edgy nocturnal encounter between two men cruising in Old St Pancras churchyard.[44] Shot at night, in black-and-white 35 millimetre film, the area is presented as a territory of possibility in a wider world of racial and sexual oppression.

As the critic bell hooks argues, the film's aesthetic is one in which 'beauty merges with death and decay, where they seem inseparable'.[45] As a place of prostitution, gay subculture and ruins, the attractions of the semi-derelict King's Cross locations to this endeavour are clear. The film also brings to mind Edensor's understanding of industrial ruins as 'a sort of modern gothic', structures that 'possess the attraction of decay and death ... and the possibilities of confronting that which is repressed'.[46] Rather than a melancholy imaginary of ruination, the urban gothic sensuality in *Looking for Langston* productively uses its settings to critically explore contemporary and historical identity politics.[47]

Deadly dirt

On 18 November 1987 a tragedy occurred that focused national attention on King's Cross, and its problems, as never before (see Figure 5.4). During the evening rush hour, a passenger lit a cigarette as she or he went up the pre-war Piccadilly Line escalator to the station's exit, and the discarded match ignited a fire that would claim 31 lives. One of the victims, 'body 115', a homeless man, was not identified (as Alexander Fallon) until 2003. In the weeks and years after the disaster, the detective work to ascertain the body's identity was frequently covered in the media, and subjected to mawkish tabloid stories.[48] In a recent book retelling the story of Fallon's body, Paul Chambers describes the fire's ignition:

> The burning match landed in a layer of grease, fluff and litter that had built up around the moving chains, cogs and wheels. The detritus was highly flammable and ignition occurred as soon as the match touched it; a small fire was created and it began to spread further along the running track.[49]

In the forensic analyses that followed, the detritus that had collected in the mechanisms of the escalator was shown to be a highly combustible composite of materials and litter including grease, scraps of paper and card, food wrappers, fluff from clothing, human and rodent hair (see Figure 5.5).[50]

Figure 5.4: *View of the scene at King's Cross on the evening of 18 November 1987.*

Rather than a chance event, however, this catastrophe was a dramatic manifestation of the neglect of the public realm, poignantly illustrating the sorry conditions of the publicly owned London Underground system. The station was suffering from staff cuts in the 1980s, which had reduced the capacity to keep its spaces and infrastructures – including the escalator mechanisms – clean and in good working order. The grease and detritus that had gathered under the escalators was highly flammable. Robert Beauregard has argued in his study of urban decline in North American cities that 'technological advances [have] raised the potential for large-scale human catastrophes'.[51] In this case, the location of the disaster in a banal urban space, saturated with somewhat outdated technology, imbued it with an uncanny horror. The event exposed the fragile infrastructural networks beneath the streets of King's Cross – the busiest underground transport intersection in London.

The worldwide news coverage of the disaster made the area notorious as a symbol of blight, under-investment and the failure of governance. Television footage featured disturbing images of the gutted ticket foyer and the station entrances acting as chimneys, smoke belching up from below. Commentaries emphasised the complexity of the area's subterranean layout, and the idea of King's Cross as a disorderly, labyrinthine place was reinforced.[52]

Figure 5.5: *Photograph of King's Cross Underground Station Piccadilly Line escalator mechanism, showing accumulation of grease and detritus on undamaged part of running track of escalator 4.*

Led by Desmond Fennell QC, the inquiry into the cause of the fire provoked intense public scrutiny of the station's layout, materials, climate and airflows, as well as its management, maintenance and cleanliness. The resulting report found that a combination of extreme overcrowding (a problem that had been acknowledged but not addressed prior to the fire), the use of flammable, solvent-based paints, the badly maintained and dirty wooden escalators, and the lack of fire safety training, were all partly responsible, although no one was ever prosecuted.[53] The arrangement of the tunnels had ventilated the fire in such a way as to produce a 'flash over' effect, so that it spread at an alarmingly fast rate, taking firefighters and passengers by surprise.

After this disaster, wide-ranging debates about privatisation, about public safety and state responsibility for urban infrastructure, arose from the specific geography and physicality of the King's Cross Underground station, with forensic attention being paid to the filth that had built up in the escalator mechanism. The report called for the radical modernisation of the station's interchange – a process that took 15 years to fully implement – and legitimised the financing of this by central government.[54] It was not until 1999 that London Underground published its plans to improve safety at King's Cross in response to the Fennell Report of 1988.

The fire occurred at the start of the third term of the Thatcher government, in the final phase of implementation of the free-market agenda that would later be picked up by New Labour under Blair. It continues to have a high profile in debates about safety, risk and state investment in the public realm, and the dangers of dirt, litter and environmental deterioration in transport systems.[55] Ironically, however, in 2002, Deputy Prime Minister John Prescott used the fire as an example of why privatisation was necessary. For Prescott, the event justified the London Underground's transference to ownership and management through a Public–Private Partnership.[56] What the fire should have emphasised more powerfully was the vast amount of effort, co-ordination and ongoing investment required to maintain complex urban infrastructures. It demonstrated that the requirements for a modern, functioning, technologically advanced city sat uneasily with the new project of privatisation and market-driven urban policy being pursued, in which the state was withdrawing from and fragmenting responsibility for the public realm. As urban historian, Rebecca Ross, has argued, the fire contributed to this intensification, and can be linked to a subsequent more systematic policing of 'abject' social groups, such as drug dealers, drug addicts, sex workers, kerb crawlers and homeless people, in the early 1990s.[57]

The 'clean up' campaign

Between 1987 and 1993, debates about the area's blight and 'wasteland' status had become more amplified within the discourses surrounding London Regeneration's Consortium proposals. A widely broadcast television documentary from 1992 charted local responses, resistance and alternatives to the proposed regeneration scheme.[58] The discussion in the documentary conveys the mood of anxiety following the fire. It also shows how architects and developers elaborated the wasteland arguments previously put forward by British Railways, as in the statement by Norman Foster, taken from the documentary and quoted at the head of this chapter (see page 105). As a hi-tech modernist architect/master-planner, Foster's role here was to provide a 'rational' scientific solution to 'all the problems of the inner city' as they were invoked at King's Cross. Yet that phrase, as the documentary suggests, referred not only to the urban environment but to the 'undesirable' people who inhabited the area.[59]

In the early 1990s there was a more intensive policing of these unwelcome social groups.[60] The police established Operation Welwyn, comprising a squad of 24 officers based at Islington Police Station and charged with the specific responsibility for tackling King's Cross 'vice'. The area was established as a temporary 'space of exception', in the terms articulated by the political philosopher Giorgio Agamben, whereby in times of crisis special powers are extended by the state, often becoming permanent.[61] In this example, new policing tactics were deployed, including undercover officers posing as drug users, and secret filming to collect evidence. By 1998, journalists reported that 800 arrests had been made, many of sex workers, and that the number of drug dealers operating in the area had been dramatically reduced.[62] That does not mean, however, that entrenched social problems were dealt with effectively rather that the aim was, as one police officer put it, to make problems 'disappear'.[63] Politicians openly encouraged the displacement of these groups through gentrification, with one local MP noting that the redevelopment would mean that the 'prostitutes and drug dealers will go and that can only be a good thing'.[64]

In spite of the well-publicised and lauded police campaign to 'clean up' the area, if anything, in the late 1990s and early 2000s, accounts became even more sensationalist in their imagery of blight and disorder, partly in justification of the redevelopment proposals.[65] In 1997, Tony Blair described King's Cross as a 'frightening place for people'.[66] With these words he reinforced the area's well-established reputation for prostitution, crime and drug dealing – evoking a simplistic image, and one unhelpful in understanding the bigger picture of what King's Cross had come to represent.

By this time, the landscape of urban regeneration in London as a whole, and in King's Cross itself, had undergone some significant changes. Planning economist and member of the King's Cross Railway Lands Group, Michael Edwards, has provided an excellent account of the complex history of the regeneration during this period, framed within a wider account of local and international urban political economy.[67] For our purposes, we will briefly review just a few of the crucial factors. In 1992, as the London Borough of Camden had been about to approve the London Regeneration Consortium's scheme, it collapsed, because the developers had gone bankrupt. This was in part the result of high interest rates, but also reflected the wider collapse of the office market in London because of over-supply. The Channel Tunnel Rail Link (CTRL) plan had also fallen through because of its cost and opposition from those who lived on the original planned route into King's Cross Station. King's Cross had been allocated £37.5 milliom of public funding in 1996 as part of the 'Single Regeneration Budget'. Then, in 1997, New Labour had come to power with their 'urban renaissance' agenda. In the same year, a new CTRL route to St Pancras was adopted, requiring the extension of St Pancras station, which was subsequently to be designed by Foster and Partners. The Greater London Authority was established in 2000, and developed a commercially oriented neoliberal vision of the area's regeneration that contrasted with the GLC's earlier plan, which had a residential focus. Finally, also in 2000, Argent were appointed by the landowners, London and Continental Railways, as the developers for the main 'King's Cross Central' site, for which Foster had previously developed the LRC plan. Argent's regeneration scheme still proceeds at the time of writing, though at a rate slower than expected because of the financial crisis that began in 2008.

Edwards evaluates the work of the King's Cross Regeneration Partnership positively in terms of the training and employment programmes they set up, but is critical of a disproportionate focus on the reconstruction of the area's image and policing. Hoardings the partnership erected with their own branding in the early 2000s, displaying multi-coloured cartoon images of idyllic

Figure 5.6: *King's Cross Partnership hoardings, King's Cross, 2001.*

parks, happy families, office workers, heritage buildings and CCTV cameras (see Figure 5.6), served both to rebrand and police. The panels invited passers-by to 'take another look' at the changing environment. However, as a micro-design intervention they were also intended to keep drug users and dealers, sex workers and squatters out of the boarded-up shop fronts of the crumbling and derelict Victorian shopping parade they concealed.[68] That the maintenance of these buildings had been neglected within the protracted regeneration process, by the developer P & O Developments, who planned to demolish them, serves to highlight the contradictions of this rebranding exercise.

Red-light drama

In 2001, the Almeida at King's Cross, a temporary theatre designed by a London-based architectural practice, Haworth Tomkins Architects, opened in a disused garage on a side street at the southern end of the Caledonian Road, very close to the King's Cross Partnership's hoardings (Figure 5.7 and

Figure 5.7: The Almeida at King's Cross, temporary theatre, external view of site before conversion, 2001.

Plate 8).[69] This project encapsulates further tensions between the regeneration strategy and the discourses and actions that accompanied it.

The theatre was in operation from 2001 to 2002, having been acquired by the Almeida to use while its base in more salubrious Islington underwent refurbishment, and after that it was demolished to make way for a private residential development. A vast building, but tucked away in the back streets between the Caledonian and Pentonville Roads, it had previously been a car and bus garage. This was run-down, functional, light industrial building stock, worn and shabby, the floors and walls stained by oil and exhaust fumes: a collection of interconnecting makeshift spaces, altered and added to piecemeal since the 1930s. Immediately before the Almeida took possession of the site, the building had acted as an ad hoc shelter for the area's homeless population, and a secluded space to which sex workers could bring clients.[70]

In essence, the Almeida scheme conformed to a classic model of culture-triggered regeneration, where an arts project or cultural building are funded because of the potential they offer for attracting visitors and economic investment to an area.[71] This was the motive underlying the King's Cross Partnership regeneration body's contribution of £250,000 to the total budget of £850,000. What is remarkable, however, is that the architects' design so explicitly reinforced the reputation of King's Cross as a run-down red-light zone. Through the programme, materials and aesthetic, the architects self-consciously emphasised the building's past industrial use and the area's seamy reputation.

The design was understated, and the design process informal, partly improvised on site. Rather than being seen as a hindrance, signs of previous occupation and low-tech industrial activity – dust and dirt, oily walls, worn floors – were sealed in, and deliberately enhanced, for effect.[72] One of the external features that stood out was a layer of turf, laid over the existing pitched and corrugated iron roof, and cladding the walls.[73] At the time, the concept of 'living' walls and roofs, now a cliché of 'sustainable' design, was a novelty. The 'grass' highlighted the temporary nature of the scheme – by the end of the theatre's short lifespan, the turf was dead and brown. Yet it also suggested that the structures had been there for so long they had been reclaimed by nature, like the decaying weed- and moss-covered industrial relics of the King's Cross railway lands nearby.

In their post-rationalisation of both projects, the architects have emphasised the limited budget as the principle reason underlying their aesthetic of urban decline.[74] Yet they also frame their work as a new performative architectural paradigm, drawn from 'the peculiar character of the theatre act'.[75] In King's Cross, as well as architectural references to the 'dirty work' that had taken place in the building, the design calculatedly evoked the image, and experience of visiting a brothel. This analogy played out through materials, lighting and signage strategies, combined with the location of the entrance at the end of a secluded backstreet. This architectural programme required theatregoers to adopt and perform a role. To find the theatre in the first place, just as to visit a brothel, one had to know and navigate the urban environment rather than follow obvious signposting, or the conventional architectural codes associated with the modern bourgeois theatre experience – typified by the neoclassical formalities of the Almeida's early-nineteenth-century theatre in Islington.[76] Only on the final approach would the visitor feel sure they were in the right place, drawn into Omega Street – a dark alley – by an illuminated plastic wall and the building's axial presence (see Plate 8). Located at the end of this backstreet, the main entrance was demarcated by a neon sign reminiscent of a sex shop. Through the plastic wall, theatregoers queuing to enter could glimpse the silhouettes of those already inside. The design, and particularly the entrance approach, revolved around theatregoers' engagement with the imagined – and, according to the theatre's management, sometimes actual – figure of the prostitute, and empathy with a client furtively approaching a brothel.[77] In the architects' photographic representations of the building, the red-light aesthetic was further enhanced through the manipulation of light, contrast and colour saturation, extending the design narrative (Plate 8).

On 1 March 2001, the Almeida King's Cross opened with a newly written version of Frank Wedekind's *Lulu Plays*, written in the 1890s.[78] The main protagonist, Lulu, is a *femme fatale* whose sexuality is defined through her relationship with the cities of Berlin, Paris and London, where she ultimately works as a prostitute in the East End, and is murdered by Jack the Ripper. Encapsulating her own abject status, before her death Lulu declares: 'I've kept my innocence all my life, only to drown in filth!'

Having planned to perform *Lulu* at the Old Vic Theatre in south London, the Almeida decided to move to their temporary accommodation in King's Cross earlier than anticipated, because of the additional resonance the play would have.[79] The move prompted direct associations between the character of Lulu and the female sex workers associated with the area in the late 1980s and 1990s, and suggested symmetries between the Victorian East End and contemporary King's Cross. The stage design by Rob Howell elaborated the design narrative with dirty and damaged glass panels and red lighting to suggest a brothel.[80] Echoing *Mona Lisa*, the staging of *Lulu* therefore consolidated the association of King's Cross with a gendered imaginary of urban disorder, embodied in the figure of the female prostitute working the streets. Theatregoers may have been challenged into more serious reflection on the plight of local sex workers; but instead of benefiting them, this particular example of state investment in regeneration saw them indirectly exploited for entertainment.

As the architectural theorist, Jane Rendell, and geographer, Steve Pile, have observed, as a modern device in nineteenth-century literature, the prostitute, like the *flâneur*, operated to suggest narratives around the metropolis, and to signify the 'unconscious' or 'underground erotic life' of the city.[81] Similarly, writing on the use of streetwalkers in late Victorian literature on urban exploration, cultural historian Judith Walkowitz argues that, 'as symbols of conspicuous display or of lower-class and sexual disorder, [prostitutes] occupied a multivalent symbolic position in this imaginary landscape'.[82] In the context of millennial King's Cross, the figure of the prostitute, and the red-light imaginary of the area, also played an important role, being invoked by the regeneration authorities to legitimise redevelopment, in real estate marketing, and here in a theatre project funded by the state regeneration authority. Interestingly, feminist theorist Elizabeth Wilson concludes her account of order, disorder and city life, *The Sphinx in the City* (1991), with a critique of the impending gentrification of King's Cross that she argued would be a consequence of the London Regeneration Consortium's proposals.[83] Yet, rather than problematising the use of the area's association with prostitution within the redevelopment rhetoric, she reinforces it. Perhaps the reason for her description of King's Cross as 'plagued by prostitution' is to counter a common romanticisation of red-light districts by male scholars in debates about urban order and disorder in the 1990s, within critiques of the perceived 'Disneyfication' of the city in debates about the diminishing value attributed to public space.[84] Yet her own description of 'local eccentrics and leafy squares' sounds quite wistful.

On one level, this temporary project turned 'urban blight into architectural lyricism'.[85] In contrast to the role of hi-tech modern architecture within the King's Cross regeneration, this was an environmentally sustainable context-specific architectural intervention, which made use of the existing built fabric at low cost, turning an industrial space into a cultural facility. However, in doing so it contributed to the gentrification of the area, reinforcing its negative reputation while capitalising on it. This is part of a wider trend: in tension with the policing campaign, as the regeneration has continued, in media discourses the 'edgy' red-light reputation has been used as a selling point – 'inner city chic' – in articles on the area's real estate potential.[86]

In their earliest publications, the appointed developers, Argent, emphasised their intention to deliver a 'mixed use' environment characterised by variation and diversity, but one with a formal logic unlike the 'very fragmented and disconnected' territory that evolved up to the end of the twentieth century.[87] This mixed-use discourse has recently been taken a step further, more read-ily embracing certain aspects of the area's gritty identity, as in the quote by developer Robert Evans at the head of this chapter (page 105 above). This shift responds to earlier criticisms of a development approach that attempted to 'sweep away' the past.[88] Evans seems to be pre-empting further criticisms that the redevelopment equates to a form of sanitisation or 'Disneyfication' – to an anti-urban environment made in some way dysfunctional through the absence of texture. However, such contextualism appears to be skin deep, and recent discourses about the regeneration prize selective heritage over any critical historical understanding of the area's earlier development and recent past. The great irony is that many 'niche venues' of the kind that Evans refers to, such as the area's lively nightclub scene, were being closed even as he made this statement about preserving the area's 'grit'.[89]

Leading a vast market-driven regeneration campaign, the developers of 'King's Cross Central' now present the area to future investors as a 'new piece of city'. The distant industrial past has real estate value as heritage. Yet the more recent and ephemeral history of King's Cross – a contested place, where creativity, charity, clubbing and queer culture appeared in the cracks of the ex-industrial cityscape – has disappeared under pristine developer-owned streets. The work of local campaigners has recently been recognised and celebrated for its positive effect on the environment that is emerging, which includes a university, and features far less office space than originally envisaged, in part because of current economic instability. Yet in the process, and accelerated by state investment, many small businesses, civil society organisations, small-scale cultural industries and members of the residential community have been displaced through rising rents and land values. Can these historical forms of ordinary urban life and creativity be fostered and sustained in the new King's Cross?

6

ORNAMENT FROM GRIME

> Everyone universally finds dirt offensive … but what counts as dirt?
> It depends on the classifications in use … Should I not allow for the
> obsessional artist whose tolerance of disorder is practically complete? His
> studio is chaotic, he sleeps there, urinates in the hand basin or out of the
> window when his passion for his work gives him no time to go to the
> wc. Everything looks wildly disordered, except on his canvas: there alone
> calm and order reign.
>
> Mary Douglas (2002)[1]

'Everyone universally finds dirt offensive.' With these words, Mary Douglas
reiterated her position in the preface to the final edition produced in her life-
time of her seminal text, *Purity and Danger: An Analysis of Pollution and Taboo*.
Although Douglas, perhaps Britain's most prominent twentieth-century social
anthropologist, stood by the definition of 'dirt as matter out of place', on
reflection she conceded that the self-consciously and creatively chaotic space
of the 'obsessional' artist's studio provided a challenge to her thesis.[2] She seems
to have had in mind the classic image of a painter at home in a chaotic studio,
whose production of beautiful works is reliant on the 'mess' of her/his lifestyle
and environment. Think of Francis Bacon, who, when questioned about his
disorderly workspace, declared: 'I feel at home here in this chaos, because
chaos suggests images to me … I think it may act unconsciously as a spur to
create order.'[3] Yet Bacon's taste for the disorderly went beyond the space of
his studio and unconventional life to challenge hegemonic notions of beauty
and ugliness themselves through the anxious aesthetics of his paintings of
contorted figures and faces. His studio was not just disorderly *per se*, but deliberately staged as such.[4] In this sense, do not the context, method and product
of his work all subvert Douglas' neat and categorical argument? Douglas'
theory has frequently been deployed in relation to art, architecture and other

spatial disciplines.[5] Moving on from her structuralist account, however, in the context of the late-modern city there is a need to explore the tensions between what sociologist, Carol Wolkowitz, terms 'postmodern/poststructural dirt … purified through abstraction' and 'the idea of "real" dirt'.[6] Furthermore, we have also seen that, in London, as elsewhere, the material and imaginary production of dirt and degradation are not 'out of place', but rather fundamental to the processes of capitalist urbanisation.

After the incorporation by modern artists of rubbish into their work as a challenge to the authority of the art object, as in the use of collage and *objets trouvés*, or as an index of the everyday, as with Marcel Duchamp's *Fountain* (1917), from the 1960s onwards there was an increasingly widespread and self-conscious exploration of the abject, waste, rubbish and ruin in Anglo-American art.[7] An elaborate 'aesthetic of recycling' also emerged, as discussed by visual culture and architectural theorist Giuliana Bruno.[8] Although useful in exploring the modernist aesthetics of hygiene and order, in the context of late-modern art and architecture, where dirt often features and can be simultaneously celebrated, critiqued and reviled, the arguments of *Purity and Danger* come to appear too rigid and self-contradictory. On the one hand, we are told that dirt is a culturally, historically and geographically specific classification, a subjective rather than an absolute value, while, on the other hand, it is said to be consistent with and equivalent to disorder across time and space, and consistently offensive.[9]

In this chapter we shall explore the 'Dirty House' (2001–2), designed by David Adjaye (Adjaye Associates) for the British artists Tim Noble and Sue Webster (see Figures 6.1, 6.2 and Plate 9). This is an example that illuminates contemporary aesthetic interests in urban degradation across architecture, art and urbanism. First, Adjaye's work will be introduced in relation to the so-called 'Gritty Brit' architects with whom he has been associated – London-based practices whose recent work focuses mainly on the East End of the capital. This leads into a discussion of the engagement of contemporary London architects with urban grime and decay, and their use of material and aesthetic strategies in eliminating or working with it. We will explore the architectural 'aesthetic of recycling', and the role of architects, such as Adjaye, in processes of cleansing and recycling in ex-industrial areas. This chapter develops from themes suggested in existing writing on Adjaye's work, attempting to tease apart some of the ideas about urban 'grit', 'dirtiness' and 'recycling' that have been evoked, and sometimes conflated confusingly, in accounts such as the exhibition *Gritty Brits: New London Architecture* (2007).[10] This exhibition,

Figure 6.1: *The Dirty House, general view of the exterior, 2007.*

and the catalogue published simultaneously with essays by the writer Iain Sinclair and curator Raymund Ryan, featured Adjaye as one of the main protagonists, and the Dirty House as a key building.[11]

Structuring an analysis of the house around its features, we can place it in a number of overlapping contexts: Adjaye's *oeuvre*, and that of the Gritty Brit architects; the site and the original factory building from which it is converted; the identities and work of the artists; and, beyond this, within precedents in architectural design and urban development. Critical frameworks suggesting different readings of the House are provided by a number of theorists from outside of the discipline of architecture, such as Bruno (the 'aesthetic of recycling'), Hal Foster ('grunge aesthetics'), Julian Stallabrass (the 'urban pastoral') and Sharon Zukin ('loft living').[12]

Creative recycling in a 'messed up' city

How have architectural critics so far conceived of Adjaye's work in relation to ideas about urban dirt and degradation, and processes of recycling, and how does he conceive of these relationships himself? For evidence of this, let us first explore some examples of documentation and criticism of the practice's output, such as the *Gritty Brits* (2007) show and catalogue, and the two monographs that have thus far appeared on the practice, before turning specifically to the Dirty House and its critical reception.[13]

Adjaye, whose high-profile work has contributed prominently to the reshaping of London's former industrial landscapes as territories of cultural production, first became known for a number of high-specification luxury houses for wealthy clients working in 'creative industries'. These houses are located in the ring of former manufacturing areas circling central London, such as King's Cross (Lost House, 2002–4), Whitechapel (Elektra House, 1998–2000) and Shoreditch (Dirty House, 2001–2). The houses reconfig-ure light industrial spaces such as warehouses, yards and small factories.[14] More recently, the practice has won a number of larger and more complex commissions for public buildings in the UK and abroad, such as the Nobel Peace Centre in Norway (2002–5), and education centres, such as the Poplar (2001–4) and Whitechapel (2001–5) Ideas Stores in east London.[15] Adjaye's houses have met with a mixed reception.[16] The intention here is to develop an extended analysis that is interdisciplinary in mode. Such an approach is necessitated by the close relationship of Adjaye's work to fine art practice, and of the Dirty House to the artists it was built for and their work; and, at a broader level, by the nature of 'urban degradation' as a multi-disciplinary thematic territory.[17]

As with Bacon's chaotic studio, Adjaye's champions have implied that his creativity is reliant on a disorderly context of production. In the 2000s, he was argued to be 'churning out stunning buildings from his studio in a run-down street',[18] with the creative act of production suggested to have been reliant in some unspecified way on the run-down street. The studio, at that time, was located in Hoxton, a former light manufacturing district which, after industrial production ceased in the 1980s, became the subject of artist-led gentrification in the 1990s; and where new art galleries now sit adjacent to degraded local authority housing and derelict industrial buildings.[19] Visiting the practice in its Hoxton studio in the mid-2000s, the street did not seem 'run-down' (this seems like the value judgment of a middle-class critic), but certainly Adjaye had chosen to locate in a predominantly working-class residential area, rather than in a 'trendier' part of the neighbourhood with a denser concentration of creative industries; and had situated the office in a building converted from industrial use.[20]

That Adjaye has embraced an image of himself that locates his original-ity in 'recycling' is highlighted in the alliterated subtitle of Peter Allison's monograph *David Adjaye Houses: Recycling, Reconfiguring, Rebuilding* (2005), a book authorised by the practice as the official documentation of its residential work, and for which they retain the copyright. In this book, Allison compares Adjaye's houses to ruins;[21] and cultural theorist, Stuart Hall, likens the Elektra and Dirty houses to 'the mud dwelling and the Berber house', remarking that

> his forms appear completely in place in the mixed environments of the contemporary city, with its dirt and grime, its secluded enclaves, boarded-up frontages and dangerous corners, its reconditioned warehouses, its parking lots, its cafés, store fronts and show rooms. His buildings fit into the shifting landscape of reconfigured and regenerated urban space without succumbing to it.[22]

What is suggested here is that, rather than imposing themselves upon or sanitising a dirty and dilapidated urban environment, Adjaye's buildings creatively and sensitively echo pre-existing forms and material qualities. The dirt, grime, enclaves, boarded-up frontages, dangerous corners and so on are naturalised, accepted as inevitable and unproblematic.

From his involvement with the *Gritty Brits* show, it seems that, at the time, Adjaye was keen to cultivate an image of himself as a 'gritty' architect. What is meant by 'grittiness' in this context? 'Grit' here has multiple meanings, referring at the same time to the economically and physically run-down, ex-industrial, environments in which these architects operate in (mainly east) London, to the physical nature and durability of the materials they use, and to a quality of persistence attributed to them (and, within British nationalist discourses, to 'Britishness' generally).[23] In the catalogue to the show, Raymund Ryan suggests a link between the quality of 'grittiness' and the 'mixed environments of the contemporary city': 'A city that is multicultural and organic, that can be messy, that is not without friction, that mixes preconceptions of high and low art. This is the new London context in which the architects here characterised as Gritty Brits operate.'[24] The Gritty Brit's architectural forms are seen to be appropriate to London's 'messy' context. 'How do you build in the oddly shaped sites, discarded warehouses and multi-ethnic communities nearby?', the show catalogue's author asks. In generic descriptions of contemporary urban 'mess', distinctions between the attributes of different areas, environments, communities and material states become unhelpfully conflated, and disconnected from the political, economic and other locally specific forces that structure and produce them.

In comments relating to his recent public buildings, such as the Whitechapel Ideas Store, Adjaye celebrates informal approaches to space and architectural typology in projects that attempt to insert new buildings sensitively into pre-existing urban contexts in London, without imposing an incongruous sense of order or cleanliness, and in ways that accept the 'contaminations' of informal and mixed uses. The implication of this approach is that it befits the rich diversity – demographic, functional, spatial, aesthetic – constituting the urban mixture of contemporary London, and in particular of the multicultural East End. As curator of *Gritty Brits*, Ryan, and the exhibition itself, make the case that the virtue of these architects is located in their approach to the organic mess of London – 'formal experimentation with gritty urban realism' on a local scale, in contrast with modernism's 'rational' and sanitising scheme to reorder the city.[25] The inside front and back covers of the exhibition catalogue have a full-page graphic showing an image of a 'butterfly bush' (*Buddleja*), a plant which we are told 'tolerates urban pollution and grows readily in inhospitable sites', drawing an analogy between the plant and the architecture on show.

The Gritty Brits

The *Gritty Brits* catalogue aligns its contributors' work with the New Brutalists but on what grounds?[26] The reasons given for this association are a common 'critical approach' to pre-existing urban contexts, the ability to fuse the principles of architectural modernism with an awareness of the everyday, and modern construction methods with consumer-focused art.[27] This alignment is interesting for two reasons. First, Adjaye, as with the New Brutalists, and particularly Alison and Peter Smithson, has forged his architectural identity in relation to fine art practice, and through collaborations with artists and artist-clients. In contemporary British architecture, this approach to architectural design positions itself as a reaction to hi-tech modernism, in which buildings are viewed primarily as products and the rational outcome of scientific and technological processes. Second, there is a similarity between the New Brutalists and the Gritty Brits in terms of their approach to materials. The New Brutalists emphasise the 'honest' qualities of 'raw' exposed materials and structures. Reyner Banham refers to this as the 'Valuation of materials for their inherent "as found" qualities'.[28] These architects and their collaborators are also suggested to draw a correlation between 'as found' materials and an aesthetic approach that is authentic or honest.

Adjaye's approach to architectural design certainly finds a precedent in the Smithsons' work, and particularly in exhibitions where they collaborated with contemporary artists such as *Parallel of Life and Art* (1953) and the installation 'Patio and Pavilion', which formed part of the exhibition *This is Tomorrow* (1956).[29] In these, the artists' and architects' interests in incorporating found and recycled objects, 'throwaway' images and industrial debris, low-grade materials and imperfect, craggy surfaces are clearly demonstrated. These approaches to materials, and the New Brutalists' general preoccupations as outlined by Victoria Walsh, with material and metaphorical ruins, decay and putrefaction and, conversely, regeneration and rebirth, resonate strikingly with Noble and Webster and Adjaye's work, particularly in the case of the Dirty House.[30]

Art from rubbish

Noble and Webster's main body of sculptural work uses recycled rubbish, of various provenances, as its primary material. Their first solo exhibition was entitled *British Rubbish* (1996).[31] The artists have focused their work on the interrelated themes of rubbish, waste and recycling in relation to their own identities. They have developed what has been termed an 'anti-aesthetic' through shadow sculptures formed by projections of light cast through assemblages of base materials, brought into alignment with base language and concepts through ironic titles, and in other works through the direct incorporation of text. The dirt and rubbish with which they work varies, from domestic refuse, to rubbish collected from the streets near to the studio, to mummified animal carcasses and taxidermy mannequins, to filthy lucre itself in the form of dollar bills. As one commentator has written: 'the duo have little regard for conventional notions of good taste, mining the aesthetics of the fairground tattoo and the Las Vegas light show, the shopping mall and the rubbish dump'.[32]

Another observer highlights their use of 'tacky aesthetics and low grade materials'.[33] In 'Dirty White Trash With Gulls' (1998), the artists arranged a pile of rubbish in the gallery space, with two taxidermy seagull models positioned as if scavenging at its base. A spotlight focused on the rubbish threw a silhouetted profile on the gallery wall, showing the two artists sitting back-to-back, one drinking a glass of wine, the other smoking: consuming, and polluting their bodies with addictive toxins. The work is abject in that someone else's domestic rubbish both repels and fascinates us, inviting us to construct a narrative about the identities of those who produced it. The viewer is teased to develop this narrative through the apparently physical, but ultimately immaterial, trace of the waste-producers – themselves – in silhouetted form. The meaning of this and similar works is ambiguous. As a whole, the body of work these artists have produced can be read variously as a critique of consumerism; a politically neutral comment on the formation of identity, or the artists' identities, in relation to commodities and their waste products; or as a celebration of consumer capitalism and kitsch – 'bad taste' aesthetics.

When they commissioned their house, Noble and Webster had an identifiable aesthetic and thematic agenda and already knew Adjaye well, and it is clear that they were proactive in shaping the design of the Dirty House. Furthermore, as residents who both work and live in the building, they have continued to mould it to their vision since occupying it. That vision was of a bespoke house/studio that would relate to, and therefore extend, the ideas in their work.[34] Making the house, like making the work, Noble and Webster describe as an 'organic' process, with many aspects of the design only being established once they were occupying the building. The name 'Dirty House' is itself derived from a meeting with Adjaye where they graffitied a model of the proposed building, making it 'dirty'.

Another sculpture by Noble and Webster, 'Falling Apart' (2001), also suggests the close relationship the artists conceived between the house and their work. Again comprised of rubbish, here the objects are an assemblage of broken personal items damaged during fights between them in the period January to March 2001, while the house was under construction. When light is projected through it, two silhouettes of the artists' heads appear on the wall. However, while recognisable as the artists, the two profiles are disturbingly fragmented, monstrous, as though their flesh were corroding. The piece records the time when the artists occupied the building before completion, producing artwork as the design and construction proceeded in order to pay for its conversion, while effectively living in a construction site. The viewer is confronted with an image of the artists' fractured subjectivities, their identities 'falling apart' in direct proportion to the coming together of their new home and studio. When we know the context in which the work was produced, it reinforces the strong presence of the artists' voices in shaping the building.

Like 'Dirty White Trash With Gulls', we can read this work on a number of levels. The piece is typical of Noble and Webster in having simultaneously a playful, infantile quality; darker, more 'adult' psychological undertones; and a level on which it operates to cement a carefully constructed image of the artists' creative identities. We imagine the events that produced this collection of broken objects and the smashed selves they represent through their meticulous arrangement. The work reinforces an image of the artists as melodramatic, highly sensitive and volatile individuals, and links this profile of disorderliness to the production of their work and the Dirty House. In *Wasted Youth* (2006), a monograph on their work, the art writer Jeffrey Deitch likens *Falling Apart* to a Bacon portrait, and the Dirty House to Bacon's studio – a comparison to which we shall return.[35]

The Dirty House and its representation

The Dirty House, for most people, exists only in elevation, by turns blank and intriguing, anonymous and yet highly idiosyncratic, plain and subtly decorative, unpretentious and yet somehow also ostentatious (see Figure 6.2). Three storeys can be read in its main façades on to Chance and Whitby Streets. Unprepossessing cobbled streets in east London just north of the City of London financial district, emphatically ordinary, they are populated mainly by small-scale brick warehouses, historically used for goods such as clothing and furniture. At the ground floor level, the outline of a front door can be traced, but, flush with the wall, it is barely delineated, matching the greyness and rough texture of the wall's coating. It is read as an industrial rather than a domestic entrance. Each façade is punctuated by four bays. On the Whitby Street elevation there is a wider service door, as if to a garage, and three square window 'openings'. At this ground level what are read as openings are, in fact, 'closings' – not just blocked, but reversed, throwing an image back out through the mirrors that cover them. This feature is decorative but understated, embellishing and simultaneously distracting from the façades. At the next level it is possible to make out that the square openings are deep window reveals, although blinds obscure the interior from view. The artists liken these recesses to eye sockets in a skull.[36] The main volume, an impressive mass highlighted by the depth of the recesses, is uniform in colour, grey with a subtle purple glow in certain lights. The surface level is consistent too. The dark paintwork provides consistency across the exterior walls. Yet closer examination reveals different strata of building activity from storey to storey, marked out by ridges, like varicose veins, in the brickwork. On the west elevation, there is a slight projection from what is otherwise legible as a rectangular plan, and this projection leads in, apparently, to a backyard. A graffitied wall and gate suggest that only a banal and uncared for space lies behind.

Looking up, which one is not particularly invited to do, it is clearer that these everyday elevations conceal something more surprising, a recent spurt of growth. At the top level, also interrupted by variously shaped geometric openings, including an arrow slit window, a floating white concrete structure can be seen to cantilever out from the walls and from an area glazed with tinted green glass. Strangely slick, what can be glimpsed of this floor is read not as an addition so much as the original building having been opened up, its lid taken off to reveal a glass pavilion, light in both senses of the word, at odds with the weighty mass of the structure below. The Dirty House is a conversion of a 1930s furniture factory, but 'conversion' here should not be taken for granted. The artist-clients and their architect did not, in this case, decide to recycle the existing industrial building based on preservationist ethics or economic pragmatism. In fact, the tax implications of refurbishment meant that it would have been cheaper to demolish the existing structure and build from scratch,[37] so the decision to work with the existing fabric, and the method of doing so, are particularly significant. Keeping the external walls of the original building, the main work of the project involved the removal of the first floor and internal columns to create two double-height studio spaces, and the construction of a new storey as a separately defined living area inside a glass pavilion, with a decked verandah enclosed within a balustrade.

The two building reviews that appeared in the architectural press at the time of the project's completion emphasise the 'experimental' nature of the building, its eccentricity, and the unconventional way in which the new design and structure related to the original building. One critic, Amanda Baillieu, concluded that the building was 'Adjaye's latest riposte to UK architecture's deep-seated conservatism … a critique of domesticity, about working in the home and the politics of privacy'.[38] Another, Peter Allison, celebrated the clever division of working and living space according to the client's needs; and the 'subtle balance between the overall organization … and the detailing of different areas'.[39] These two articles are notably enthusiastic about the house, especially given the criticism of some of Adjaye's other residential projects, described by one mainstream newspaper critic as 'vast, opaque containers' out of context in their neighbourhoods.[40] How far, in this building, did Adjaye actually move away from 'architecture's deep-seated conservatism'?

As well as referencing Noble and Webster's interest in rubbish and stigmatised, low-grade materials, the name 'Dirty House' also signals the most idiosyncratic visual feature of the exterior – the 'dirty' rough surface of its black anti-fly-posting textured coating, which design journalist Caroline Roux

Figure 6.2: *The Dirty House, 2002.*

refers to as simultaneously 'tantalizing and repellent'.[41] Made by a company called Clean Streets, the coating is normally used, along with anti-climb paint, to sanitise the city, preventing fly-posting and the other incidental aesthetics of urban grime that Noble and Webster, like many of their contemporaries, celebrate in their work.[42] This matt coating is mixed with crushed marble aggregates. Physically, it is extremely hard-wearing, beyond any reasonable practical requirements for the building's exterior. It is a solvent-based paint with a highly volatile organic content – a type that will soon be banned by EU law because of the toxic emissions made when the paint dries, which, in still, sunny conditions, react with nitrogen oxide to produce smog.[43]

Evocative and tactile, used here in a decorative way elevated from its day-to-day functional context, the gritty surface carries extended references to contemporary ideas about urban pollution and sanitisation beyond those that might be gleaned through the first encounter. It seems to suggest, simultaneously, sanitisation or grime, according to whether or not one recognises it as anti-fly-posting paint. This is a ubiquitous coating for street furniture – lamp-posts, railings, bicycle stands, parking meters, bollards and so on – in London and elsewhere, associated with the functional 'background noise' of the urban fabric: things people are generally meant to ignore. In daily use it functions ostensibly to keep maintenance costs down by preventing posters being glued to the surface of these objects, and is therefore part of the everyday processes of upkeeping the city, undertaken by local authorities. However, encountering this surface without recognising its function (it is so banal as easily to go unnoticed), its colour and aggregated texture would read perhaps not as dirtiness exactly, but as drabness, an effect that is increased when the building is wet and streaky.

Thinking back to Hall's comment on Adjaye's forms appearing 'completely in place in the mixed environments of the contemporary city', the paint seems to act as a camouflage, concealing any newness or effort in its design. Located in a neighbourhood where prestige properties sit alongside local-authority-owned housing that often looks, and is, the worse for wear, this camouflage could be read as a tactic to play down the contrast. As the artist-residents point out, if it registers at all, the paint suggests unpretentiousness rather than ostentation. It is likely to be read as inexpensive, in spite of its real cost, or the effort required in applying it.[44] Rather than celebrate the industrial as ruin or quasi-ruin, the anti-fly-posting coating both signals that the building is 'new', and that its current phase takes precedence over any fussy preservation of its past. The durability of the material defies any notion of the building surrendering to ruin in the future, through its apparent strength, and the fact that it protects the structure from the elements and from human traces. It is a simple gesture, but one that can be read either as a romanticist defiance of what might be perceived as the draconian sanitisation of contemporary London, where 'orderliness' as defined by the city authorities produces a drab and anxious aesthetic; or as a commodification of the functional aesthetics of the everyday city, and a camouflage for gentrification.

The curator of the *Gritty Brits* show selected an image of the Dirty House as the main image for the exhibition flyer. This suggests that the building epitomises the Gritty Brits' approach (and it is a loose approach, including the East End location of many of their buildings, which is suggested as the primary bond between the group, rather than any coherent aesthetic style). Adjaye was therefore positioned as a key player within this 'new generation of architects', this being reinforced by his delivery of the exhibition's opening lecture. The photograph chosen for the flyer was taken by Lyndon Douglas, an architectural photographer who has a close association with Adjaye Associates, having photographed other buildings by the practice and exhibited with Adjaye. The same image is used in the entry for the Dirty House in *David Adjaye: Houses* (2005) (see Plate 9). Appearing to have been taken at dawn, in the half-light, it actively develops the building's 'shabby chic' narrative. The façade of the house is punctuated by the illuminated mirrored windows at ground level, with the dark voids of the window recesses on the storey above just visible. The colours that saturate the photograph have been manipulated to increase their intensity, and the contrast has been heightened. The red-brick Victorian railway arches reflect a glow that bleeds into the uneven surfaces of the pavement and street. Beyond the house there is a construction site, a structure covered in scaffolding and draped in theatrically-lit plastic sheeting, with disorderly temporary fencing at its base.[45]

'Architectural photography', as the architectural critic Robin Wilson has recently argued, 'has long been dominated by a tendency to depict the architectural object only in its finished state, free of signs of process or occupation'.[46] New buildings are conventionally represented through a mode of photographic sanitisation in what Wilson refers to as a 'pristine state', empty of occupation, divorced from any sense of real time. Photographic records are, as art historian John Tagg asserts, 'construed as impartial, objective, clean, compelling and modern', yet it is the passive and uncritical reception of the architectural photograph that Wilson problematises, rather than the dominant mode of photography itself.[47] In Douglas' image of the Dirty House, however, we are aware of the presence of the photographer's decision making in constructing the scene, both at the time of the image being taken and in its editing. In this, objects and features that might normally be erased using editing software in the official photographs of a new building, such as a bag of rubbish or parked car, are retained. Furthermore, in photographer Timothy Wray's photographs (see Figure 6.1), a rainy day has left the building wet, so that what might normally be considered imperfections in the surface texture are emphasised and aestheticised. In taking a series of photographs of the building, Wray chose not to suppress imperfections in the photographs themselves, such as smears caused by rain drops on the lens. This is in keeping with the aesthetic of the house, as well as a rejection of the sanitising conventions of architectural photography.[48]

In the Douglas photograph used for the flyer, and others used in the practice's documentation of the building, a concrete wall to the left of the house has been used, perhaps, the viewer imagines, in retaliation against the anti-vandal coating covering the house itself, as a canvas for a dialogue in graffiti. Next to the tag of 'Spanky', 'WOMAN ARE REVOLTING' has been crossed out, and 'NOT TRUE!', a second voice declares. This graffitied wall appears in other photographs of the house around the time of completion.

On further investigation, Tim Noble concedes responsibility for the first daubs of graffiti, suggesting collusion between the artists and architect in staging the location as a shady place. The edgy photographic representation of the neighbourhood is paralleled and extended in the anecdotes both artists and architect narrate about the building. For example, in the opening lecture to the *Gritty Brits* show, Adjaye recounted an anecdote, presumably to enhance the sense of the building's 'edgy' location, in which he described local prostitutes writing graffiti in lipstick on the mirrored ground floor windows.

Modernist industrial aesthetics purposefully evoke ideas about order, cleanliness and sterility, emphasising the rational and scientific basis of production, as well as countering the presence or threat of material pollution. In the case of the Dirty House, the name, and the exterior design, not only reference but also exaggerate the building's former industrial use, capturing the building's, and the area's, degraded aesthetic after de-industrialisation, rather than its functional operation as an industrial district. Fluctuating between a sense of contamination and sanitisation, this ambiguous effect is cemented in the building's representation, largely controlled by the architect. While Norman Foster, Nicolas Grimshaw, Richard Rogers and other hi-tech London-based architects celebrate the refined industrial processes and technology of late capitalism in the imagery of their buildings, Adjaye's architecture more often draws out associations with an earlier and shabbier low-tech industrialism.[49] Tidying the different phases of brickwork by applying one uniform coating, the use of anti-fly-posting paint does not entirely conceal these different phases, so that the building's 'organic' regeneration is visible. Instead of preserving industrial features, or reworking them so that the building's new functions are apparent, the exterior suggests a contemporary, or even a future, industrial aesthetic, where the building itself has to be coated in a chemically-produced protective surface. The name and the 'toxic' paint suggest industrial contamination above and beyond what we might expect of a light industrial building in a former furniture manufacturing district, taking our imaginations to the more hazardous landscapes and toxic structures associated with large-scale industrial manufacture; landscapes where chemical pollutants have become engrained in the environment, climate and built fabric.

The boundary from the street is marked by a doormat stencilled with the words 'Welcome Muthafuckers' – an ironic take on suburban pleasantries. On crossing this threshold there is a double-height lobby area, painted white and startlingly light in contrast to the drab exterior. This acts as a buffer between the street and the studios, reached via an office, a space with functional continuity from the building's former life as a furniture factory. Among the various images that cover the office walls, a calendar with a 'dirty' picture of a 'page 3 girl', and one of pop singer Samantha Fox, remain from the earlier period before production ceased, creating a self-conscious association between the artists and the 'bad taste' of the workers who once occupied the space.[50] Through the office are a smaller studio, for lighter activities, a compact courtyard garden, and the massive second studio for creating larger sculptural works. Webster refers to these respectively as the 'clean' and 'dirty' studios, in reference to the nature of production located in them.

Taking the stairs up from the front lobby, past a spare bedroom at first-floor level, one reaches the main, open-plan living area. Paradoxically, given the close association between context and house in the representation of the building, in spatial, aesthetic and experiential terms, the living area is defined through complete separation from the street outside and from the studio spaces at ground floor level. Again, the contrast with the mass of the industrial-strength exterior is stark. The metaphor for this space suggested by Noble is of a tree house.[51] This gives a sense of the feeling of secretive and protected isolation the architecture induces; a lofty position where one can survey one's surroundings in safe anonymity. The feeling of isolation from the outside world is intensified in the secluded bedroom. When the doors, painted white and flush with the white walls, are shut, this room completely disappears from view. Within its intimate boundaries the lines of conventional domestic privacy and personal hygiene are (modestly) redrawn through, on Noble's suggestion, the placement of a bath next to the bed.

In the original state after the building's completion, the living area and verandah were floored with the same timber decking, placed upside down, the grooves of its underside exposed. With such materials and other features in the house and studio – exposed concrete, strip lights, the timber decking of the floors – Adjaye creates a simple aesthetic, of elements easily sourced, if not recycled. The decking created a direct relationship between the interior and the immediate exterior of the verandah. Placing it upside down suggested a desire to subvert convention (modestly, again) in the use of materials. However, this proved impractical, as the grooves required painstaking cleaning with a tooth-brush – the inhabitants of the Dirty House appear to have been less tolerant of 'real' dirt than its postmodern index. As a result, the artists have since replaced the timber floor with an exuberantly colourful mock-wood grain vinyl, one designed by Richard Woods. This has a dramatic effect in animating the space, in keeping with the ironic use of materials elsewhere in the design.

The high balustrade surrounding the verandah, stipulated by Noble and Webster, increases the sense of separation, framing a panoramic view to nearby skyscrapers in the City of London financial district, allowing surreptitious views to the street beneath, while preventing anyone on the street from seeing in. An arrow-slit window above the white concrete kitchen top has a similar effect. Such features are perhaps why one critic referred to the house as a 'private fortress'.[52] There is a parallel between this sense of den-like security and the artists' playfully infantile corruption of the wall outside with graffiti.

Frugal pastoral and grunge aesthetics

Since the late 1980s, a theoretical discourse has developed on the aesthetics of waste in cinema and the visual arts. For example, in 1987, writing about the film *Blade Runner* (1982), Giuliana Bruno argued: 'Postindustrialism recycles; therefore it needs its waste. A postmodern position exposes such logic, producing an aesthetic of recycling.'[53] Given that the conversion of former industrial space has become one of the dominant modes of architectural practice in late-modern cities, and a self-conscious 'aesthetic of recycling' one of its principal modes, one might expect to find a more developed discussion about this aesthetic within architectural discourse, in relation to late-twentieth-century and contemporary architecture. Spatial and material recycling have, of course, always been part of the production of architecture. However, in the context of late modernity, for a combination of economic, ethical and aesthetic reasons, architectural design echoes visual arts practice in self-consciously embracing and reconfiguring already-used and worn materials and spaces, and in 'distressing' new materials.

A coffee-table publication entitled *New Loft Living* (2002), essentially a step-by-step guide to a successful loft development, outlines some reasons for incorporating recycled materials and elements in loft interior design as follows:

> A loft, which is essentially a salvaged space, provides the perfect home for reclaimed materials and salvaged fittings and fixtures ... Most, but not all, salvaged materials are cheaper than new, and they generally have the rugged authenticity that comes from decades of wear and tear, a characterful patina that is almost impossible to simulate. Salvage also scores high on ecological grounds.[54]

In the self-conscious lifestyle consumerism of loft living, residents happily buy into the fictional authenticity of 'rugged' materials, whose narrative may either enhance or distort the building's or location's actual history. Recycling is recommended here, therefore, on a combination of practical, economic, aesthetic and ecological grounds. The notion of 'rugged authenticity' connects loft living with other architectural traditions of expressing 'truthfulness' through exposed or old materials, notably in the work of the New Brutalists, and their 'frugal pastoral' approach, with which the Gritty Brits have been associated.

The cultural geographer Sharon Zukin's *Loft Living: Culture and Capital in Urban Change* (1982) provides the most extended and original critical account of 'loft living' and the recycling of former industrial space, and therefore sets up a valuable historical and theoretical framework for interpreting the Dirty House. Focusing on New York's SoHo district in the 1970s, Zukin analyses the conversion of former industrial and former commercial spaces into combined studio-home 'lofts' for artists. She traces from these pioneers the development of a broader cultural phenomenon of 'loft living', a lifestyle genre of urban development that, as she demonstrates, soon became popular with a broad cross-section of urban professionals who, to different degrees and for different ends, wished to associate with artists and their lifestyles. Such developments continue to have a high profile in property markets in New York and other cities, including London, where a decline in manufacturing left suitable office, warehouse and factory spaces vacant and therefore ripe for conversion. 'The residential conversion of manufacturing lofts confirms and symbolizes the death of an urban manufacturing center', writes Zukin.[55] Loft living is not restricted to such spaces, however, with new-build developments often mimicking industrial architecture in their exterior design and loft-like interiors. The loft has become a branded form of urban development.[56] Zukin's analysis suggests that 'recycling' in this context should be understood as a multi-layered process: a renegotiation of value at once physical, aesthetic, conceptual and economic, to be understood in relation to broader frameworks affecting property markets and urban restructuring, such as the planning system and the media.

How does the house-studio, built for Noble and Webster in a former industrial space, fit with Zukin's model? In this case, unlike in Zukin's examples from 1970s Manhattan, architectural and spatial recycling are not based on preservationist ethics. Yet, in many ways, Noble and Webster's aspirations and requirements do seem similar to those of the American Abstract Expressionists and Pop Artists that Zukin explores. The more explicit of these needs are practical: light, airy, spacious properties suited to the production of, often large, artworks. Other requirements, while pragmatic, are underpinned by more nuanced motives, such as the close life–work association that loft developments provide. As Zukin suggests, this has a practical function in that it gives artists freedom in their patterns of work, while also contributing to the construction of their status as cultural producers, through projecting ideas about their creativity and industry to their audiences and potential buyers.[57]

While Noble and Webster's acquisition of their building as a run-down shell suggests that they, like Zukin's artists, were seeking the maximum space for the minimum price, in developing the Dirty House financial restraints do not seem to have been an issue. Rather, they simply produced more work in order to finance the development of the building to meet their vision. On certain aspects of the design where their views conflicted with Adjaye's, they even advocated a more expensive option than the one suggested by the architect.[58] The modernist 1930s factory they chose to develop was emphatically plain and ordinary, far less ornamental in its façades than the nineteenth-century industrial buildings described by Zukin that, despite also being mass produced, were adorned with cast ironwork and sculptural elements. This 'blank canvas', and the artists' economic power, allowed Noble and Webster the freedom to realise their vision of the Dirty House as an expression of themselves and their work. In the process, the building itself has become a symbol of their economic success.

The interior of the Dirty House fits with Zukin's argument in the sense that lofts challenge a suburban domestic model and are more suited to 'alternative lifestyles'. As discussed earlier, reviews of the building have highlighted its 'critique of domesticity' and the 'politics of privacy'. However, the case for this seems overstated when we consider that lofts have been a mainstream form of urban development for over 30 years, and when we compare Robert Rauschenberg's lifestyle and living arrangements in 1950s New York with those embodied in the Dirty House.

Unlike the very early pioneers of loft living, such as Rauschenberg, to whom Zukin refers, Noble and Webster have no romantic pretence to 'live poor', or in dirty, unheated, uncomfortable surroundings lacking running water. While the exterior is not ostentatious, those 'in the know' are able to identify the Dirty House as an architect-designed building for wealthy clients. Instead, the sense of frugality and association with industrial dirt have become aestheticised in the building's design and in the choice of materials, sanitising the 'uncultivated' industrial space while retaining what the artists and architects perceive as its excitements. With its gutted interior, and fastidiously detailed pavilion, the Dirty House is closer, perhaps, to the phenomenon of new-build residences designed to look like lofts, than to the industrial conversions discussed in *Loft Living*. In Zukin's examples, the artists (and other cultural entrepreneurs) benefit from the 'cultural capital' attached to loft spaces, both from the creative edginess associated with industrial architecture, and their value as objects of nostalgia. This is a major cultural shift, requiring the 'metamorphosis of industrial sweat shops into "beautiful spaces"'.[59] In the Dirty House, the artists and architects also capitalise on the association with industry, with the workers who once populated the factory, and with the 'urban chic' of a down-at-heel location. The literature that has emerged around the reconfiguration of 'brown-field' – that is, previously developed – sites and ex-industrial buildings does not account for their glamorisation, for the aesthetic value and cultural kudos attached to abandoned and seemingly contaminated, or poor and run-down spaces associated with working-class communities.

Urban pastoral

In art history, Julian Stallabrass has pursued a neo-Marxian approach to the representation of degraded urban environments in his critique of the 'Young British Artists' and their use of the 'inner city'.[60] Stallabrass suggests that a pastoral trope formerly focused on the representation of rural landscapes and their inhabitants has re-emerged in depicting the inner city and impoverished urban dwellers, commenting that the work 'is about seeing something valuable in something trivial associated with the less advantaged sections of society, and bringing that to the attention of art lovers'.[61] He suggests that this mode is touristic or 'quasi-anthropological', operating through repeated, formulaic, patterns. It focuses attention on particular 'raw', degraded or seamy urban environments, encouraging a fascination with and a desire to venture into such places. Importantly, Stallabrass notes that 'gentrification and the cultural celebration of urban debasement are closely connected', and that in late-twentieth-century British art the pastoral is generally 'more to do with artefacts and the appearance of the urban environment than with its inhabitants'.[62]

Stallabrass' account is confined to two-dimensional visual artworks that represent the urban, typically displayed in the highly codified environment of the gallery. Is the Dirty House, or the photographs chosen by the architect to represent it, an example of an abstract kind of 'urban pastoral' in contemporary architectural design? Certainly, they refer us indirectly to the workers who once occupied the factory; and to the working-class residents of this 'gritty' but now gentrified urban district. The image presented through the building's exterior aesthetic, and through its photographic presentation, is of an area that is both 'raw' and threatening to an acceptable degree, recalling the work of German photographer, Rut Blees Luxemburg. In *Meet Me in Arcadia* (1996), analysed by Stallabrass, Blees Luxemburg photographs a low-rise modernist council housing estate at night, and from above, using a long exposure. The stigmas and state of repair of such estates are concealed by a glamorising photographic veil. As Stallabrass argues, they show 'run-down, perhaps threatening urban landscapes about which the speculation of polite viewers can run wild'.[63] He continues by observing that: 'The grime and dereliction of the environment, safely distanced ... acts as an alluring patina, endowing the otherwise alienating geometric modernist lines with character. Modernism in ruins takes on a strongly Romantic and sublime character.'[64] In relation to work in this mode – and thinking back to the photographs of the Elephant and Castle produced by residents that we discussed in Chapter 2

– we may ask, as Jane Rendell does in critiquing Blees Luxemburg's stylised photographs of modernist council housing: 'Is this a vision that only someone removed from the realities of living in these poorly maintained environments could afford to have?'[65]

A final important context for thinking about the Dirty House can be found in debates about the early architecture of Frank Gehry and, in particular, Gehry's own home in Santa Monica (1977–8). Indeed, referencing critical work on Gehry is particularly appropriate, given that Adjaye holds him in high esteem ('Look at Gehry. We can do anything now').[66] The art critic, Hal Foster's, critique of Gehry identifies a number of characteristics of his early architecture that fit well with the Dirty House and its relationships to its urban context. For example, a comparison can be drawn because, according to Foster, Gehry's innovation lies primarily in his inventive use of everyday, inexpensive materials, resulting in an unfinished, provisional, 'funky', 'edgy', 'gritty' aesthetic appropriate to the 'restless transformations' of Los Angeles, and aesthetically resistant to that city's glossier aspects.[67] However, there are two main criticisms that Foster then proceeds to make. One is that Gehry's self-conscious attempt to create a 'grungy', low-grade, 'pop' aesthetic became clichéd, with his cardboard furniture eventually becoming a kind of 'homeless chic'; moving, that is, from an inventive 'frugal pastoral' to something more like the 'urban pastoral'. The second is that the claim of Gehry's architecture to respond sensitively to its urban context is exaggerated, and based on superficial imagery.

Reflecting on the fact that Gehry began developing his grunge aesthetic in the 1970s challenges the originality of Adjaye's aesthetic strategies and use of materials, emphatically stated by some critics.[68] In formal terms, Adjaye is certainly far more modernist in approach: the Dirty House does not stray far from the geometries of the original 1930s factory. Gehry positions himself equidistantly between the stigmas of modernism and postmodernism; while Adjaye works with postmodern tropes of irony and architecture-as-image within – quite literally, in the case of the Dirty House, but also at a more general level – a modernist framework. Where the two architects are most similar is in their playful approach to, and use of, 'recycled' or 'low grade' materials. It is this aspect of the house that strays furthest from architectural modernism. In both Gehry's and Adjaye's work, this is part of a strategy to develop an urban vernacular suited to the context.

Called 'dirty', this house actually turns out to have a complicated relationship with the sanitisation of the city, jeopardising the alluring simplicity and categorical certainty of Mary Douglas' arguments that 'dirt is matter out of place' and 'everyone universally finds dirt offensive'. This is an example that enables us to bridge across the aesthetics and discourses of urban dirt and degradation in contemporary architecture and art. In the design, a self-conscious aesthetic plays on an instability in the boundary between dirtiness/cleanliness, developing narratives prompted by Noble and Webster's work, and capitalising on the area's associations. As far as Adjaye and the Gritty Brits are concerned, reviewers of their practice conjure confused images of urban grit and associations with dirt all too readily, without critical reflection on how such associations are constructed through material and aesthetic strategies, and in relation to preconceptions about the contexts of the work. Like Noble and Webster themselves, Adjaye responds to the urban degradation that forms the context and content of his practice, from a comfortable distance. He celebrates the informal and aesthetically diverse city even while participating in its elimination, reinforcing the conservatism his critics claim he wants to subvert.

7

BURIAL AND BIOREMEDIATION

Stephen Gill has learnt this: to haunt the places that haunt him.

Iain Sinclair, quoted on Stephen Gill's website (accessed 2011)[1]

[T]here is something to be gained in focusing explicitly on an archaeology of the present, on an archaeology that engages with the here and now.

Victor Buchli and Gavin Lucas (2001)[2]

In the mid-2000s, London-based photographer, Stephen Gill, published a number of special edition photographic books under his own imprint, Nobody.[3] Eight of these contain photoworks documenting Hackney Wick and the London 2012 Olympic Park area before its reconfiguration as such.[4] Here, I consider one example, *Buried* (2006), featuring photographs Gill took of Hackney Wick, and subsequently buried and exhumed. We shall consider which sites Gill chose to document like this, and why. What does the act and metaphor of burial mean in relation to this contested site? What are the implications for understanding the manner in which this mega-event-led redevelopment for the Olympic Games progressed? In addressing these questions we shall consider some contexts in which *Buried*'s methods and motifs can usefully be situated.

Gill combines low-tech equipment and simple photographic formats with the labour-intensive process of burying and retrieving his photographic prints. The resulting images engage the photographer and viewer in more dynamic exchanges with the sites they depict than the utilitarian photographs typically produced by professionals involved in urban change – those of construction contractors, architects and archaeologists. As a series, Gill's photographs and books constitute an archive, making visible people that have been displaced, and structures and spaces that have since been demolished, removed or assigned to new uses in the area's restructuring. The Games involved the biggest compulsory purchase order (CPO) in UK history.[5] The stories of those who were evicted from their homes and businesses as the London Development Agency (LDA) acquired the land have been played down in the mainstream media, but carefully recorded by artists and activists.[6] Documenting some of the spaces and people from the site, in *Buried*, Gill also produced an image from – materialised – the properties and movement of the land. This is significant because the 'bioremediation' of the soil was central in justifying the need for the Olympic-led regeneration, taking us back to the more literal biological meaning of that term, as well as evoking its usual metaphorical overtones.

The dirtied photographs of *Buried* pointedly contrast with the slick idealistic 'photo-real' simulations and architectural photographs circulating according to the official communications agendas of the Olympic development process. Such images are highly controlled at the macro scale of master-planning, as at the micro scale of specific architectural schemes. The writer, Iain Sinclair, one of the most vocal critics of the Olympics, evokes the projective renders associated with the redevelopment as 'CGI [computer-generated images] smears on the blue fence', drawing attention to their abstracting tendency, and suggesting their potential to blur reality in disorientating and deceptive ways.[7] The fence he refers to is itself an image as well as a physical boundary. It encircled the perimeter of the construction zone when demolition began in the summer of 2007, and it quickly became an especially contentious boundary for many artists and photographers. They had previously wandered freely in this area, recording it as they wished, but were now prevented from doing so as this large piece of the city was 'locked down'.[8]

Early on in the construction phase the Olympic Delivery Authority (ODA) anticipated criticism of a lack of visual accessibility to the site, installing 20 webcams streaming live footage of the construction zone to their website. The ODA's top public relations priority was to communicate the progress of the site towards its idealised future – the Olympic dream. Aware of the power of images, the ODA prioritised spending on visual communications, and the production of a photographic and film archive to record the site as work proceeded.[9] The webcam images and time-lapse photographs, and the 'CGI smears' Sinclair refers to, were precisely intended to 'bury' certain things, closing down the area's pre-existing identity and history, neutralising any sense of controversy about the form of redevelopment, suggesting 'transparency' while keeping spectators and unauthorised image-makers at a safe distance.

Of course, numerous other professional groups have produced their own archives of the site as part of their day-to-day work. These kinds of photographic documentation normally serve to fix and stabilise an urban area in the throes of physical and social transformation, making sense of it as works progress, rationalising it. Photographs 'clean up' an architectural or archaeological site, freezing time in order that it can be understood (see page 139). Within the proliferation of publicly available images, produced by built environment professionals associated with the Olympic redevelopment, we hardly encounter any that depict a sense of process or the messy realities of construction. As the work towards the Games reached completion, idealised architectural photographs became the norm.[10] This is what makes Gill's photographs so unusual.

Taken and disseminated during the pre-construction phase, Gill's work emphasises process, chance, and a subjective and intimate understanding of the area's qualities prior to its possession by the ODA. Traces resulting from the burial of the original prints expressively record the photographer's material interaction with the place he was photographing, as well as the physical influence of the site on the photographs. Marks, smears, scratches and dirt take the 'witness' aspect of documentary photography to a new dimension. If the original images provided the illusion of a window onto reality, these blemishes communicate the process of their production and – in the original photographs at least – a direct index of the site's materiality.

Dirty surfaces

Buried is a slim A5 book, packaged in a stone-coloured cardboard slipcase: self-consciously nondescript and earthy (see Figure 7.1). As well as the book itself, inside there is a plain envelope containing a photograph, as if perhaps a treasure hunt clue. In edition number 007 this is a snapshot of an overgrown and mossy concrete verge: a definitively urban-manufactured feature reclaimed by wild plants and flowers. The format and proportions of the image and frame recall an over-sized Polaroid photograph. The slipcase also contains the book itself, smeared with earth, actual abject dirt: evidence of its recent burial.

The book's title, *Buried*, is in a version of a rounded serif font – Cooper Black – eroded underneath, as is the name of the author, Stephen Gill. The positive and negative images of the letters suggest simultaneously a pile of dirt

151

Figure 7.1: *Cover of* Buried, *2006.*

and an excavated trench. The colour of the text hovers between grey, brown and black. The author's name is obscured by actual dirt, so one would have to pick at it to reveal it.

Inside are 27 images that echo the format of the enveloped one. In contrast to that pristine print, here the images and their white borders are damaged and distorted. Three explanatory paragraphs include the information that 'the photographs in this book were taken in Hackney Wick and later buried there'. They were deposited at various depths and positions, for variable lengths of time.[11] The suggestion is that the reader should take the single unblemished photograph and bury it themselves, joining a collaboration with the authors, identified as 'Stephen Gill and Hackney Wick'.

Buried is a C-type – chromogenic colour – print book, designed by Melanie Mues, and is one of a series of photobooks published with the intention of 'making the book the finished expression of the photographs, rather than just a shell in which to house them'.[12] This method gives Gill maximum possible control over the presentation of his photographs, and has meant that the many he has taken of Hackney Wick have been disseminated in publications printed and bound in the area. Close identification with place, and with Hackney and Hackney Wick in particular, have been consistently important for Gill. He has become well known for his methodical documentation of everyday urban sites and lives, through understated, self-consciously low-tech snapshots, revealing patterns and complexity in ostensibly simple and familiar scenes, objects and city features.

Gill took the photographs in *Buried* with a second-hand plastic Coronet camera, bought for 50 pence in a market local to the sites they depict. How are we to read the frugal use of such low-tech equipment, and the sparse understated quality of the work? The camera lacked focus and exposure controls, and knowledge of this communicates the virtue of unpretentious yet skilful craftsmanship and an association with everyday amateur photography. Though as mannered as it is modest, the act of recycling a discarded piece of obsolete equipment could suggest creativity and pragmatism in Gill's approach to photographing an area rich with history as a 'landscape of production' and industrial innovation.[13] This same area was portrayed as derelict in the regeneration discourses, and contaminated from its previous uses for industry and landfill beyond remediation, except in the most dramatic – *tabula rasa* – form, intended to transform it into a 'landscape of consumption'. Reinforcing this transition, in the spectacle of the opening night ceremony for the 2012 Games, directed by Danny Boyle, the stadium at first appeared as a pastoral scene from feudal Britain, then was transformed through a dramatic re-enactment of the Industrial Revolution.

Gill's attitude to the Olympics is equivocal, but much of his work appears to lament what has been or will be lost. On his website he comments:

The games ... will bring many good things to the area: new transport links and much-needed infrastructure. But there will be losses, too. There is another side to Hackney Wick. Away from the noise and chaos nature has somehow managed to find and keep a place for itself. The canals and rivers and secret allotments (known only to their dedicated gardeners) are home to many birds and animals. These hidden paradises have a vibrancy of their own which will soon be muted by the dust that will cover them.[14]

This statement indicates Gill's interest in a poetics of dust and burial, and in the forms of urban nature that existed in this industry-saturated environment prior to the Olympic redevelopment. The photographs in *Buried* depict a range of views that highlight the area's complex metropolitan nature. Two pylons, iconic landmarks conveying manufactured power and energy, are shot from below, set pictorially against a grey sky in an overgrown park (see Figure 7.2). They appear as harmonious outcrops rather than incongruous eyesores. As we move through the book we view industry and infrastructure, street scenes, workers, workspaces, snapshots of local residents, discarded objects, scrapyards, and the anonymous interstitial background architecture of industrial parks, alongside blurry close-ups of plants and flowers, allotments and their guardians.

Each visual fragment coheres within the series through a common presentation format, and the consistent interruptions of scratches, specks of dirt, stains, watermarks, fingerprints and other traces, indexing the burial of the original prints. The degree to which these disrupt the image varies. Some photographs are just lightly speckled, but towards the book's centre the original subject matter becomes virtually unrecognisable, erupting into kaleidoscopic explosions of psychedelic colour, with alien forms that bleed, bubble and blur into one another (see Plate 10). These result from the emulsion on the original photographs' surfaces breaking down in contact with the water and chemicals in the soil.

If the link between reality and the photograph was inscribed when Gill originally pressed the shutter, the blemishes record a second interaction with the site, analogous to the exposure of light on film, more direct and literally grounded in the site's materiality, yet less controlled and predictable to the photographer. In one image, the process has produced a new multi-coloured coral-reef-like landscape. Another shows a jumping dog, seemingly bursting through intensely orange layers of flame that spontaneously combust the picture plane. In the shot of the two pylons, the clouds of the overcast sky float

Figure 7.2: *Extract from* Buried *series, 2006.*

into the white border. An image of a man inspecting a marrow on his allot-
ment has a dirty frame: added realism, involving us in the scene, surrounded
as he is by piles of earth. At the same time, these supplements to the photographs – as with the collages of plants in his later *Hackney Flowers* photobook
– disrupt the conventional photographic illusion of reality, making us aware
of the photograph as a material artefact.

Although the sites featured often seem low-key, definitively ordinary, as a group they represent a number of important locations in the controversies encircling the area's Olympic-led redevelopment. The pylons were among the first features removed from Hackney Marshes, replaced by power-lines buried neatly underground at high cost. Another shot shows water bursting through a lock in the Lea Navigation system. The management of these waterways since the ODA took over has been challenged by those who argue that the area's already rich ecology, and its natural bioremediation following the closure of heavy industry, is being destroyed in favour of a sanitised biodiversity that better fits a managerial, neoliberal image of the good city.[15] The photograph of the man inspecting a marrow is presumably taken at Manor Gardens allotments, from which the owners were evicted in 2007.[16]

Sometimes Gill's strategies are pictorial, as when a shot of a bridge over the River Lea in another of his photobooks, *Archaeologies in Reverse*, echoes Claude Monet's *Bridge over a Pond of Waterlilies* (1899). At other times, less so: urban nature is also represented impressionistically but here it has an edge, rather than being pretty; it can be disorderly and unfinished rather than formally laid out. In *Buried*, a cormorant sits in front of a graffitied concrete wall. A grassy bank has been sectioned off with plastic construction safety fencing: surgery imminent. Water streams through mossy canal gates and wildflowers bloom through chain-link fences.

Gill's photo assemblages of artefacts, organisms and settings suggest a subtle understanding of the city as an environment with its own nature, the meaning of which is constructed dialectically between manufactured and natural conditions, images and objects. Here is a pre-existing biodiversity at odds with the ODA's vision of formal parklands, which might not be economically productive, but which Gill (and others) celebrate as a positive and meaningful feature of the city, and a space for creativity and imagination.

Dirt as context

Gill belongs to a line of artists and writers who have highlighted the urban everyday, running from the surrealists and situationists to the psychogeographers of present-day London, including Sinclair, and, in photography, Richard Wentworth and Mark Atkins. Gill, like Atkins, has collaborated with Sinclair. Both have engaged with Hackney in a sustained way through multiple projects with overlapping motifs. Gill's work, rather than taking a formalistic approach to the built environment, is rather a kind of intuitive documentary: 'suggestive of how buildings and cities are occupied and acquire a personal, emotional resonance'.[17] He displays a psychogeographer's interest in the flows of life, energy and entropy that collectively shape the experience of the area: what he calls the 'spirit' of place.[18] He also emphasises the process of photography as one of 'reaction to place' rather than straightforward documentation.[19] As in Wentworth's photographic series *Making Do and Getting By* (1974–ongoing), Gill often identifies and highlights formulaic patterns in urban and material culture – as in his series of the back of advertising hoardings, ATM machines: and lost people in *A Book of Field Studies* (2005). The rigid structure and repetition involved in such work contrast, on the surface at least, with the writings of Sinclair, who also highlights value in interstitial spaces and familiar things, but through ambulatory connections.

Roger Luckhurst's critique of the contemporary London literary psychogeographic tradition is helpful in thinking about Gill's work, given his direct association with the authors Luckhurst discusses.[20] In the quotation at the head of this chapter, Sinclair comments that Gill has learnt 'to haunt the places that haunt him', and thus suggests how the photographer's investigations of east London connect with what Luckhurst describes as a 'master trope' of the uncanny, and a 'contemporary London Gothic'.[21] Pursuing spectral themes that invoke Jacques Derrida's *Spectres of Marx* (1993), the literary exponents of this mode share a number of characteristics with Gill, and specifically with *Buried.*[22] They use motifs of haunting as a mechanism to 'excavate' repressed traumatic memories, and lost or threatened histories. They focus on banal or degraded spaces and structures – conduits through which overlooked histories and mythologies erupt into, and disrupt, the present.

Contemporary regeneration – and in particular the form of *tabula rasa* approach typified by the Olympic redevelopment, and encapsulated in the ODA's 'Demolish Dig Design' slogan – either denies, fictionalises or neutralises the past. Driven by what Derrida calls 'archive fever', it may construct specific reductive historical imaginaries that legitimise – or at least do not conflict with – the forms and directions it pursues.[23] The implicit political strategy underlying the gothic imaginaries of ruination, burial and exhumation at work in London's contemporary psychogeographic practices instead reveal the city as a complex 'polytemporal assemblage' – in which different timeframes collide. For Derrida, according to Luckhurst, 'hauntology' was a way of thinking through the 'ghosts' of Marxism – its association with totalitarian regimes – in relation to his philosophy of deconstruction.

In the London context, Luckhurst observes, 'the buried Gothic fragment ... operates as the emblem of resistance to the tyranny of planned space'.[24]

This approach has the potential to reveal forgotten times and repressed histories in order to critically intervene, stimulating alternative imaginaries, countering a collapse of imagination in urban development.[25] Yet Luckhurst raises a number of important limitations: first, 'the generalized structure of haunting is symptomatically blind to its generative loci'; second, the 'deadpan mythology' of its authors makes their political intent ambiguous; third, the celebration of London's ineffability tends towards an aestheticising 'supernaturalisation', distancing us from the city's shifting political structures; and finally, the mode itself, even if it is subversive, is 'necessarily occluded and interstitial, passed on only between initiates'.[26] Gill's intent is implicit rather than explicit. The language and mode he uses are more readily available to a cultural elite familiar with the wider body of recent London psychogeographic work than they would be to anyone else. However, his 'collaboration' with the site certainly addresses the first of Luckhurst's critiques. The soil powerfully brings to mind the physical, political and economic restructuring taking place in a specific place.

Gill's interest in 'degraded' working-class urban environments and the people who live in them has echoes with the approaches of other artists and architects we have explored. However, in his case, the quasi-anthropological 'urban pastoral' (see pages 146–47) mode moves into the quasi-archaeological, connecting with a body of recent London-based artists, such as Wentworth, who have adopted archaeological methods and metaphors in their work.

Sifting the soil

The acts of physically burying these photographs and photobooks, and metaphorically burying the people and places that are their subjects, moves photography beyond the passivity and neutrality of official site documentation, instigating a necessarily more involved encounter with the land 'in motion'. Instead of flat images or records of places that have since been lost, or of the processes of demolition or construction themselves, the energy – both creative and destructive – and physical substance of urban change are made manifest. The architectural photographer's conventional play between distant overviews, involved but partial fragments, and constructed boundaries, are supplemented by visual and tactile information added through contact with the site, and extending beyond the picture plane.

These are what the archaeological photographic theorist, Michael Shanks, terms 'photoworks' rather than straightforward photographs, in the sense that that they are explicitly interpretative, and highlight the photographic image as a material artefact, comprised of paper and emulsion. The materiality of photography is reasserted at a time when, through digital technologies, photographs are being detached from the material and chemical processes that once defined their limits. The chance actions of soil, air, water and other elements in the ground shape each image as a unique artefact. Like archaeological photographs, the 'truth' of these images can only be understood in relation to multiple temporal and spatial scales. In *Buried*, photographic time pertains to the presence of the past of each site recorded, the present of each original photographic act, and each burial and retrieval. Also the viewer's present, the moment of reading, with or without a knowledge of the site's transformed condition. At present, there are ongoing debates about the legacy of the Games and the nature of the changes that are happening, though the place is already radically different from what it was when the photographs were taken.

To prepare for the Games, between 2007 and 2008 over 500,000 tonnes of earth were processed through a Soil Treatment Centre.[27] The ODA have very successfully communicated this in the media as a vital benefit of the redevelopment process. Indeed, this was a key feature of the Olympic regeneration narrative; and anyone who visited the site during the construction would have been impressed by the massive mounds of earth around the site, reminiscent of the dust heaps of nineteenth-century London, in the process of being filtered through decontamination machines. That Gill's photographs have been influenced by the chemical properties of the soil, and thus draw our attention to it, is fitting, given the expense and complexity of this process of 'bioremediation'.

The justification for washing the soil was to remove hydrocarbons and heavy metals: indicators of the site's industrial use, mainly as landfill. However, critics have suggested that much of the landfill buried in the area had been safely secured under 2–3 metres of topsoil since the 1970s; and that, ironically, the recent excavations and soil treatment works have had a hazardous effect on local people, subjecting them to dangerous dusts and high levels of radioactivity.[28] Furthermore, contaminated waste is still buried beneath the velodrome and other sporting venues. Local activists, such as Paul Charman and Mike Wells, have done extensive research on the kinds of contamination on the site and the way it has been treated.[29] The contaminants they detail include decaying refuse and its associated production of methane; radioactive waste buried in 1953 after the demolition of a chemical plant, and asbestos. Some of the remaining waste is now only buried to a depth of 60 centimetres beneath the surface, capped by a prophylactic layer of Terram 1000 plastic sheeting – a so-called 'geo-textile' usually used to separate layers of material for functions such as drainage.[30] In this case, the material is coloured orange as a warning sign to future excavators, and it covers most of the Olympic site. Charman and Wells are critical, in particular, of the disturbance of contaminated material during the construction process, and of the use of contaminated material as landfill within the redevelopment. They argue that the site remains contaminated – and potentially dangerous in the future – in spite of the high-profile emphasis the ODA have placed on the redevelopment as a clean-up operation.

In this context the act of burying the photographs and books raises important questions beyond the artist's own statement, which appears on the surface to be quite politically neutral – that his intention was simply to collaborate with the site, and introduce a chance element to his practice. This is dirt (soil) drawn into the circulation of capital in complex ways – first as the site of industry, then for landfill, and now cleansed for re-use within the spectacle of regeneration and afterwards as a site for cultural consumption. The same soil is used by Gill to narrate place, embodying the area's history through chemical traces. Rather than being simply 'natural' or 'unnatural', the land has its own historically and geographically specific nature formed through a unique mixture of properties: minerals, decomposing organic material, chemicals and industrial pollutants.

In Gill's work, dirt is introduced as a material not simply for its potential to create 'distress' aesthetics.[31] He makes high art from base matter, and the 'damage' to the photographs indexes the effects of time and wear. Through burying the photographs, Gill highlights the materials, site, means of production and labour in his own practice, as well as those of the Olympic development process. In the process of his work, Gill changes the value of the dirt in which he buries his photobooks. This brings to mind the most fundamental 'regeneration' taking place: not only the mechanised bioremediation of the soil, but its revaluation as an asset, and the transfer of its ownership, from local residents and businesses, and the state, to elite private investors.[32]

An excavation

As a project in conceptual archaeology, *Buried* emphasises that the discipline of archaeology itself – as with the 'heritage industry' more generally – is inextricably bound to neoliberal redevelopment, and limited in its critical possibilities. In contrast to the archaeological work taking place within the contractual frameworks of the Olympic development, Gill's archaeological metaphor is more akin to experimental 'archaeologies of the contemporary past'.[33] In the 1990s, such projects sought to destabilise the archaeological production of knowledge, and the scientific distancing of archaeology's object of inquiry – the past – through performative archaeological acts intended to scrutinise present-day ('contemporary past') material culture, and emotionally charged situations. Similarly, in the context of Gill's work, burial and excavation refer us to the processes through which information and criticism have circulated, or have been prevented from circulating – buried, suppressed, repressed – within the regeneration discourses.

In discussing repression and the operations of image and archaeological metaphors within psychoanalytic thought, the art historian Griselda Pollock observes:

> Repression at once erases and encrypts traumatic memories. They are buried and thus preserved like relics in the unconscious which is, as Derrida has helped us to recognise, the Freudian archive. Analysis is not only excavation; it is at the same time something more shocking: exhumation. In this double form, analysis does not, however, aim at merely re-archiving relics in the psychic museum.[34]

Taking her lead from Freud's archaeological metaphors, Pollock thus sees psychoanalysis as an archaeological method of exhuming and 'working through' traumatic memories. This therapeutic analogy could apply equally to the potential of contemplating the traumas enacted on the various sites and communities in the Olympic Park development through the medium of Gill's photoworks. In the context of a *tabula rasa* redevelopment, buildings and other structures are razed to the ground, returned to dust. The soil becomes an archive, with archaeology being the only means of extrapolating the knowledge it contains. In burying images of the area's everyday architecture and inhabitants, Gill appears to want to preserve a set of memory-images. Once retrieved, their interactions with the land have lent them primal, elemental qualities. They have changed dramatically, quickly, and now seem like evidence of a long-lost culture, its customs and rituals quite alien. As with memories, when the images are recovered they have partly been distorted or erased, some seem banal, while others are intense, vivid or traumatic. They form a dream-like sequence of flashbacks rather than a coherent narrative.

Gill's work prompts us to think about the different and conflicting 'place images' of the area – the active imaginaries, rather than passive representations – through which individuals and groups have identified with it as a materially, empirically and perceptually knowable entity. The fact that the photographs and books have been buried and ornamented with dirt from the area complicates a binary understanding of reality versus representation. The strategy adopted is the antithesis of the developers' own highly codified 'photo-real' CGI imaging of the site. Gill has created an archive featuring aspects of the area that have been overlooked or actively denied – buried – within the official discourses of the regeneration. He has then put that archive at risk, subject to chance chemical reactions, damage and decomposition. The photobook containing the archive is a 'fetish object' in a psychoanalytic sense – that is, an object that stands in totemically for displaced traumatic memories. Like a trauma from the past that re-emerges to the surface when prompted by new events in the present, *Buried* takes on new meanings, beyond Gill's original intentions, as the redevelopment proceeds, and as the soil becomes increasingly significant in terms of the restructuring taking place.

In Gill's photoworks, there is an excess of image, overflowing from the frame. The method highlights conventional photography's limits – its lack of power to properly represent the ways that architecture and cities are made, the difficulty of documenting the complexity of social, spatial and material restructurings of urban space, and the necessarily reductivist, abstracting tendency of all kinds of photography.

Critical fine art photography still has the power to reveal aspects of urban change that officials might not necessarily want people to see, and to prompt us to question its processes and the authorities' own use of images. Gill's contextual, literally bottom-(ground)-up images are presented to us in a situation where visual rhetoric has played a powerful role in promoting and implementing redevelopment. Gill's situated approach contrasts with the form of business-led managerial planning that has characterised this process. His photoworks poetically and forensically open up urban transformation in all its emotional, material, spatial and temporal complexity.

CONCLUSION

A regeneration supernova is currently exploding across Newham,
London.

Newham Council (2010)[1]

In 2010, Newham Council used a film and brochure to project the image
of a 'regeneration supernova' exploding across the borough.[2] As one of the
London 2012 Olympic Games host boroughs, the area formed part of an
'arc of opportunity'. The intention was to market the potential of places
designated for regeneration – such as Stratford, with the Olympic Park under
construction – as real estate to investors in the Far East at the Shanghai
Expo. The British Pavilion at the Expo itself was, of course, a promotional
fanfare designed to attract Chinese capital. Within this context, the film and
brochure constructed an image of Newham focused on its ongoing reconfiguration through the Games. The borough is presented as a place of resources
– plentiful 'empty' developable land, connectivity ('the new heart of London',
'connected to the world') and labour ('a youthful, energetic and growing
workforce'). Interviewed when the film was released, in 2010, Newham's
Executive Director of Regeneration, Property and Planning, remarked that
Newham is 'literally a platform waiting for things to happen'.[3]

These artefacts of Newham's and London's regeneration strategies emphasise that here the role of local government in regeneration is primarily one of
facilitating private sector investment to instigate urban change. Its function is
to market the potential of land and labour in order to attract global capital.
It is easy to understand the desperate tone of the marketing effort when one
considers that Newham is a borough that faced extraordinary challenges in
2010, and still does after the Games: poverty, unemployment, overcrowding
of poor quality private rented housing, a transient population. In this area,
which was bypassed by the wealth that flowed through London in the boom

years of the 2000s, local politicians and planners have to manage the borough's high levels of debt and its massive housing waiting list within the context of government welfare cuts. In response, gentrification strategy is only very thinly veiled as regeneration strategy, focused on raising land values, opening new markets, and attracting the 'right' kind of businesses and residents to settle – with the assumption of a trickle down effect in which this new wealth will benefit at least some of the existing communities.

The idea of a regeneration supernova – a catastrophic explosion forming a new star – is a projection of London that neatly encapsulates urbanisation proceeding at a rapacious rate, and the dynamic between degradation and regeneration that we have explored in this book. As a spectacular metaphor it mixes the spiritual, celestial and biological, evoking an exciting scale and moment, but also a violent one. As a pitch for redevelopment it works because it is sufficiently abstract and preposterously grand, both full and empty of meaning, leaving potential investors to imagine what could be there in the future. Apart from its definition in astrophysics, there is a long tradition of using 'supernova' figuratively – for example, in science fiction. It can suggest brilliance, explosiveness, collapse, success or excess (a supernova ego).

The corporate graphic style of Newham's film and brochure are the visual mode that perhaps, of all those we have considered, best encapsulates the rhetoric of twenty-first-century neoliberal urban regeneration in London. The film uses excitable editing to bombard spectators with word clouds and image grids: logos, hierarchically organised texts and tables of quantitative information; photographs with graphics superimposed; specially drawn maps and diagrams; CGI illustrations; and 'photo-real' renderings. Some are from commercial 'stock' image libraries, others from architectural offices: visualisations of possible new buildings, a cast of diverse citizens, tourist icons, heritage buildings, green spaces and other images of benevolent urban nature. Unlike the situation in some of the other cases of regeneration we have considered, there is no need here for direct reference to existing degradation because the message is that investors will be given a clean slate.

As we have seen throughout this book, the imaginaries of decline and regeneration constructed in London from the twentieth century to the present work through rhetoric that is multi-layered, and increasingly in tension with its stated goals. Discourses of urban degradation are constructed as the inevitable underside of large-scale redevelopment, and in symbolic forms it is configured into complex relations with material conditions on specific sites. It is important for us to understand how ideas about decline and regeneration operate in different cultural forms because of the crucial role they play in justifying and facilitating particular modes of urban transformation; and because they actively influence peoples' identification with place, their feelings of empowerment or alienation from the processes of urban change, and from the environments that result. As redevelopment intensifies at particular moments we observe how these ideas are construed through various media and act back on the city. Groups of citizens, artists and others have developed their own powerful imaginaries of regeneration, creatively putting these into action in order to critique, resist and offer alternatives to the hegemonic discourses and structures of transformation.

There are tensions between the perspectives and languages deployed by different agents of urban change, and across different representational media. In these contested locales language is powerful, with official discourses often silencing the voices of the communities that are the 'object' of regeneration, in the process forcing a more hardened polarisation of perspectives. Forms of language and representation often distort the understanding of particular locales and communities in unhelpful ways; or constrain the agency and imagination of those who receive them uncritically. Technological advances in the capacity to depict visions of the future city, and the new proliferation of images that inform and effect urban change, appear to be exacerbating rather than resolving the disconnect between built environment and other regeneration professionals and urban communities.

From poverty, slum clearances and pest control in the early twentieth century, to deprivation, mega-event-led redevelopment and the washing of contaminated soil in the 2000s, we have seen how the restructuring of London has been consistently legitimised by the need to tackle abject matter and conditions, and dangerous or disorderly manifestations of nature, and thus produce a healthier, more orderly and socially equitable city. Yet, in the development of visions of improvement, degradation has typically been conceptualised as existing outside of capitalist urbanisation – the undesirable object of its endeavours – rather than fundamental to its processes of 'creative destruction' and its attendant discourses. The cleansing of the soil within the Olympic regeneration serves both a spectacular function, and a practical one, recycling material already exhausted during one phase of industry back into a new cycle of capital production and accumulation.

In all the phases of London's transformation that we have considered, we observe processes akin to abjection, proceeding from the desire for a cleaner and more orderly city, but often resulting in displacements – economic, political, social, psychological – of the communities who are intended to benefit. Displacement in this sense is not only physical, but involves the imposition of elite perspectives on what a 'good' or 'world class' city is, and its accompanying social structures, proper functions and aesthetic attributes. Regeneration often fails to take into account the ways that people already identify in positive ways with the places subject to change – even if these places are deemed unproductive, derelict, or dysfunctional from a certain perspective.

We are better able to approach these problems if we take an inter-disciplinary and multi-scalar approach, looking panoramically across the treatment of different spaces of abjection. In our investigations we have there-fore considered slums, war ruins, dirt-clogged infrastructures, contaminated and ruinous industrial wastelands, red-light zones, 'sink' estates, 'sick' and derelict buildings. In these contexts, projections of urban change, from micro-architectural design interventions to citywide plans, implicitly and explicitly reveal attitudes towards the places, forms of degradation and communities that they address, or purportedly address.

In the cases we have explored, 'regeneration' has consistently been envisioned through representational strategies that seek to detach and decontextualise places from their existing histories, identities and communi-ties. There is therefore a need to reconnect regeneration to the imaginaries of those communities it purportedly sets out to benefit. Surprisingly, given the unpopularity of *tabula rasa* strategies of mid-twentieth-century modernist urban development, more recent models echo these approaches, with sites described as empty platforms for development, in need of total reconstruction rather than incremental improvement. The potential economic value of land overrides the desire or practical potential to better the existing built fabric, flawed and poorly maintained as it might be. We also see selective uses of history to legitimise particular development strategies, or history flattened into apolitical constructions of heritage. It is apparent that working-class areas and post-war housing are rarely thought important to conserve under this banner. A challenge emerges, across the examples we have explored, of how to connect urban and architectural history to regeneration practice more success-fully, linking the understanding of contested sites in the present to the earlier phases of urbanisation through which they were formed.

In this book we have concentrated on clusters of contested sites and their associated communities over extended periods of time. The consistent focus on certain places – sites of major reconstruction – suggests less of a rupture between the modern and late-modern city than we might imagine, and high-lights that it is useful to elucidate continuities as well as shifts. It is helpful to understand the present-day counterparts of the material pollutions associated with the industrial city and its processes of urbanisation; and contemporary regeneration against the backdrop of the restructuring of the city driven by public health imperatives and housing need in the nineteenth and early-twentieth centuries.

We began our investigation by considering a community-centred form of regeneration driven by the urgent need for housing reform in Somers Town in the 1920s and 1930s. In this example, the desire to improve material condi-tions and the environment, and to tackle unwanted natural occurrences, were central. A spectacle of decline, imaginatively communicated, played an impor-tant role in attracting attention to, and investment in, the work of reform. In this context, the power dynamics between the professionals regenerating the area, and the community who lived there, were unequal. Yet the experts and church leaders involved at least situated themselves within the community, directly addressing their needs, and using their own capital and elite perspec-tive to give residents a voice.

The next examples we considered, in the Elephant and Castle from the 1940s to the 1960s, revealed the narratives of reconstruction and modernisa-tion from the post-war period, when the planning system and Welfare State were established and extended, and planning was centralised. Through these examples, we examined a new interest in representing the everyday lives of working-class Londoners living in conditions of poverty. The particular cases we explored highlighted ambiguities and contradictions in representations of specific communities and the degraded spaces they inhabited, and the ways in which particular representational modes and motifs served multiple purposes – serving social reform and reconstruction discourses while also providing a spectacle of poverty.

We also saw how the set-pieces of redevelopment that formed part of the post-war vision, and resulted from *tabula rasa* development, themselves quickly became seen as irretrievably abject, as the modernist project and the Welfare State made way, from the mid-1970s onwards, for the gradual adop-tion of neoliberal strategies of regeneration. These approaches, continue to intensify in varied forms today, as in the mega-event-led redevelopment asso-ciated with the 2012 Olympic Games. We also examined how constructions of urban blight were crucial, shaping the restructuring of the city during and after de-industrialisation. In the late twentieth century we saw how art and architectural design have converged to express narratives of post-industrial decline centred on urban squalor and recycling in regeneration zones.

Now, more than ever before, there is an acute tension between market-led approaches to regeneration that fragment the city they set out to cohere, and democratic processes for the achievement of community-led collective visions of urban improvement. If we reflect back on Paul Hirst's critique of visionary modernist architects for washing away the spirit of the city, imposing top-down visions of order and cleanliness (see page 1), we may be inclined to think that late-modern regeneration has continued this trend. Present-day strategies strive towards an unattainable idealised and sanitised city of steel, glass and granite, in denial of the need for the ordinary and the informal, suffocating diversity, and displacing degradation to the periphery.

NOTES

Introduction

1 Hirst, Paul, 'Modernism's fear of dirt', unpublished keynote lecture, *Cleanliness, Dirt and Women's Roles*, Symposium, The Women's Library (London: 2002).

2 Duffy, Ellie, 'Dirty rotten scoundrels', *Building Design* 1556 (15 November 2002). See: http://www.duffydesign.com/downloads/hirst.pdf (accessed 1 July 2008). The bathhouse conversion, transforming the building into premises for The Women's Library (formerly the Fawcett Library), Guildhall University, was undertaken by Wright and Wright architects and completed in 2002, winning a number of architectural awards.

3 This was a significant year in the history of public health in Britain, given that it saw the appointment of the first Medical Officer of Health: Markus, Thomas A., *Buildings and Power: Freedom and Control in the Origin of Modern Building Types* (London: Routledge, 1993).

4 The Heritage Lottery Fund was set up by Parliament in 1994 to distribute funds raised through the National Lottery for Good Causes in order to 'sustain and transform' heritage. The fund operates as a non-departmental public body reporting to Parliament via the Secretary of State for Culture, Media and Sport. Policy is steered by the government but funding decisions are made independently of it. See: http://www.hlf.org.uk/aboutus/Pages/OurBackground.aspx (accessed 20 July 2012). At the time of writing, The Women's Library's custodians, Guildhall University, have said that they can no longer fund it. It is to re-open in 2013 as part of LSE.

5 Rogers, Richard, *Towards an Urban Renaissance: The Report of the Urban Task Force Chaired by Lord Rogers of Riverside* (London: Urban Task Force, 1999); Rogers, Richard, *Towards a Strong Urban Renaissance: Urban Task Force* (London: Urban Task Force, 2005), p. 2.

6 *Oxford English Dictionary*. See: http://www.oed.com (accessed 1 March 2012). For an excellent discussion of the uses of regeneration as a metaphor in urban policy see Furbey, Robert, 'Urban "regeneration": reflections on a metaphor', *Critical Social Policy* 19(4) (1999), pp. 419–45.

7 The *Oxford English Dictionary* cites the following early example of 'regeneration' in reference to place: "Regeneration, *n.*", 1 b. In extended use: renaissance;

renewal, spec. of a geographical area by the improvement of its economic and social conditions, 1567, W. Painter, *Palace of Pleasure* II. xxij. f. 166v, "The further he went, the greater he saw the increase, & almost a regeneration, or as I may say, a new birth of rare things, which made yt littlenesse of the place more stately and wonderfull", *Oxford English Dictionary*. See: http://www.oed.com (accessed 1 March 2012). On large-scale nineteenth-century slum clearance programmes in London and the displacements of communities that accompanied them, see Stedman-Jones, Gareth, *Outcast London: A Study in the Relationship Between Classes in Victorian Society* (Oxford, UK: Oxford University Press, 1971).

8 Mayor of London, *The London Plan: Spatial Development Strategy for Greater London* (London: Greater London Authority, July 2011).

9 The dataset is produced by the Social Disadvantage Research Centre, University of Oxford. The first index was produced in 2000, covering 33 variables for 8,414 wards in England. It was championed by the New Labour government for the purpose of identifying areas most in need, so that resources could be targeted towards them. Further indices were published in 2004 and 2007, with increasing specificity to particular locales: HM Government, *Index of Multiple Deprivation*. See: http://data.gov.uk/dataset/index-of-multiple-deprivation (accessed 20 July 2012); Communities and Local Government, *The English Indices of Deprivation 2007*. See: http://www.communities.gov.uk/documents/communities/pdf/733520.pdf (accessed 20 July 2012).

10 See, for example, Colomb, Claire, 'Unpacking new labour's "urban renaissance" agenda: towards a socially sustainable reurbanization of British cities?', *Planning, Practice & Research* 22(1) (2007), pp. 1–24; Davidson, Mark, 'Love thy neighbour? Social mixing in London's gentrification frontiers', *Environment and Planning A* 42(3) (2010), pp. 524–44; Edwards, Michael, 'King's Cross: renaissance for whom?', in John Punter (ed.), *Urban Design, Urban Renaissance and British Cities* (London: Routledge, 2010), pp. 189–205; Imrie, Rob, Loretta Lees and Mike Raco (eds), *Regenerating London: Governance, Sustainability and Community in a Global City* (London: Routledge, 2009); Porter, Libby and Kate Shaw (eds), *Whose Urban Renaissance? An International Comparison of Urban Regeneration Strategies* (London: Routledge, 2009).

David Harvey defines 'neoliberalism' as follows: 'Neoliberalism is in the first instance a theory of political economic practices that proposes that human well-being can best be advanced by liberating individual entrepreneurial freedoms and skills within an institutional framework characterized by strong private property rights, free markets and free trade ... Furthermore if markets do not exist (in areas such as land, water, education, health care, social security, or environmental pollution) then they must be created, by state action if necessary': Harvey, David, *A Brief History of Neoliberalism* (Oxford, UK: Oxford University Press, 2005), p. 2.

11 For a discussion of the context for the Abercrombie plan, see Hebbert, Michael, *London: More By Fortune Than By Design* (Chichester: John Wiley and Sons, 1998).

12 For a recent discussion of the health advantages of living in cities, see Rydin, Yvonne *et al.*, 'Shaping cities for health: complexity and the planning of urban environments in the 21st century', *The Lancet* (London: The Lancet Commission and UCL, 2012).

13 Porter and Shaw (eds), *Whose Urban Renaissance?*; and see note 10 above.

14 In the case of London, see Imrie *et al*, *Regenerating London*. Through a wide range of case studies this collection demonstrates how regeneration is primarily shaped by, and in the interests of, politicians, policy-makers, business elites and built environment professionals.

15 Ennis, Nick and Gordon Douglass, 'Culture and regeneration – what evidence is there of a link and how can it be measured?', *GLA Economics Working Paper*, 48 (2011), p. 2. For Edwards' evaluation of the work of the King's Cross Regeneration Partnership, see Mutale, Emmanuel and Michael Edwards, *Monitoring and Evaluation of the work of the King's Cross Partnership: Final Report* (London: Bartlett School of Planning, UCL, 2003). For a recent discussion of culture-led 'creative city' strategies of urban economic regeneration, see Harris, Andrew and Louis Moreno, *Creative City Limits: Urban Cultural Economy in a New Era of Austerity* (London: UCL Urban Laboratory and the Arts and Humanities Research Council, 2012).

16 Edwards, Michael, 'London for sale: towards the radical marketisation of urban space', *Urban Constellations* (Berlin: Jovis Verlag, 2011), p. 56. In architectural criticism, compare this with Littlefield, David (ed.), *Architectural Design: London (Re)generation* (London: John Wiley, 2012): 'property development is not the same thing as regeneration. Nor is change … We would do well to remember that the city does not actually heal or regenerate itself; it relies on the active agents (people, policy-makers) within that organism to provoke change' (p. 9).

17 Hatherley, Owen, *A Guide to the New Ruins of Great Britain* (London: Verso, 2010), p. xv; see also Hatherley, Owen, *Militant Modernism* (Winchester: Zero Books, 2008).

18 Hatherley: *A Guide to the New Ruins of Great Britain*, pp. xii–xiii.

19 Littlefield, *London (Re)generation*, p. 9.

20 See, for example, Southwark Notes, 'Regeneration? Gentrification?'. See: http://southwarknotes.wordpress.com/what-is-regeneration-gentrification/; Games Monitor. See: http://www.gamesmonitor.org.uk/; Save Carpenters. See: http://savecarpenters.wordpress.com/ (all accessed 1 July 2012), King's Cross Railway Lands Group. See: http://www.kxrlg.org.uk/history/timeline.pdf (accessed 30 April 2007).

21 Beauregard, Robert, *Voices of Decline: the Postwar Fate of U.S. Cities* (London: Routledge, 2003), p. x.

22 For comparison, on discourses of urban decline in the UK see, for example: Baeten, Guy, 'Hypochondriac geographies of the city and the new urban dystopia', *City* 6/1 (2002), p. 111; Hastings, Annette, 'Discourse and urban change: introduction to the special issue', *Urban Studies* 36/1 (1999).

23 For example, Hastings, 'Discourse and urban change'.

24 For interesting uses of the term 'imaginary' in geography and urban history see Shields, Rob, *Places on the Margin: Alternative Geographies of Modernity* (London: Routledge, 1991), p. 6; and Ross, Rebecca, 'Picturing the profession: the view from above and the civic imaginary in Burnham's plans', *Journal of Planning History*, forthcoming.

25 Lacan, Jacques, *Écrits: A Selection* (London: W. W. Norton, 2003, first published 1966).

26 Castoriadis, Cornelius, *The Imaginary Institution of Society* (Cambridge: Polity Press, 1987, first published 1975).

27 Castoriadis, *The Imaginary Institution of Society*, p. 127.

28 Castoriadis, *The Imaginary Institution of Society*, p. 127.

29 Castoriadis, *The Imaginary Institution of Society*, p. 146.

30 Kerr, Joe, 'Introduction' in Joe Kerr, Andrew Gibson and Mike Seaborne (eds), *London: From Punk to Blair* (London: Reaktion, 2003), pp. 11–22, 12.

31 Raban, Jonathan, 'My own private metropolis', *Financial Times*, 8 August 2008.

32 Raban, 'My own private metropolis'.

33 See, for example: Robson, Garry, 'Class, criminality and embodied consciousness: Charlie Richardson and a south east London habitus', *Critical Urban Studies: Occasional Papers* (London: Goldsmiths College, 1997), p. 7; Walkowitz, Judith, *City of Dreadful Delight: Narratives of Sexual Danger in Late-Victorian London* (London: Virago, 1992), pp. 17, 21.

34 For example, architectural historian Diane Ghirado narrates the story of architecture after modernism through an account of the post-industrial transformation of London's Docklands from 'wasteland' to financial services centre: Ghirado, Diane, *Architecture after Modernism* (New York: Thames and Hudson, 1996), pp. 176–94; see also Hamnett, Chris, *Unequal City: London in the Global Arena* (London/New York: Routledge, 2003); Kerr *et al.*, *London from Punk to Blair*.

35 Kristeva, in Kelly Oliver (ed.), *The Portable Kristeva* (New York: Columbia University Press, 1997), pp. 209–10.

36 Laporte, Dominique, *History of Shit* (Cambridge, MA: MIT Press, 2000).

37 Kristeva, Julia, *Powers of Horror: An Essay on Abjection* (New York: Columbia University Press, 1982). Kristeva writes: 'It is thus not lack of cleanliness or health that causes abjection but what disturbs identity, system, order. What does not respect borders, positions, rules. The in-between, the ambiguous, the composite' (p. 4).

38 Bataille, Georges, 'L'Abjection et les formes misérables', in Georges Bataille (ed.), *Essais de sociologie, oeuvres complètes* (Paris: Gallimard, 1970).

39 Douglas, Mary, *Purity and Danger: An Analysis of the Concepts of Pollution and Taboo* (London: Routledge, 2000, first published 1966), p. 2. For discussion of Mary Douglas' theory of dirt in relation to the city see, Campkin, Ben, 'Placing matter out of place: *Purity and Danger* as evidence for architecture and urbanism', *Architectural Theory Review* 18(1), forthcoming 2013; and Campkin, Ben and Rosie Cox (eds), *Dirt: New Geographies of Cleanliness and Contamination* (London: I.B.Tauris, 2007).

40 Steve Pile describes the process of abjection thus: 'Children learn to displace dangerous or unwanted feelings onto others – others who are perceived to be different. These feelings are simultaneously social, bodily and spatial ... In abjection, senses of revulsion over bodily materials and feelings are established. The subject wants to expel whatever is reviled, but is powerless to achieve it: thus, for example, the desire to be completely clean all the time cannot be achieved, purity cannot be maintained. Abjection, then, is a perpetual condition of surveillance, maintenance and policing of impossible "cleanliness"': Pile, Steve, *The Body and the City: Psychoanalysis, Space and Subjectivity* (London: Routledge, 1996), p. 90.

41 Kristeva quoted in Kelly, *The Portable Kristeva*, p. 372.

42 Robinson, Jennifer, 'Feminism and the spaces of transformation', *Transactions of the Institute of British Geographers: New Series* 25/3 (2000), pp. 285–301.

43 Lahiji, Nadir and Daniel S. Friedman, 'At the sink: architecture in abjection', in Nadir Lahiji and Daniel S. Friedman (eds), *Plumbing: Sounding Modern Architecture* (New York: Princeton Architectural Press, 1997); McClintock, Anne, *Imperial Leather: Race, Gender and Sexuality in the Colonial Contest* (London/New York: Routledge, 1995); Penner, Barbara and Olga Gershenson (eds), *Ladies and Gents: Public Toilets and Gender* (Philadelphia: Temple University Press, 2009); Robinson, Jenny, 'Feminism and the spaces of transformation'; Sibley, David, *Geographies of Exclusion: Society and Difference in the West* (London: Routledge, 1995); Wilton, Robert D., 'The constitution of difference: space and psyche in landscapes of exclusion', *Geoforum* 29/2 (1998), pp. 173–85; Urbach, Henry, 'Closets, clothes, disClosure', in Jane Rendell, Barbara Penner and Iain Borden (eds), *Gender Space Architecture* (London/New York: Routledge, 2000), pp. 342–52.

44 The social, aesthetic and other contradictions inherent within the different forms of urban change explored in this book suggest that 'abjection' is a more useful term than Freud's conception of the 'urge to cleanliness' as part of 'proper' evolutionary development. For Freud, along with order and beauty, cleanliness constituted one of the three prerequisites for the progress of civilisation. He writes: 'There is an unmistakable social factor in the cultural striving for cleanliness ... which is later justified on grounds of hygiene, but manifested itself before this connection was appreciated.' See Freud, Sigmund, *Civilization and Its Discontents* (London, 2002, first published 1930, p. 41, n. 1). The transformation from 'anal eroticism' and reliance on olfactory stimuli, and the 'urge for cleanliness', accompany man's evolution into an upright posture, setting him apart from animals. The emergence of responses of shame and disgust to excrement – 'organic repression' – provide key components of proper development of the libido. See Bersani, Leo, *The Freudian Body: Psychoanalysis and Art* (New York: Columbia University Press, 1986), p. 17. For recent discussions of Freud's ideas on cleanliness and order in psychoanalytic architectural theory, see Holm, Lorens, 'eS aitcH eYe Tee', *The Journal of Architecture* 12/4 (2007), p. 428; Lahiji *et al.*, 'At the sink: architecture in abjection', p. 42.

45 Vidler, Anthony, *The Architectural Uncanny: Essays in the Modern Unhomely* (Cambridge, MA: MIT Press, 1992); Picon, Antoine, 'Anxious landscapes: from

the ruin to rust', *Grey Room* 1/Fall (2000), pp. 64–83; Williams, Richard, *The Anxious City: English Urbanism in the Late Twentieth Century* (London: Carlton Books, 2004).

46 Kristeva, 'Approaching abjection', in Oliver (ed.), *The Portable Kristeva*, p. 230.

47 On abject art, see Krauss, Rosalind, 'The destiny of the informe', in Rosalind Krauss and Yve-Alain Bois (eds), *Formless: A User's Guide* (New York: Zone Books, 1997), p. 235; Kelly, M., *The Uncanny* (Cologne: König, 2004); Vidler, *The Architectural Uncanny*. For a recent discussion of the uncanny in neo-Marxian urban analysis, see Kaïka, Maria, *City of Flows: Modernity, Nature and the City* (Abingdon, UK/New York: Routledge, 2005).

48 Freud, Sigmund, 'The uncanny', in G. Williams (ed.), *The Gothic* (London, 2007, first published 1919), pp. 168–73.

49 Vidler, *The Architectural Uncanny*, p. 3.

50 Jameson, Fredric, *Postmodernism, or, the Cultural Logic of Late Capitalism* (London: Duke University Press, 1991), pp. 32–3.

51 Baeten, 'Hypochondriac geographies of the city and the new urban dystopia'; 'The uses of deprivation in the neoliberal city', in N. Lakides (ed.), *Urban Politics Now: Re-Imagining Democracy in the Neoliberal City* (Rotterdam, NAi Publishers, 2007); Gandy, 'The Paris sewers and the rationalization of urban space', *Transactions of the British Institute of Geographers* 24/1 (1999), pp. 23–24; Gandy, *Concrete and Clay: Reworking Nature in New York City* (Cambridge, MA: MIT Press, 2002); Gandy and Alimuddin Zumla, *The Return of the White Plague: Global Poverty and the 'New' Tuberculosis* (London and New York: Verso, 2003); Kaïka, *City of Flows;* Kaïka and Erik Swyngedouw, 'Fetishizing the modern city'; Swyngedouw and Kaïka, 'The environment of the city ... or the urbanization of nature', in Bridge, Gary and Sophie Watson (eds.), *The Blackwell Companion to the City* (Oxford: Blackwell, 2000), pp. 567–80.

52 Marx, Karl, 'Economic and philosophical manuscripts', in Karl Marx, *Early Writings* (London: Penguin/New Left Review, 1992, first published 1844), pp. 359–60.

53 Wuthnow *et al.* write that: 'For Mary Douglas the artifact is simple, obvious and everyday, much like Marx's commodity and Durkheim's totem': Wuthnow *et al.*, *Cultural Analysis*, p. 85.

54 Kaïka and Swyngedouw, 'Fetishizing the modern city', p. 136.

Chapter 1: Slum Spectacle

1 Anon, 'The rise and fall of Somers Town', *Estates Gazette*, 22 November 1930.

2 Origin Housing was formed in 2010 as an amalgamation of St Pancras Housing Association, the Humanist Housing Association (formed in the 1930s) and Griffin Homes (formed in 1974 to provide housing for London Transport staff).

3 Holmes, Malcolm J., *Housing Is Not Enough: The Story of St Pancras Housing Association* (London: St Pancras Housing Association, 1999), p. 10. Jellicoe

served as leader from 1922 to 1927. The St Pancras House Improvement Society was connected to the local Mary Ward Settlement through individuals such as Mrs Edith Neville, one of the Society's committee members and warden of the Mary Ward Settlement in the early 1920s. See: http://www.magd.ox.ac.uk/college/societies/trust (accessed 31 March 2009); Beauman, Katherine Bentley, *Women and the Settlement Movement* (London: Radcliffe Press, 1996), p. 148.

4 Although the Society was officially non-denominational, in practice it was essentially an Anglo-Catholic organisation.

5 Members of the Garden Cities and Town Planning Association (GCTPA) were directly represented on the Society's committee; and the rules of the Society were based on those of the Association: Holmes, *Housing Is Not Enough*, pp. 11, 13. The Society also contributed to publications on housing with other individuals and organisations associated with the Garden Cities movement. However, in many ways, building flats in densely-populated urban areas was the antithesis of GCTPA principles, with their focus on planned, self-contained communities, encircled by greenbelt, and with designated areas of housing, industry and agriculture. Bridget Cherry and Nikolaus Pevsner later dismissed the Society's classification of their Sydney Street Estate as a 'miniature garden city' as 'optimistic': Cherry, Bridget and Nikolaus Pevsner, *Buildings of England. London 4: North* (London: Penguin, 1998), p. 380.

6 Barclay, Irene, *The St Pancras Housing Association in Camden: What It Is and Why: A History 1924 to 1972* (London: St Pancras Housing Association, 1972), p. 5; Holmes, *Housing Is Not Enough*, p. 16.

7 Holmes, *Housing Is Not Enough*, p. 11.

8 McManus, Ruth, 'Public utility societies, Dublin Corporation and the development of Dublin, 1920–1940'. See: http://www.ucd.ie/gsi/pdf/29-1/pus.pdf (accessed July 2012).

9 Barclay, *The St Pancras Housing Association in Camden*, p. 9.

10 Darling, Elizabeth, 'To induce humanitarian sentiments in prurient Londoners: the propaganda activities of London's voluntary housing associations in the inter-war period', *London Journal* 27/1 (2002), p. 43. This had already been a complaint of philanthropic model housing schemes of the 1880s, which neglected the 'worst class in Somers Town', critics argued. See John Hollingshead, quoted in Porter, Roy, *London: A Social History* (London: Hamish Hamilton, 1994), p. 273.

11 Anon, 'Interesting remarks on present day problem', *Litchfield Times*, 24 January 1930.

12 Blake, Ernest George, *The Protection of Buildings against Vermin. With a Comprehensive Description of the Most Effective Methods that Can Be Adopted for the Extermination of Rats, Mice and Various Insects* (London: Crosby Lockwood & Son, 1926), pp. 1–2.

13 According to the London Borough of Camden's chief pest control officer, at the beginning of the twenty-first century, infestations were exacerbated by the poor quality of construction, just as they were in the 1920s and 1930s: 'Modern

[contemporary] buildings present the biggest problems ... There are more void areas, partition walls, gaps for insulation, trunking and cabling areas, electricity cupboards etcetera and when holes are drilled they are not drilled to size but are too big for their purpose. These factors create perfect environments to host pests such as rodents'. Interview with Dave Coleman, Environmental Health Pest Controller, London Borough of Camden, 8 April 2008.

14 Hwang, Stephen W., Tomislav J. Svoboda, Iain J. De Jong, Karl J. Kabasele and Evie Gogosis, 'Bed bug infestations in an urban environment', *Emerging Infectious Diseases* 11/4 (2005), p. 533. In Swedish, the plural for bedbugs is 'vägglöss', which translates literally as 'wall bugs'.

15 For film and photographic footage see also Crockford, Sue (dir.), 'Somerstown' (UK: People to People, 1984).

16 Henry Mayhew refers to a 1503 report of the insects in Mortlake: Mayhew, Henry, *London Labour and the London Poor* 3 (London: Constable, 1968, first published 1861), p. 34.

17 Campkin, Ben, '"Terror by night": bedbug infestations in London', in Matthew Gandy (ed.), *Urban Constellations* (Berlin: Jovis Verlag, 2011), pp. 139–44.

18 Kaïka, Maria and Erik Swyngedouw, 'Fetishizing the modern city' Gandy, *Concrete and Clay*; Gandy and Zumla, *The Return of the White Plague*; Gissen, David, 'Atmospheres of late-modernity: the urban production of indoor air in New York City, 1963–2003', unpublished PhD dissertation, Department of Geography, University College London, 2007; Gissen, David, *Subnature: Architecture's other Environments* (New York: Princeton Architectural Press, 2009); Swyngedouw and Kaïka, 'The environment of the city'.

19 Gandy, *Concrete and clay*, p. 2.

20 Swyngedouw and Kaïka, 'The environment of the city', p. 136.

21 Gissen, *Subnature: Architecture's Other Environments* , p. 21–22.

22 Orwell, George, *Down and Out in Paris and London* (London: Penguin, 2003, first published 1933). On the use of military metaphors in hygienism, see Forty, Adrian, *Objects of Desire: Design and Society since 1750* (London: Thames & Hudson, 1986), p. 168.

23 For example, in *The Cherry Orchard*, which opened in 1904, Anton Chekov's character Trofimov describes how 'the workers eat abominably, sleep without pillows, thirty or forty to a room, and everywhere there are bedbugs, stench, dampness, and immorality'. See Beck, Bernard, 'Bedbugs, stench, dampness, and immorality: a review essay on recent literature about poverty', *Social Problems* 15/1, Summer (1967), pp. 101–14.

24 Gandal, Keith, *The Virtues of the Vicious: Jacob Riis, Stephen of the Slum* (New York: Oxford University Press, 1997).

25 This phrase, derived from the French 'nostalgie de la boue', is used by cultural historian Michael Collins to describe the observations of middle-class commentators, including Orwell, on working-class life in south London: Collins, Michael, *The Likes of Us: A Biography of the White Working Class* (London: Granta, 2004), p. 110.

26 Irene Barclay had become the first female chartered surveyor in 1922.

27 Hamilton, Ian, Irene T. Barclay and Evelyn E. Perry, 'The truth about bugs', in Kathleen M. England (ed.), *Housing: A Citizen's Guide to the Problem* (London: Chatto & Windus, 1931), pp. 73–7. Hamilton *et al.* trace the etymology of *Cimex lectularius* to 'a Celtic word signifying ghost or goblin' because of the terror caused by its nocturnal attacks.

28 Darling quotes a slum tenant, a Mr Norwood, speaking directly about his living conditions in the film *Housing Problems* (1935). The quote communicates very clearly his sense of anger at living in a dwelling 'overrun with bugs', mice and rats: Darling, *Re-forming Britain*, pp. 158–9.

29 Forty, *Objects of Desire*, p. 158.

30 Darling, *Re-forming Britain*, p. 52.

31 Forty, *Objects of Desire*, p. 156.

32 Hamilton *et al.*, 'The truth about bugs', p. 77.

33 Barclay, Irene, *People Need Roots: The Story of the St Pancras Housing Association* (London: St Pancras Housing Association, 1976), pp. 18, 26.

34 Barclay quoted in Crockford, 'Somerstown'.

35 Barclay, *People Need Roots*, p. 23.

36 Architect and theorist, Jonathan Hill, has recently explored the 'immaterial' in architecture in an effort to disrupt conventional notions of architectural materiality as 'solid, stable and reassuring': Hill, Jonathan, *Immaterial Architecture* (London: Routledge, 2006), pp. 2–3. Reinhardt, Klaus and Michael T. Siva-Jothy discuss the noxious smell associated with bedbugs: Klaus Reinhardt and Michael T. Siva-Jothy, 'Biology of the bed bugs (*Cimicidae*)', *Annual Review of Entomology* 52 (2007), p. 363.

37 In discussing industrial ruins, geographer Tim Edensor has remarked that 'animals and plants are always waiting in the wings, ready to transform familiar material environments at the slightest opportunity': Edensor, Tim, 'Waste matter: the debris of industrial ruins and the disordering of the material world', *Journal of Material Culture* 10/3 (2005a), p. 319.

38 Hamilton *et al.*, 'The truth about bugs', p. 75.

39 Darling, *Re-forming Britain*, p. 21. Further incentives to build new blocks of flats were the prohibitive cost of converting and renovating the slum houses; and the organisation's commitment to rehouse the slum tenants in new homes on the sites of their existing ones, rather than displace anyone. Holmes, *Housing Is Not Enough*, p. 18.

40 Darling, 'To induce humanitarian sentiments in prurient Londoners', p. 45; Darling, *Re-forming Britain*, p. 22. The SPHIS was not unique in this respect. For example, Kensington Housing Trust also made documentary films about slum life. However, the SPHIS were perhaps the most experimental.

41 Clarke, Linda, *Building Capitalism: Historical Change and the Labour Process in the Production of the Built Environment* (London: Routledge, 1991), plate 20, p. 264.

42 Clarke, *Building Capitalism*, pp. 214, 264.

43 Social historian Roy Porter also discusses the 'meanness' of proportion in the area's highly standardised and low-grade Georgian town houses in his account of Somers Town's development. Architect of Regent's Park John Nash complained of the threat of more 'houses of such a mean sort as have been built at Somers Town' being built further north: Porter, *London*, p. 217.

44 Clarke, *Building Capitalism*, p. 214. See also Dennis, Richard, 'Review of Linda Clarke, 'Building capitalism: historical change and the labour process in the production of the built environment', *Journal of Historical Geography* 18/4 (1992), p. 486.

45 Suitably flammable, cardboard and straw are identified as the materials used in the construction of the models in a newspaper report of the event: Anon, 'Clearing the slums: brighter homes in St Pancras', *Westminster Chronicle*, 6 February 1931.

46 The striking photographs of the incineration of the vermin models have previously been published without commentary in two historical accounts and one photographic history of Somers Town: Clarke, *Building Capitalism*; Holmes, Malcolm J., *Somers Town: A Record of Change* (London: London Borough of Camden, 1989); Holmes, *Housing Is Not Enough*.

47 The St Pancras Housing Association's architect, Ian Hamilton, was the nephew of General Sir Ian Hamilton who ignited the vermin effigies: Barclay, *People Need Roots*, p. 22.

48 Anon, 'Slum clearance in Somers Town', *The Times*, 30 January 1931.

49 Anon, 'Slum clearance in Somers Town'; Anon, 'The "burning" of slumland', *The Sunday Times*, 25 January 1931; Scott, Nigel, 'A peaceable habitation', *House Happenings* 8 (1931), pp. 20–2.

50 For example, as Chairman of the LCC, Lord Monk Bretton dynamited a group of slum buildings in January 1930: Anon, 'Dynamiting of slums by Lord Monk Bretton', *The Daily Chronicle*, 24 January 1930.

51 Holmes, *Housing Is Not Enough*, p. 16.

52 The caption to one of the photographs of the event published in the Society's magazine *House Happenings* reads: 'The Criminals ready for execution before the funeral pyre was lighted': Scott, 'A peaceable habitation', p. 24.

53 Holmes, *Housing Is Not Enough*, p. 98.

54 Darling, 'To induce humanitarian sentiments in prurient Londoners', p. 52.

55 Belmont, Gerard E. and Leonard A. Day, *Paradox City* (22.34 minutes) (London: St Pancras House Improvement Society, 1934).

56 Cranston, Ros, 'Paradox city' (London: BFI Screenonline, undated). See: http://www.screenonline.org.uk/film/id/1168236/ (accessed 1 May 2009).

57 A lost film, *The Terror That Waketh in the Night*, is likely to have focused specifically on bedbugs. A montage of the Society's films in Sue Crockford's *Somerstown* (1984) shows footage of infestations and live insects: Crockford, 'Somerstown'.

58 Scott, Nigel (ed.), *House Happenings* 7 (1930); Scott, 'A peaceable habitation'.

59 Scott, 'A peaceable habitation', p. 21.

60   Scott, 'A peaceable habitation', p. 21.
61   Ivor Novello, 'Keep the Home Fires Burning' (1914). See: http://www.first-worldwar.com/audio/keepthehomefiresburning.htm (accessed 21 April 2008).
62   Anon, '"Burning" down the slums, A miniature garden city arising in the heart of Somers Town', *St Pancras Chronicle*, 30 January 1931.
63   Barclay quoted in Crockford, 'Somerstown'.
64   Anon, 'The "burning" of slumland' (1931).
65   Scott, 'A peaceable habitation', p. 8.
66   Barclay, *People Need Roots*, p. 28. Fumigation was common practice as part of the process of moving slum tenants to new housing, and became formalised as part of municipal slum clearances in a report published on *Management of Municipal Housing Estates* (1938). See Anon, *Moving from the Slums: Seventh Report of the Housing Management Sub-Committee of the Central Housing Advisory Committee* (London: Her Majesty's Stationery Office, 1956). Fumigation targeted mainly bedbugs, with furniture being treated using hydrogen cyanide gas inside removal vans, and bedding being steam-cleaned. The scientific bases of these practices were later laid out in Medical Research Council, *Report of the Committee on Bedbug Infestation* (1935–40): Anon, *Moving from the Slums* (1956).
67   Holmes, *Housing Is Not Enough*, p. 18.
68   Matthew Gandy writes: 'much of the public health discourse of the modern era has drawn on racialized and class-based caricatures of cleanliness and hygiene, stressing behavioural admonitions to the poor in place of any real challenge to the patterns of property ownership and official neglect that underpin the persistence of slum housing': *Concrete and Clay*, p. 3.

       Similarly, historian Nan H. Dreher has examined the moral panics that emerged in London about the use of parks by 'verminous persons', mostly vagrants and others perceived to be carriers of vermin and disease. This study shows how verminous metaphors were used to denigrate particular social outcasts in urban debates. Informed by new knowledge about disease transmission and prevention, class discrimination against workers and the poor shifted, Dreher argues, 'to a new form of exclusion that emphasised individual behaviour rather than inherited status ... Discrimination against verminous persons ... made the respectable citizenry seem purer, cleaner, and healthier in comparison'. In this context marginal social groups were portrayed as vermin-carrying and vermin-like; and the discourses around vermin control stigmatised the poor, rather than identifying or alleviating the conditions that produced their poverty: Dreher, Nan H., 'The virtuous and the verminous: turn-of-the-century moral panics in London's public parks', *Albion* 29/2 (1997), p. 260.

Chapter 2: Life in the Ruins

1   Forshaw, John H. and Patrick Abercrombie, *County of London Plan. Prepared for the London County Council* (London: Macmillan and Co., 1943), p. 135.

2 Hardy won an Encyclopaedia Britannica photography award for the series. For context, on the wider politics of *Picture Post*, Hardy's work for the magazine, its account of the social transformation of Britain from 1938–57 and its layout, see Hall, Stuart, 'The social eye of *Picture Post*', in Glenn Jordan (ed.), *Down the Bay: Picture Post, Humanist Photography and Images of 1950s Cardiff* (Cardiff: Bluetown History and Arts Centre, 2001), pp. 67–74; Anon, 'A record of the symposium held to celebrate the 150th birthday of photography', *Makers of Photographic History* (Bradford: National Museum of Photography, 1990a); Hallett, Michael, *The Real Story of Picture Post* (Birmingham: ARTicle Press, 1994); Weightman, Gavin, *Picture Post Britain* (London: Collins & Brown, 1991).

3 Lloyd, A. L. and Bert Hardy, 'Life in the Elephant', *Picture Post* 42/2, 8 January 1949, pp. 10–16, p. 15. On the regulation of streets and traffic as constituent of urban modernisation, see Dennis, Richard, *Cities in Modernity: Representations and Productions of Metropolitan Space, 1840–1930* (Cambridge, UK: Cambridge University Press, 2008), esp. pp. 113–43.

4 Interview with Sheila Hardy, widow of Bert Hardy and former picture researcher at *Picture Post*, Bert Hardy Photographic Studio, London, 29 October 2006.

5 Although there are various versions of how the area got its name, it is generally thought to have derived from the Elephant and Castle inn, located on the site of the present Michael Faraday Memorial, and established in the mid-seventeenth century. The inn occupied the site of a former smithy and a cutler's. The cutlers' guild had an elephant with a castle on its back as its heraldic emblem.

6 Hardy, Bert, *Bert Hardy: My Life* (London: G. Fraser, 1985), p. 105. The magazine was known for its strong page layouts, whereby pictures were arranged strategically together to produce a dynamic visual story that, once it had caught the reader's attention, would lead to the captions and articles.

7 Hardy used a 35 mm Leica camera and was known for his skill in using natural light to dramatic effect. The unfiltered Leica lens produced prints with startling flare, which were more subdued after they had been reproduced in magazines. Sarah McDonald refers to the Elephant, and Hardy and Lloyd's earlier Gorbals photo-essay, as 'classics' in McDonald, Sarah, '*Picture Post*' – Essay for *Encyclopaedia of Twentieth Century Photography* (2004). See: http://corporate.gettyimages.com/masters2/press/articles/BWP_Picture_Post.pdf#search=%22sarah%20mcdonald%20picture%20post%22 (accessed 1 August 2006).

8 Robson, 'Class, criminality and embodied consciousness', p. 7; Reilly, Leonard, *Southwark: An Illustrated History* (London: London Borough of Southwark, 1998), p. 67.

9 Collins, *The Likes of Us*, p. 10.

10 Humphrey, Stephen, *Southwark in Archives* (London: London Borough of Southwark, 2000), pp. 30, 32.

11 Robson, Garry, *No One Likes Us, We Don't Care* (Oxford: Berg, 2000), p. 51.

12 Anon, 'Elephant and Castle – a history of change', Southwark Council (2008). See: http://www.elephantandcastle.org.uk/history-of-change (accessed 5 May 2009).

13   Anon, 'Improving the Elephant', *London*, 16 December 1897.

14   Anon, *Opening of the Elephant and Castle subways by the Mayoress of Southwark (Mrs. A. J. Wilson) on Thursday the 1st June, at 3.0 pm. Programme* (London: Metropolitan Borough of Southwark, 1911). The subways were jointly funded by the LCC, the Baker Street and Waterloo Railway Company, and the Metropolitan Borough of Southwark.

15   Forshaw and Abercrombie, *County of London Plan*, pp. 14, 19. For the Elephant, recovery from the air raids that devastated the environment in the early 1940s was slow. Many buildings remained in a ruined state until 1956, when clearance began in earnest. The redevelopment was so slow that it was out of sync with need, with a road scheme designed in 1948 only being fully implemented in the 1960s, by which time car use had massively increased: White, Jerry, *London in the Twentieth Century* (London: MIT Press, 2008), p. 51.

16   Jacobs, Jane, *The Death and Life of Great American Cities* (London: Pimlico, 1961).

17   Anon, 'L.C.C.'s big reconstruction scheme. Redevelopment of the Elephant and Castle area', *The Municipal Journal and Local Government Administrator*, 25 October 1946.

18   Hall, 'The social eye of *Picture Post*'.

19   Jordan, *Down the Bay: Picture Post, Humanist Photography and Images of 1950s Cardiff*, p. 28; Sontag, Susan, *On Photography* (London: Penguin, 1979), pp. 7, 9.

20   Collins, *The Likes of Us*, p. 129.

21   Hallett, *The Real Story of Picture Post*, p. 1.

22   Hall, 'The social eye of *Picture Post*', p. 71.

23   Hall, 'The social eye of *Picture Post*', p. 71.

24   On humanist photography as a mode with both poetic and social ambitions, see Gautrand, Jean-Claude, 'Looking at others: humanism and neo-realism', in Michel Frizot (ed.), *A New History of Photography* (London: Konemann, 1998), pp. 614, 619.

25   Riis, Jacob A., *How the Other Half Lives* (London: Penguin Classics, 1997, first published 1890).

26   Thomson, John, *Victorian London Street Life in Historic Photographs* (New York: Dover Publications Inc, 1994).

27   Gandal, *The Virtues of the Vicious*, p. 8.

28   Gandal, *The Virtues of the Vicious*, p. 12.

29   Gandal, *The Virtues of the Vicious*, p. 17.

30   Gandal, *The Virtues of the Vicious*, p. 9.

31   Sontag, *On Photography*, p. 11.

32   Sontag, Susan, *Regarding the Pain of Others* (New York: Farrar, Straus and Giroux, 2003), p. 6.

33   Tamar Y. Rothenberg discusses the *National Geographic Magazine*'s conventions of representation, editorial and readership before the Second World War: Rothenberg, Tamar Y., 'Voyeurs of imperialism: the *National Geographic Magazine* before World War II', in Anne Godlewska and Neil Smith (eds), *Geography and Empire* (Oxford: Blackwell, 1994), pp. 155–72.

34 Note also Brian Dillon's assertion that the ruin 'casts us forward in time', in Brian Dillon (ed.), *Ruins* (London: Whitechapel Gallery, 2011), pp. 11, 23–24.

35 Hopkinson, Tom, *Bert Hardy: Photojournalist* (London: Arts Council of Great Britain, 1975), p. 7. Reinforcing this idea, Jordan argues that Hardy, 'the product of a poor, working-class community', identified with the 'poor and maligned – as a result of shared experience': Jordan, *Down the bay*, p. 19.

36 Sheila Hardy, Hardy's second wife, describes his first wife as the daughter of the 'boss' of a local gang. Interview with Sheila Hardy (see note 4 above).

37 This account is verified by that of his unpublished diary (1948) shown to me by his widow, Sheila Hardy. Interview with Sheila Hardy.

38 Sontag, *Regarding the Pain of Others*, p. 9.

39 Lloyd and Hardy, 'Life in the Elephant', p. 15.

40 While Jordan argues that the magazine was 'anti-racist', the story fits with wider post-war discourses in its apparent nationalism. However, the final selection of images would have been determined by the quality of the photographs and the constraints of the page spread, so it is impossible to fully explain any specific omissions. Jordan, *Down the Bay*.

41 Sontag, *Regarding the Pain of Others*, p. 29.

42 Lloyd and Hardy, 'Life in the Elephant', p. 12.

43 Lloyd and Hardy, 'Life in the Elephant', p. 10.

44 Lloyd and Hardy, 'Life in the Elephant', p. 14.

45 Williams, Raymond, *The Country and the City* (London, 1973), pp. 156, 158.

46 Such as Thomas Hardy's vision of London as 'a monster whose body had four million heads and eight million eyes': Hardy, in Williams, *The Country and the City*, p. 216.

47 Lloyd and Hardy, 'Life in the Elephant', p. 10.

48 Lloyd and Hardy, 'Life in the Elephant', p. 15.

49 Lloyd and Hardy, 'Life in the Elephant', p. 15.

50 Lloyd and Hardy, 'Life in the Elephant', p. 7; Hardy, *Bert Hardy*, p. 105.

51 No such couple appeared in the *Picture Post* story as published, but the contact sheets for the shoot include negatives of a rather stiff and not particularly young-looking couple gazing into each other's eyes underneath a lamp-post. The negatives are lodged in the Hulton Archive, Getty Images, London.

52 This is surprising, given the importance Hardy places on Maisie in 'giving us ideas and telling us where to find the things we wanted': Hardy, *Bert Hardy*, p. 105. As discussed above, examining the negatives of the sequence as a whole it is interesting to see which pictures were omitted during the editorial process. Some of the most intimate scenes which, assuming they are not staged (a possibility discussed below), must have been the most challenging to shoot were not included – those of patients being examined in the doctor's surgery; of men at the barber's mid-haircut; of the occupants of a Salvation Army hostel getting undressed, and asleep in their dormitory at night among a sea of beds.

53 The images bring to mind Rothenberg's discussion of the fetishising and objectifying photographic depiction of African women in *National Geographic Magazine*

in the early twentieth century. Differentiated from the magazine's 'civilised' female readers, such women, Rothenberg argues, were presented as uncivilised and mysterious, alluring and 'other', just as were the remote and unexplored territories they came to represent. In this way, photography operated as a colonising practice. 'Romanticization and exploration of native populations went hand in hand', Rothenberg argues: Rothenberg, 'Voyeurs of imperialism', pp. 157, 165.

54   Gautrand, 'Looking at others', p. 617.

55   Hardy, *Bert Hardy*, p. 185.

56   Sontag, *Regarding the Pain of Others*, p. 18.

57   Interview with Sheila Hardy.

58   Jordan, *Down the Bay*, p. 15.

59   Interview with Mark Chilvers, photographer and Heygate Estate resident, London, 1 August 2006.

60   Interview with Sheila Hardy.

61   The setting up of photographs is still an accepted practice in British press photography, with the photographer influencing a scene in order to get the best possible photograph. In other countries, such as the USA, however, such interventions are more regulated or illegal.

62   There are approximately 1,050 surviving images in the Getty Images archive, London.

63   A selection of Hardy's *Picture Post* photographs were digitised in the early 1990s, making the images available to a global market. Figures on image sales are not available, but Sarah McDonald, Curator at Getty Images, attests to their continuing popularity for commercial use. Interview with Sarah McDonald, Curator, Getty Images, London, 22 August 2006.

64   Twenty-two prints from Hardy's series were purchased by Southwark's Cuming Museum, funded by a Heritage Lottery grant. However, there was subsequently a dispute over their authenticity as original prints (interview with Keith Bonnick, Curator, Cuming Museum, London Borough of Southwark, 2006). Chilvers' project produced a digital archive of images of the area taken in 2005, later lodged in the Cuming Museum, and a series of portraits of residents of the Heygate, for which he was the sole photographer. The images used in the Hardy and Chilvers exhibition can be viewed at: http://www.southwark.gov.uk/info/200162/the_cuming_museum/1157/previous_exhibitions/7 (accessed 1 July 2012). For other recent photographic projects documenting the area, also initiated by Southwark Council, see Sutherland, Patrick (ed.), *Community: The Elephant and Castle* (London: London College of Communication, 2006); Sutherland, Patrick (ed.), *Home: The Elephant and Castle* (London: London College of Communication, 2008).

65   Chilvers lived on the Heygate for 12 years. Interview with Mark Chilvers.

66   At the time the first draft of this chapter was written, in 2007, planned completion was estimated between 2014 and 2016, but Southwark Council's website in 2012 states that the regeneration will take place 'over the next 15 years'. Up-to-date details of the Elephant and Castle regeneration scheme from the developers'

and Southwark Council's perspectives, including development frameworks, can be found at: http://www.elephantandcastle.org.uk/ and http://www.southwark.gov.uk/YourServices/RegenerationSection/elephant/ (accessed 1 July 2012).

67 Horn, Chris, 'Delivering sustainable communities: the challenge at the Elephant and Castle' (undated). See: http://www.resource05.co.uk/presentations/day3/Chris%20Horn.pdf (accessed 1 July 2012).

68 At the time of writing, 'registered social landlords' (RSL) are defined as 'government-funded not-for-profit organisations that provide affordable housing. They include housing associations, trusts and cooperatives. They work with local authorities to provide homes for people meeting the affordable homes criteria. As well as developing land and building homes, RSLs undertake a landlord function by maintaining properties and collecting rent'. However, this idea of 'affordable' housing, which is defined only loosely, is a fallacy, since it now effectively means 80 per cent of market-level rent. See: http://www.idea.gov.uk/idk/core/page.do?pageId=7175736 (accessed 1 July 2012).

69 Southwark Council, *Cleared for Action. Elephant and Castle Regeneration: A Guide to the Programme* (London: London Borough of Southwark, 2005).

70 See 'Down and out in Elephant and Castle underpass' by Mujib Rahman, reproduced in Campkin, Ben, 'Dirt, blight and regeneration: a study of urban change in London', unpublished PhD thesis (London: UCL, 2009), fig. 6.8.

71 Porter, *London*, p. 358.

72 See: http://www.southwark.gov.uk/info/200162/the_cuming_museum/1157/previous_exhibitions/7 (accessed 1 July 2012). The residents who were interviewed were asked questions, some more leading than others, such as: How long have you lived here? What are your memories of when you first moved here? How has it changed? Are you looking forward to moving? Will you be sad to leave? Interview with Mark Chilvers.

73 In the ongoing online exhibition of the images the photos are not credited individually, though they were in the physical exhibitions of the work. See: http://www.southwark.gov.uk/info/200162/the_cuming_museum/1157/previous_exhibitions/7 (accessed 1 July 2012).

74 The Lend Lease and Southwark Council Elephant and Castle regeneration plans website states that 'the revolutionary ideas of the 1960s have not stood the test of time. Instead, the developments have, on the whole, made life more difficult for local residents'. See: http://www.elephantandcastle.org.uk/pages/elephant_castle/89/challenges.html (accessed 27 July 2012).

Chapter 3: Regeneration ad nauseam

1 Cousins, Mark, 'The ugly (Part 1)', *AA Files* 28 (1994), pp. 61–6, p. 63.

2 Anon, 'Minister attacks prison-like buildings', *Evening Standard*, 17 October 2001, p. 6. This was the year in which Tony Blair, as prime minister, instituted the

Prime Minister's Better Public Building Award, sponsored by the Commission for Architecture and the Built Environment (CABE), which had been established in 1999 during the first term of the New Labour government.

3   Arnott, Jake, 'Jumbo plans for Elephant. Jake Arnott reports on a scheme to raze London's ugliest landmark', *The Sunday Times*, 30 September 2001.

4   Sherwin, Adam, 'Foster to tackle ugly Elephant', *The Times*, 27 June 2000.

5   Coren, Giles, 'Dragon castle', *Times Online*, 22 July 2006. See: http://www.timesonline.co.uk/tol/life_and_style/food_and_drink/eating_out/giles_coren/article690242.ece (accessed 5 May 2009).

6   Arnott, 'Jumbo plans for Elephant'.

7   See: http://www.london-se1.co.uk/news/view/4753 (accessed 1 July 2012).

8   Watanabe, Haruko, 'The Elephant and Castle post-war development: a critical analysis of the perceived failure', Unpublished dissertation (London: UCL, 1995); Cousins, 'The ugly (Part 1)', pp. 61–6; Cousins, 'The ugly (Part 2)', *AA Files* 29 (1995a), pp. 3–6; Cousins, 'The ugly (Part 3)', *AA Files* 30 (1995b), pp. 65–8. In an architectural biography of 2004, Nigel Warburton also refers to the debates about the building's ugliness and conversion. See Warburton, Nigel, *Ernö Goldfinger – the Life Of An Architect* (Abingdon: Routledge, 2004), pp. 181–5.

9   Cousins, 'The ugly (Part 1)', p. 63.

10 Cousins, 'The ugly (Part 1)', p. 62.

11 Leonard Hamburger, has examined the use of the category 'ugly' in architectural discourses around All Saints, Margaret Street, London. He discusses Prince Charles' repeated use of the word ugly in attacking buildings such as the National Theatre and British Library around the time of his 'monstrous carbuncle' speech: Hamburger, Leonard, 'A deliberate preference of ugliness', unpublished dissertation, University College London, 1997. Watanabe also discusses the way in which Prince Charles' 'monstrous carbuncle' comment was repeated in the press and used to refer more generally to the perceived failures of modern architecture: Watanabe, 'The Elephant and Castle post-war development'. Prince Charles recently updated his critique of 'the Modernist experiment' through metaphors of monstrosity, describing modernist buildings as 'mechanical, or even genetically modified' – as opposed to 'organic' architecture with 'natural patterns and rhythms': BBC, 'Prince attacks flawed design', *BBC News*, 12 May 2009. See: http://news.bbc.co.uk/1/hi/uk/8046946.stm (accessed 12 May 2009).

12 Banham, Reyner, *The New Brutalism* (London: The Architectural Press, 1966); Whiteley, Nigel, 'Banham and "otherness": Reyner Banham (1922–88) and his quest for an architecture *autre*', *Architectural History* 33 (1990), pp. 188–221.

13 Porter, *London*, p. 359.

14 Forty, Adrian, 'The material without a history', in Jean-Louis Cohen and Martin Moeller, Jr. (eds), *Liquid Stone: New Architecture in Concrete* (New York: Princeton Architectural Press, 2006), p. 37; 'Concrete and memory', in Mark Crinson (ed.), *Urban Memory: History and Amnesia in the Modern City* (New

York: Routledge, 2005), pp. 75–95; *Concrete and Culture: A Material History* (London: Reaktion Books, 2012).

15 Goldfinger, Ernö, 'A talk to the Architectural Association on the 21st February 1962 prior to a site visit', *Architectural Association Journal*, April 1962, pp. 244–9, p. 244.

16 The scheme as designed was described by Goldfinger in *The Architectural Review*. Goldfinger, Ernö, 'Offices: Elephant and Castle, London', *Architectural Review* volume 127, January (1960), pp. 40–3.

17 Anon, 'Goldfinger's Italian piazza', *Manchester Guardian*, 14 July 1959; Anon, 'Italian piazza look for South London', *The Sunday Times*, 10 January 1960.

18 Bar-Hillel, Mira, 'New threat over hated building', *Evening Standard*, 21 July 1988, p. 11.

19 Warburton, *Ernö Goldfinger*.

20 Bar-Hillel, 'New threat over hated building', p. 11; see also Bar-Hillel, Mira, 'New granite face of the Elephant and Castle', *Evening Standard*, 1 August 1991; Katz, Ian, 'Land of pink and white elephants', the *Guardian*, 16 August 1991.

21 Raw, G. J., 'Sick building syndrome: a review of the evidence on causes and solutions', *HSE Contract Research Report* 42 (London: Her Majesty's Stationery Office, 1992).

22 Goffe, Leslie, 'Sixties' concrete complex loses plea for listed status', the *Guardian*, 6 August 1988.

23 Thanks to Adrian Forty for relaying this anecdote to me. Interestingly, Alexander Fleming House was also described as 'Stalin's buildings as they should have been'; while at around the same time Goldfinger's contemporary building, the Elephant and Castle Odeon Cinema (begun 1963; demolished 1988), was compared with 'Hitler's concrete bunker'. See Collins, *The Likes of Us*, p. 160; Warburton, *Ernö Goldfinger*, p. 182.

24 O'Neill, Paul, 'Leisure centre inquiry delay', *South London Press*, 5 July 1994.

25 Imry, quoted in Holliday, Richard, 'Selling of the "cool" Elephant', *Evening Standard*, 23 June 1997, pp. 4–5.

26 Allen, Richard, 'Blot is saved', *South London Press*, 7 July 1992.

27 In 1994, the rent for the 'unlettable' offices was £313,137 per annum, with a further estimated £500,000 per annum of maintenance and security costs: Blunkett, David, 'Alexander Fleming House. Written answers', House of Commons debate 241, c177W, 13 April (1994). See: http://hansard.millbank-systems.com/written_answers/1994/apr/13/alexander-fleming-house (accessed 1 February 2009).

28 Two separate proposals were submitted which involved re-cladding the exterior in white aluminium and mirrored glass. Both were rejected: Paget, Sarah, 'Beauty or beast?', *South London Press*, 4 November 1988, p. 4; Powell, Kenneth, 'Sixties "monument" in mirror glass row', *Daily Telegraph*, 31 March 1989; Anon, 'Alexander Fleming House – soon to go?', *Southwark Sparrow*, 12 April 1991, p. 7.

29 Anon, 'Alexander Fleming House – soon to go?' (1991).

30 Bar-Hillel, 'New granite face of the Elephant and Castle'.
31 Even before the DHSS moved out, when the building was already vulnerable to refurbishment or demolition, modernist heritage lobbyists and conservationists had rallied to its defence. For example, in 1988, architect James Dunnett led a 'Save Alexander Fleming House' campaign to protest plans for a '£25m facelift' that would threaten the building's status as a 'masterpiece' of Constructivism: Bar-Hillel, 'New threat over hated building'.
32 Dunnett, James, 'Save Centre Point, the tower we loved to hate', *The Independent*, 21 February 1990, p. 19; Warburton, *Ernö Goldfinger*, p. 184.
33 Glancey, Jonathan, 'It's very clever, but it's still a concrete block', *The Independent*, 15 May 1991, p. 19.
34 Anon, 'Goldfinger's Italian piazza' (1959); Anon, 'Italian piazza look for South London' (1960).
35 One of the recurrent lines of contemporary and subsequent criticism of the 1950s and 1960s redevelopment of the Elephant centred on a perceived obliteration of history and social identity. For example, a 1959 *Time* editorial bemoaning recent urban transformations across Europe commented: '[i]n the name of progress … [t]o make way for a new road junction, London's urban planners recently decreed the destruction of The Elephant and Castle, a fabled 200-year-old pub, which lent something of the raffish, robust flavor of 18th century England to the whole London district of Southwark'. Writing from the USA, the author caricatures an authentic 'rough-but-real' English social texture that, it is suggested, the planners are in the process of concreting over, erasing history and social identity in favour of modernisation: Anon, 'Progress of a sort', *Time*, 30 March 1959b.
36 Katz, Ian, 'Land of pink and white elephants', the *Guardian*, 16 August 1991.
37 Goffe, Leslie, 'Sixties' concrete complex loses plea for listed status', the *Guardian*, 6 August 1988.
38 Shonfield, Katherine, *Walls Have Feelings: Architecture, Film and the City* (London: Routledge, 2000), p. 3; Whiteley, 'Banham and "otherness"', p. 196.
39 Goldfinger, 'A Talk to the Architectural Association', p. 244.
40 Goffe, 'Sixties' concrete complex loses plea for listed status'; Chester, Lewis, 'Inside story: high and mighty', the *Guardian*, 16 July 1994, p. 28.
41 The conversion did not satisfy the building's supporters, who described it as 'ham fisted': James Dunnet in Warburton, *Ernö Goldfinger*, p. 182.
42 Anon, 'Green light for massive homes plan', *South London Press*, 11 October 1996; Hutchinson, 'Alexander Fleming House approval'.
43 The brochure can be downloaded as a PDF from: http://metrocentralheights.com/files/original%20MCH%20marketing%20brochure%201997.pdf. See also Anon, '£20m urban village plan for Alexander Fleming House', *Architects' Journal*, 27 June 1996; Anon, *Metro Central: London SE1*, Knight Frank International and St George Developments Ltd (London: 1996).
44 Harvey, David, *Spaces of Hope* (Edinburgh: Edinburgh University Press, 2000), p. 148.
45 Holliday, 'Selling of the "cool" Elephant'.

46   Personal correspondence with a former resident of Metro Central Heights, 18 July 2012.

47   See Harnack, Maren, 'London's Trellick Tower and the pastoral eye', in Gandy, Matthew, *Urban constellations* (Berlin: Jovis Verlag, 2011), pp. 127–31; Lambon, Henry, 'London illustrated: Manhattan, here we come?', *Independent on Sunday*, 27 April 2003.

48   There were 36 entries in total. The other architects included Goldfinger and Owen Luder, another British architect whose work has been at the centre of controversies regarding brutalist architecture.

49   Anon, *Elephant and Castle Comprehensive Redevelopment Scheme: New Shopping Centre: LCC Press Bureau*, Press Conference, 14 July 1960, p. 2; and quoted in Marriott, Oliver, *The Property Boom* (London: Hamish Hamilton, 1967), p. 250.

50   Marriott, *The Property Boom*, pp. 247, 252.

51   Parnell, Tom and Ryan Kisiel, 'Elephant and Castle regeneration: struggling but still open for trade', *South London Press*, 1 May 2007, pp. 12–13.

52   Harvey, *Spaces of Hope*, p. 168.

53   Ghirardo, *Architecture after Modernism*; Sorkin, Michael, *Variations on a Theme Park: The New American City and the End of Public Space* (New York: The Noonday Press, 1992).

54   Anon, 'The Elephant and Castle', the *Guardian*, 28 January 1963, pp. 12–13.

55   McAuslan, Fiona, 'Elephant & Castle Shopping Centre – the elephant graveyard', *Time Out*, 6 September 2006.

56   Anon, 'The Elephant and Castle' (1963), p. 12.

57   Anon, 'The Elephant and Castle Shopping Centre, promotional brochure', Mathers Public Relations for the Willett Group (London: *c.* 1963).

58   Marriott, *The Property Boom*, p. 267.

59   Anon, 'Another "Piccadilly Circus" at the Elephant', *Evening Standard*, 21 March 1947.

60   Anon, '*2nd Birthday, Spring '67*', Elephant and Castle Shopping Centre (London, 1967).

61   Marriott, *The Property Boom*; Richardson, Tim, 'E&C CDA: Elephant and Castle: an analysis of the redevelopment of the Elephant and Castle 1955–1965', unpublished dissertation, Architectural Association (London: Architectural Association, 1979); Anon, 'The Elephant and Castle' (1963).

62   Sibley, *Geographies of exclusion*, pp. ix–xviii.

63   Richardson, 'E&C CDA'.

64   Robson, 'Class, criminality and embodied consciousness', p. 8. This reputation for social disorder continued. In 1977, in response to 'gangs of hooligans intimidating shoppers and shopkeepers', the pedestrian routes through the centre were reclassified from private land to public walkways so that they could be policed under Section 18 of the *Highways Act* (1971). More recently, the building was again associated with social disorder in the press after fighting broke out at the inquiry into the murder of Stephen Lawrence, which took place in Hannibal House, the

office block above the shopping centre: Anon, 'Elephant Shopping Centre hooligans warned', London Borough of Southwark press release, 29 April (1977).

65 Parnell, Tom and Ryan Kisiel, 'Elephant and Castle regeneration: struggling but still open for trade', *South London Press*, 1 May 207, pp. 12–13. In 2004, Southwark Council decided to demolish the building as part of the wider regeneration. First scheduled for 2010, it was subsequently postponed to 2012. The building is now owned by Key Property Investments, and they expect to submit a planning application imminently (mid-2012).

66 McAuslan, 'Elephant & Castle Shopping Centre'.

67 Anon, 'The big smoke – readers' poll', *Time Out*, 7 June 2007.

68 Anon, 'The big smoke – readers' poll'.

69 Anon, 'Tickled pink!', *The Trumpet*, advertising supplement, August 1990. It was later painted red for the charity event Comic Relief 'Red Nose Day' in 1999.

70 Anon, 'Tickled pink!'.

71 Falconer, 'Up the Elephant'.

72 McAuslan, 'Elephant & Castle Shopping Centre'.

73 McAuslan, 'Elephant & Castle Shopping Centre'.

74 Cozens, Claire, 'Levi's goes up the Elephant and round the Castle', the *Guardian*, 9 August 2002.

75 Powell, *City Reborn*, p. 7.

76 Anon, *'Elephant and Castle Shopping Centre', Terms and Conditions of Lease for Standard Shop Tenant* (undated, c. 1963).

77 'Charles', Elephant and Castle Shopping Centre, 'London destruction' blog (2007). See: http://www.geocities.com/londondestruction/ (accessed 5 May 2009).

78 Brand, Stewart, *How Buildings Learn* (London: Viking, 1997); Woodward, Tim, 'The Elephant reborn: a miraculous transformation in south London', *Radio Times*, 12–18 July 1997; Ouseley, in Anon, 'Elephant and Castle BME [black and minority ethnic] traders' newsletter', August (2006). Between September 2004 and February 2005, Ouseley had chaired an independent review of Southwark Council's equality and diversity framework. This review looked in particular at the concerns of black and minority ethnic small businesses with regard to the ongoing regeneration, in response to claims that they had been treated unfairly. The report identified a number of weaknesses in the council's policies, a lack of trust between the BME traders and the council, and a need for better structures to involve the borough's most deprived communities in decision-making processes linked to the regeneration: Ouseley, Lord Herman, *Independent Review of the Council's Equality and Diversity Framework*, February (London: London Borough of Southwark, 2005). According to local activist Patrick Anderson (Planning Aid for London and Black Planners Network), 80 per cent of the traders in the shopping centre are from ethnic minorities.

79 Sennett, Richard, *The Uses of Disorder: Personal Identity and City Life* (London: Allen Lane, 1971), p. 83.

80 Harvey, *Spaces of Hope*, p. 153.

Chapter 4: Sink Estate Spectacle

1   Hatherley, Owen, *Militant Modernism* (Winchester: Zero Books, 2008), p. 13.

2   See: http://www.southwarkfilmoffice.co.uk/ (accessed 14 December 2008).

3   According to Lees, approximately 17 per cent of dwellings have been purchased through the 'right-to-buy' scheme: Lees, Loretta, 'The urban injustices of New Labour's "new urban renewal": the case of the Aylesbury Estate in London', undated manuscript, p. 2. See: http://www.enhr2011.com/sites/default/files/Session4-PaperL.Lees-_0.docx (accessed 29 April 2012).

    For a summary of New Labour's approach, see Hodkinson, Stuart, 'Housing regeneration and the Private Finance Initiative in England: unstitching the neoliberal urban straightjacket', *Antipode* 43/2 (2011), pp. 358–83. On the effects of the Coalition's spending cuts on the Aylesbury Estate, see Fulcher, Merlin, 'Spending cuts: Aylesbury estate regeneration loses £20m', *The Architects' Journal*, 21 June 2010. See: http://www.architectsjournal.co.uk/news/daily-news/spending-cuts-aylesbury-estate-regeneration-loses-20-million/8601822.article (accessed 2 February 2012).

4   Newman, Oscar, *Defensible Space: People and Design in the Violent City* (New York: Macmillan, 1972); Coleman, Alice, *Utopia on Trial: Vision and Reality in Planned Housing* (London: Hilary Shipman, 1990/1985). Coleman was employed by the Joseph Rowntree Foundation, and later by the Conservative government under Margaret Thatcher.

5   For a recent critique, see Minton, Anna, *Ground Control: Fear and Happiness in the Twenty-first Century City* (London: Penguin, 2009), esp. pp. 61–82.

6   David Hepher's paintings of the Aylesbury Estate have recently been on sale in London's Flowers Gallery, at prices up to £80,000. Hepher uses building sand with paint for added 'realism', and 'insists he is not interested in the political or social connotations of his subject'. See: http://www.flowersgalleries.com/uploads/David-Hepher-press-release.pdf (accessed 25 February 2012).

7   It actually ran over this budget by about £1.5 million.

8   There was a housing waiting list of approximately 12,000 in Southwark. See Toller, Robert, 'Did Groucho Marx invent the cost yardstick?', *The Architect*, April 1975, pp. 30–3.

9   Cherry, Bridget and Nikolaus Pevsner, *Buildings of England. London 2: South* (London: Penguin, 2001), p. 562.

10   Cherry and Pevsner, *Buildings of England. London 2: South*, p. 562.

11   For example, three journalists referred to Pevsner's analysis in the same week in September 2005. Descriptions of the estate often echo Pevsner's in their vocabulary. For example, see Barker, Paul, 'Ever get that sinking feeling?', *The Times*, 28 September 2005, p. 18; Muir, Hugh, 'End of London's most ambitious post-war housing project', the *Guardian*, 22 September 2005, p. 11; Raymond, Clare, 'Death of an urban dream', *The Mirror*, 29 September 2005, pp. 24–5.

12   London Borough of Southwark Department of Architecture and Planning, 'Aylesbury Redevelopment', design brief, undated; and 'Aylesbury

Redevelopment', brochure, undated. A few post-war housing developments were retained, with the intention of their being integrated into the Aylesbury scheme.

13   Interview with Timothy Tinker, UCL Urban Laboratory, 21 March 2012.

14   Interview with Timothy Tinker. An undated newspaper article from *c.* 1970 reports the clearance of an estimated 3,000 slums: Anon, 'Clear-slums drive gets underway' (undated, *c.* 1970).

15   Forty notes that Corbusier's *Unité* had defects in the concrete, but these were accepted and incorporated by the architect as a design feature: Forty, *Concrete and Culture*, p. 38.

16   The younger members of the team included John Crallan, Don Genassi, Fred Guest, Rick Mather and John Nichols.

17   Interviews with Timothy Tinker, and John Crallan and John Nichols, UCL Urban Laboratory, London, 21 and 23 March 2012.

18   Interview with John Crallan and John Nichols, UCL Urban Laboratory, 23 March 2012. Most of the design work took place between September and December 1965. The Aylesbury was under way by 1966, and largely complete by 1972.

19   In the UK, the concept of 'streets in the sky' was first developed by the New Brutalist architects, Alison and Peter Smithson, in their widely published entry for the Corporation of London's Golden Lane Competition (1951). The Aylesbury's snake-like blocks, linked by raised walkways known as 'pedways', find a precedent in the 'streets in the sky' of Park Hill, designed by Ivor Smith and Jack Lynn, completed in 1961. Park Hill also became a site for debate about Oscar Newman's theory and the relationship between design and crime. See Mawby, R. I., 'Defensible space: a theoretical and empirical appraisal', *Urban Studies* 14 (1977), pp. 169–79. Some of the Aylesbury Estate architects had visited Park Hill, while a lead figure in the team for the Heygate, Timothy Tinker, had worked with the Smithsons. Interview with John Crallan and John Nichols, UCL Urban Laboratory, 23 March 2012.

20   Aylesbury Development Area Opening Ceremony, pamphlet, 11 April (1970).

21   Anon, 'Aylesbury development area, opening ceremony', press release, 11 April, London Borough of Southwark (1970); Anon, 'Estate is not just an ugly duck-ling', *South London Press*, January 1975. The image of a 'concrete jungle', and the stigmatised materiality and greyness of concrete in general, have played a consistent part in the negative discourses about the estate over time. In discussing the iconography of concrete, Forty has argued that 'nature-suppressing qualities' constitute one of the primary characteristics of concrete, and are the reason for both its attraction and unpopularity. The numerous references to the estate's monotony and greyness can be placed within a wider semantics of concrete in which this material is frequently described as 'dense, dull, grey, monotonous or soulless': Forty, 'Concrete and memory', pp. 78, 94.

22   McKee, Will, 'London 2062 housing symposium', University College London, 2012.

23 Anon, 'Showpiece estate criticised', *The Times*, November (1970); Frank, Douglas, 'The greatest happiness of the greatest number?', *The Architects' Journal*, 27 May 1970, p. 1288.

24 Interview with John Crallan and John Nichols, The Bartlett School of Architecture, UCL, 23 March 2012.

25 Interview with John Crallan and John Nichols.

26 For a contemporary discussion of the problems of LPS in relation to the Aylesbury Estate, see Anon, 'Systems swansong', *Building*, 10 September 1976, pp. 74–5.

27 See Blunden, Mark, 'Why pull down a perfectly good housing estate, asks its architect', *London Evening Standard*, 10 March 2011. See: http://www.thisislondon.co.uk/news/why-pull-down-a-perfectly-good-housing-estate-asks-its-architect-6575907.html (accessed 1 May 2012).

28 Interview with Timothy Tinker, UCL Urban Laboratory, 21 March 2012. Tinker notes that at the Heygate more thought and financial investment were directed towards the circulation spaces and planting, for example, and the use of the Jespersen system was more consistent. The monolithic nature of the estate was, he argues, a symptom of architects' and planners' attempts to keep the borough engineers, who had responsibility for road layout, out of the decision-making.

29 See: http://southwarknotes.wordpress.com/heygate-estate/ (accessed 29 July 2012).

30 Toller, 'Did Groucho Marx invent the cost yardstick?', p. 32; interview with John Crallan and John Nichols, The Bartlett School of Architecture, UCL, 23 March 2012.

31 Toller, 'Did Groucho Marx invent the cost yardstick?', pp. 31, 33.

32 Mansfield, J.M. (dir.), *Horizon: The Writing on the Wall*, BBC, video, 50 minutes approx. (1974).

33 In the UK, *Defensible Space: People and Design in the Violent City* was published by the Architectural Press in 1972, just prior to the related publication of a collection on vandalism, edited by Colin Ward. It also intersects with the argument of James Wilson and George Kelling's influential essay, 'Broken windows', published a decade later in *Atlantic Monthly*: Ward, Colin (ed.), *Vandalism* (London: The Architectural Press, 1973); Wilson, James Q. and George L. Kelling, 'Broken windows', *Atlantic Monthly*, March 1982. See: http://www.theatlantic.com/doc/198203/broken-windows (accessed 25 June 2009).

34 Anon, 'Future slum? Is the Aylesbury Estate our very own home grown Pruitt–Igoe?', *Building Design*, 17 May 1974, pp. 20–1.

35 Toller, 'Did Groucho Marx invent the cost yardstick?', p. 30.

36 For an excellent discussion of the contemporary securitisation of UK housing, with an explanation of Newman's theory, see Minton, *Ground Control*.

37 Newman, *Defensible Space*, p. 3.

38 Newman, *Defensible Space*, pp. 14, xiii.

39 Newman, *Defensible Space*, p. 50.

40 Newman, *Defensible Space*, p. 4.

41 Newman, *Defensible Space*, p. 11.

42 Jacobs, *The Death and Life of Great American Cities*; Rainwater, Lee, *Behind Ghetto Walls: Black Families in a Federal Slum* (Harmondsworth: Penguin, 1970). Newman's concept of 'stigma' derives from the work of Erving Goffmann: Goffmann, Erving, *Stigma: Notes on the Management of Spoiled Identity* (New York, Simon & Schuster, 1963).

43 Minton observes that, while Jane Jacobs and Richard Sennett's arguments about interactions between strangers as a fundamental and healthy part of urban life have been given the status of seminal texts in urban theory, policy-makers have favoured Newman's thinking about strangers as a potential danger and cause of disorder. See Minton, *Ground Control*, p.142.

44 While, on the one hand, Newman sees the bounding and vigilant defence of private property as a desirable aspiration, he is at the same time critical of the increasing social and spatial isolationism of 'high-rise security-guarded fortresses of semiluxury' that constitute 'middle class ghettos': Newman, *Defensible Space*, pp. 14, 18, 19.

45 Residents' responses were varied, of course, and this was reflected in newspaper coverage of the estate's opening. While some were said to 'weep for their slums', others were reportedly pleased with the new flats and environment: Anon, 'The children of Walworth weep for their slums', *South London Press*, 12 December (1967); Anon, 'Showpiece estate criticised' (1970). These estates required people to adjust to a completely new way of living, so mixed feelings were inevitable. The actual process of moving could also be traumatic as, for example, residents' furniture, bedding and other belongings had to be disinfested before being moved, or thrown away.

46 Anon, 'Future slum?' (1974).

47 Coleman has continued to be referenced by Conservative politicians; for example, in debates on the *Sustainable and Secure Buildings Act* (2004). See: http://www.publications.parliament.uk/pa/cm200304/cmstand/c/st040303/am/40303s03.htm (accessed 1 February 2012).

48 Coleman, *Utopia on Trial*, p. 150.

49 Coleman, *Utopia on Trial*, p. 2.

50 Coleman, *Utopia on Trial*, pp. 170, 3.

51 Coleman, Alice, 'The psychology of housing'. See: http://www.singleaspect.org.uk/?p=2363 (accessed 30 January 2012).

52 *Utopia on Trial* is illustrated with a photograph of an entrance to a block on the estate, which has no door and graffiti on the concrete and brick surround. The caption complains of a 'gaping aperture, which leads into a twisted passage without proper visibility, and offers a short cut through the block for outsiders': Coleman, *Utopia on Trial*, pp. 34–5, 41.

53 Dreher, Nan H., 'The virtuous and the verminous: turn-of-the-century moral panics in London's public parks', *Albion* 29/2 (1997), pp. 246–67.

54 Hillier, Bill, 'In defense of space', *RIBA Journal* (journal of the Royal Institute of British Architects) 80/11 (1973), pp. 539–44.

55 Hillier, 'In defense of space', p. 542.

56 Hillier, 'In defense of space', p. 543.

57 Hillier, 'In defense of space', p. 543.

58 Banham, *The New Brutalism*; Bottoms, Anthony, 'Review of *Defensible Space* by Oscar Newman', *British Journal of Criminology* 14 (1974), pp. 203–6.

59 Bottoms, 'Review of *Defensible Space* by Oscar Newman', p. 204.

60 Bottoms, 'Review of *Defensible Space* by Oscar Newman', p. 205.

61 In the book's preface Newman explains that the research examined New York City Housing Authority projects because of the 'limited variation in the social characteristics' of residents as compared with 'extreme variations' of social characteristics in private sector housing: Newman, *Defensible Space*.

62 Coleman, Alice, 'Design influences in blocks of flats', *The Geographical Journal* 150/3 (1984), p. 351.

63 Katherine Bristol notes this in relation to Newman's work. See Bristol, Katharine G., 'The Pruitt–Igoe myth', *Journal of Architectural Education* 44/3 (1991), p. 167.

64 Harvey, David, *Social Justice and the City* (Oxford: Basil Blackwell, 1988, first published 1973), p. 46.

65 Newman, *Defensible Space*, p. 13.

66 See, for example, repeated references to Alice Coleman's work in parliamentary debates in 1999 and 2004 in relation to the Sustainable and Secure Buildings Bill, and 2008, in attacks on Labour's historically 'Utopian' views on housing. See: http://www.publications.parliament.uk/pa/cm199293/cmhansrd/1992-11-03/Debate-4.html (accessed 30 January 2012).

67 Coleman, 'The psychology of housing'.

68 Bristol, 'The Pruitt–Igoe myth', p. 170; Jencks, Charles, *The Language of Postmodern Architecture* (London: Academy Editions, 1977).

69 Bristol, 'The Pruitt–Igoe myth', p. 167. This argument concurs with Loïc Wacquant's more recent analyses of 'hyperghettoisation' and public disorder as 'violence from below' in response to 'violence from above'. See Wacquant, Loïc, *Urban Outcasts: A Comparative Sociology of Advanced Marginality* (Cambridge, UK: Cambridge University Press, 2008).

70 Rainwater, *Behind Ghetto Walls*. Quoted by Newman, *Defensible Space*, pp. 107–8.

71 Rainwater, *Behind Ghetto Walls*, p. 4.

72 Interview with John Crallan and John Nichols, UCL Urban Laboratory, London, 23 March 2012.

73 Minton, *Ground Control*, p. 72. For an earlier discussion of the securitisation of space as part of the privatisation of public spaces in London, see Borden, Iain, 'Thick edge: architectural boundaries in the postmodern metropolis', in Iain Borden and Jane Rendell (eds), *Intersections: Architectural Histories and Critical Theories* (London: Routledge, 2000), pp. 221–46.

74 Anon, 'Wardens' good practice guidance notes: case study – Aylesbury Estate security patrol, Southwark', *Factsheet 7* (Great Britain: Neighbourhood Renewal Unit, 2002).

75 The Faraday Sub Ward (E01003972) is 'average' compared with the rest of England and Wales, as at December 2011, and it was average in 2010/11, with little variation over the year, and slightly lower figures than for Southwark as a whole. See: http://maps.met.police.uk/.

76 New Deal for Communities National Evaluation (Sheffield Hallam University, 2009). See: http://extra.shu.ac.uk/ndc/ndc_data.htm (accessed 8/12/12). Thanks to Adrian Glasspool for pointing me to this data.

77 Power, Anne, *Estates on the Edge: The Social Consequences of Mass Housing in Northern Europe* (London: Macmillan, 1999), p. 114.

78 This is based on a survey of over 100 newspaper articles in the local, national and international media, identified through the LexusNexus database using the search term 'Aylesbury Estate', and searching up to July 2008. Lees has argued that the 1980s was the key period of decline, but in terms of press coverage the estate had a lower profile than it had when it opened, or than it would do later, around the time of Blair's visits. However, there were nonetheless some exceptions in the late 1980s as, in 1987, *The Times* reported on squatting, describing an environment littered by 'rubbish, broken windows and graffiti'. and in 1988 the *Guardian* published an article that graphically evoked an unpleasant 'strangely empty' environment characterised by 'a distinctive smell of cooking, urine, and rubbish', 'filthy graffiti', and buildings 'leaking, crumbling, flooding and peeling'. See Warman, Christopher, 'Tenants welcome plan for more say on homes', *The Times*, 20 May 1987; Rusbridger, Alan, 'Guardian tomorrows: a place in Peckham – after the planners', the *Guardian*, 17 February 1988; Lees, Loretta, 'The urban injustices of New Labour's "new urban renewal": the case of the Aylesbury Estate in London', undated manuscript, p. 1. See: http://www. enhr2011.com/sites/default/files/Session4-PaperL.Lees-_0.docx (accessed 29 April 2012).

79 Anon, 'Howard: why I will keep all my pledges', *The Express*, 14 April 2005, p. 8; Harris, Andrew, 'Branding urban space: the creation of art districts in contemporary London and Mumbai', unpublished PhD dissertation, University of London (London: 2005); Muir, Hugh, 'Hugh Muir asks why, when the media visit a "sink" estate, does it ignore the good news?', the *Guardian*, 18 May 2005, p. 11.

80 Kirk, Jon, 'Estate that came back from hell', *The People*, 24 June 2007, p. 22.

81 Anon, 'Howard' (2005a).

82 The need for structural reinforcement is debated by professionals who know the buildings well, and who note that strengthening of the original construction took place in the wake of the Ronan Point collapse in 1968, and also that new criterion were introduced at a late stage in the process of determining the feasibility of refurbishment. Interview with John Crallan and John Nichols, UCL Urban Laboratory, 23 March 2012.

83 Blair, Tony, 'The will to win', Aylesbury Estate, 2 June (London: Office for the Deputy Prime Minister, Social Exclusion Unit, 1997).

84 Blair, 'The will to win'.

85   Power, *Estates on the Edge*, p. xxiii.

86   Lees, 'The urban injustices of New Labour's "new urban renewal"', p. 2.

87   Walkowitz, Judith, *City of Dreadful Delight: Narratives of Sexual Danger in Late-Victorian London* (London: Virago Press, 1992), p. 19.

88   Pilger, John, 'A great betrayal: ordinary people had the right to expect that after 18 years of the Tories, Tony Blair would be different', *The Mirror*, 30 April 2002, pp. 6–7.

89   Two years after Blair's speech, the tenth annual Eton geography field trip to the estate, with Prince William in attendance, attracted further attention to the 'infamous', 'vast' and 'sprawling', 'rundown' estate, and its 'serious drug and crime problems'. Coverage of this event focused on the reaction of an elderly resident of the estate's Taplow House who had shown the schoolboys her flat after they had toured the estate by coach. Once again, there were echoes of historic royal slum visits: Kay, Richard, 'How William sampled life in a tower block', *Daily Mail*, 13 February 1999, p. 29; Turner, Lucy, 'Wills came to visit my council flat; but I didn't even recognise him', *The Mirror*, 13 February 1999, p. 18.

90   Moyes, Jojo, 'Even the stairwells were perfumed for Blair's visit', *The Independent*, 3 June 1997, p. 3.

91   For example, Deans, John and Nick Hopkins, 'The premier chooses one of Britain's bleakest housing estates to launch his drive to make the single mothers pay their way', *Daily Mail*, 3 June 1997, pp. 12–13; Hamilton, Alan, 'Blair meets apathy walking on the wild side', *The Times*, 3 June 1997; Lauder, Lorraine, 'Resident's plea for derided estate', the *Guardian*, 15 August 1997, p. 4; Young, Alf, 'Workers in the shadows', *The Herald*, 3 June 1997 (Glasgow), p. 17.

92   See, for example, Sky News and Channel 4's television news broadcasts for 25 June 2007.

93   Barker, 'Ever get that sinking feeling?'

94   Hartley-Brewer, Julia, Colin Freeman and Saba Salman, 'Blair pledges to flatten "sink estates" that shame the nation', *Evening Standard*, 15 September 1998, p. 5; Hughes, David, 'I'll lay foundations of hope in these ghettoes, says Blair', *Daily Mail*, 16 September 1998, p. 13.

95   Anon, 'Voice of the people: to hell and back', *The People*, 24 June 2007, p. 8.

96   Welshman, John, 'The concept of the unemployable', *The Economic History Reveiew* 59(3), 2006, pp. 578–606; Stedman-Jones, Gareth, *Outcast London: A Study in the Relationship between Classes in Victorian Society* (Oxford, UK: Oxford University Press, 1971).

97   Lahiji, Nadir and Daniel S. Friedman, 'At the sink: architecture in abjection', in Nadir Lahiji and Daniel S. Friedman (eds), *Plumbing: Sounding Modern Architecture* (New York: Princeton Architectural Press, 1997), p. 39. See also Gabrys, Jennifer, 'Sink: the dirt of systems', *Environment and Planning D: Society and Space* 27/4 (2009), pp. 666–81.

98   *Daily Mail*, 4 October 1972; the *Guardian*, 17 October 1972; *New Society*, 365/2, 18 November 1976.

99 The parliamentary debates, Hansard, official report, vol. 531.

100 Baeten, 'Hypochondriac geographies of the city', p. 111.

101 Stallabrass, Julian, *High Art Lite: British Art in the 1990s* (London: Verso, 1999), p. 259; Rendell, Jane, *Art and Architecture: A Place Between* (London and New York: I.B.Tauris, 2006), p. 89. See Campkin, Ben, 'Finding treasure in "trash": representations of London's Aylesbury and Heygate Estates', e-proceedings of the day conference organised by Docomomo's International Specialist Committee on Urbanism and Landscape (2007): http://www.archi.fr/DOCOMOMO/docomomo_electronic_newsletter7.htm (accessed 14 December 2008).

102 Kerr, Joe, 'Blowdown: the rise and fall of London's tower blocks', in Joe Kerr, Andrew Gibson and Mike Seaborne (eds), *London: From Punk to Blair* (London: Reaktion, 2003), pp. 189–97. A film documenting one such demolition can be viewed at: http://www.hackney.gov.uk/housing-blowdown-nightgale03.htm (accessed 14 December 2008).

103 Talkback TV productions used the estate repeatedly for filming *The Bill* in 2007 and 2008. Source: Southwark Council Film Office data.

104 A related example can be identified in a recent Sony Bravia TV commercial, directed by Jonathan Glazer, in which a tower block in Toryglen, Glasgow, was covered in blasts of brightly-coloured paint, set to Rossini's overture, *The Thieving Magpie*.

105 Stallabrass, *High Art Lite*, p. 259.

106 The single was internationally successful and reached No. 3 in the UK singles chart: Adams, M. (dir.), 'David Guetta vs. The Egg', *Love Don't Let Me Go/Walking Away* (2006). See: http://www.youtube.com/watch?v=E6e3R-aA2LA (accessed 29 July 2012).

107 Borden, Iain, *Skateboarding, Space and the City: Architecture and the Body* (Oxford: Berg, 2001), p. 29.

108 Saville, Stephen J., 'Playing with fear: parkour and the mobility of emotion', *Social & Cultural Geography* 9/8 (2008), pp. 891–914.

109 Edensor, Tim, *Industrial Ruins: Spaces, Aesthetics and Materiality* (Oxford: Berg, 2005b), p. 25.

110 Compare this with the 'ethos of adventure' in slum photography, discussed in Chapter 2: Gandal, *The Virtues of the Vicious*, p. 17.

111 See: http://www.youtube.com/watch?v=_lfOHndPQFw (accessed 29 July 2012).

112 Correspondence with former Channel 4 employee, 2008.

113 See: http://www.moving-picture.com/index.php?option=com_content&view=article&id=341&catid=47&Itemid=105#id=album-13572&num=3 (accessed 1 November 2008).

114 Blackman, Oona, Gary Jones and Rosie Dunn, 'Poverty shock report: forgotten families; hungry and sick, Leah, 3, lives with her mother in abject poverty on a squalid, violent estate', *The Mirror*, 30 October 1998, pp. 33–5.

115 Channel 4 won a number of awards, including a prestigious DA&D Golden Pencil, for the series, which has since influenced other UK terrestrial channels to create similar ident sequences.

116 Correspondence with former Channel 4 employee, 2008.

117 Hastings, Rob, 'South London estate residents bar filming', *Independent*, 6 February 2012. See: http://www.independent.co.uk/news/uk/this-britain/south-london-estate-residents-bar-filming-6579551.html.

118 Concurrently there have been many ethnographic photographic projects documenting the lives of residents, as represented by the London College of Communication's collections: for example, see Sutherland, *Home: The Elephant and Castle* and *Community: The Elephant and Castle*, London, London College of Communication, 2008.

119 See Hatherley, *Militant Modernisation*, p.2. In response, Hatherley has been criticised for nostalgically overlooking the brutalising tendencies of brutalist architecture. See Self, Will, 'It hits in the gut', *London Review of Books* 34/5, 8 March (2012). See: http://www.lrb.co.uk/v34/n05/will-self/it-hits-in-the-gut (accessed 1 May 2012).

120 Stewart, Heather, 'PFI under attack from both left and right', *The Observer*, 4 September 2011. See: http://www.guardian.co.uk/business/2011/sep/04/pfi-private-finance-initiative (accessed 2 February 2012); Hodkinson, 'Housing regeneration and the Private Finance Initiative in England'.

Chapter 5: Crisis and Creativity

1 Norman Foster in Crockford, Sue (dir.), *King's Cross: David and Goliath*, (1992).

2 Evans in Hatcher, David, 'Save the last dance: what impact will Argent's redevelopment have on King's Cross's club scene?', *Property Week*, 8 February 2008.

3 Battle Bridge was the area's previous name, given to the crossing of the Fleet – fabled as the site of a battle between the Romans and the Iceni tribe, led by Boudica.

4 Gray, Robert, *A History of London* (London: Hutchinson, 1978), p. 261; see also Weightman, Gavin and Steve Humphries, *The Making of Modern London* (London: Sidgwick & Jackson, 1983).

5 Stedman-Jones, *Outcast London*, p. 163. Given that Somers Town, as it is defined today, was not demolished completely at this time, Stedman-Jones is presumably referring to the wider boundaries of historic Somers Town, including the land north of Euston Station but west of Eversholt Street; and including Agar Town, south of Camden. These demolitions increased overcrowding in the slums of the core area of Somers Town, as defined today, occupying the space bounded by Eversholt Street, Euston Road, Crowndale Street and Pancras Road.

6 Weightman and Humphries, *The Making of Modern London*, p. 50.

7 King's Cross voices, 'A brief history of King's Cross'. See: http://www.kingscross-voices.org.uk/History_of_Kings_Cross.asp (accessed 2 October 2008).

8 Townend, Peter Norman, *Top Shed* (Shepperton, UK: Ian Allan Ltd, 1989), p. 4.

9 This sentiment is paralleled in mid-twentieth-century debates about the psychological effects of dirty work on construction labourers: Anon, 'The environment

of the building operative: psychological research in industry', *The Builder* 176/5540 (1949), pp. 499–500. In these discussions, beyond the unpleasantness and danger to public health of dirt, workers from dirty industries complained about the perceived detrimental effects of a dirty appearance on social standing.

10 Kerr in Kerr *et al.* (eds), *London: From Punk to Blair*, p. 19.

11 For example, Boseley, Sarah, 'A public nuisance cruising slowly in a private car', the *Guardian*, 4 February 1985.

12 Under the *Railways Act* (1993), British Rail was eventually split up and sold off. By November 1997 it had shed all its operating railway functions.

13 Thanks to Michael Edwards for bringing these photographs to my attention. I have been unable to source the original photographs or the full archive of the BRPB. See www.picturingplace.net (accessed 7 December 2012) for Edwards' commentary on the image. BRPB was set up to manage the land and assets of BR. On this, see Edwards, Michael, 'How should we manage the land resources of state railways? Lessons from London', in Gaston Ave and Franco Corsico (eds), *Urban Marketing in Europe* (Turin: Incontra, 1994), pp. 869–76.

14 King's Cross Railway Lands Group. See: http://www.kxrlg.org.uk/history/time-line.pdf (accessed 30 April 2007).

15 Picon, 'Anxious landscapes', p. 65.

16 Edensor, *Industrial Ruins*; 'Waste matter: the debris of industrial ruins and the disordering of the material world', *Journal of Material Culture* 10/3 (2005a), pp. 311–32.

17 Edensor, *Industrial Ruins*, p. 8.

18 Porter, Henry, 'The uplifting power of ingenious design enhances our daily lives', the *Guardian*, 25 March 2012. See: http://www.guardian.co.uk/commentisfree/2012/mar/25/henry-porter-kings-cross-new-concourse (accessed 30 July 2012).

19 Edwards, Michael, 'Fear and loathing at King's Cross', unpublished paper, University College London, 2003; Edwards, Michael, 'King's Cross: renaissance for whom?', in John Punter (ed.), *Urban Design, Urban Renaissance and British Cities* (London: Routledge, 2009). See: http://discovery.ucl.ac.uk/14020/1/14020.pdf.

20 Bartlett School, 'King's Cross second report', University College London (1990), p. 37; quoted in Catterall, Bob, 'Informational cities: beyond dualism and towards reconstruction', in Gary Bridge and Sophie Watson (eds), *A Companion to the City* (Oxford, UK: Blackwell, 2000), p. 198; Fainstein, Susan, *The City Builders: Property Development in New York and London, 1980–2000* (Lawrence, KS: University of Kansas, 2001), p. 122.

21 Edwards, Michael, 'A microcosm: redevelopment proposals at King's Cross', in Andy Thornley (ed.), *The Crisis of London* (London: Routledge, 1992), pp. 168, 170; Edwards, 'How should we manage the land resources of state railways?'; Edwards, 'Fear and loathing at King's Cross'.

22 In subsequent phases of the regeneration in the 2000s, the developers have promoted institutionalised and commercially sponsored art and culture more

actively, as an essential aspect of the area's regeneration. For example, King's Place, designed by Dixon Jones architects, opened in 2008 as a venue that accommodates a mix of offices, concert facilities and gallery space. In 2012, Carmody Groarke architects converted a former petrol station into an arts and restaurant venue, The Filling Station. See: http://www.artatkingscross.com/ (accessed 29 April 2009).

23 Catterall, 'Informational cities', p. 200; Crockford, *King's Cross*.

24 Catterall, 'Informational cities'.

25 See: http://www.kingscrosscentral.com/camley (accessed 29 July 2012).

26 Jordan, Neil (dir.), *Mona Lisa*, Handmade Films, 104 minutes (1986).

27 The film was shot on location in King's Cross and behind Liverpool Street station.

28 Sarler, Caroline, 'Thou shalt not…', *The Sunday Times*, 6 October 1991.

29 'Over the past 10 years the Goods Way has become one of the most sordid and notorious vice areas in London, harbouring a trade that used to be plied in residential streets south of the station until the police cleansed them. The sex acts that can be bought, at a price of £20 to £100, from the women loitering there must be among the most unpleasant possible: quick, cold, anonymous and dehumanising. In the film Mona Lisa it was a symbol of sexual degradation'; Sarler, 'Thou shalt not…'.

30 Young, Lola, 'A nasty piece of work: a psychoanalytic study of sexual and racial difference in "Mona Lisa"', in Jonathan Rutherford (ed.), *Identity: Community, Culture, Difference* (London: Lawrence & Wishart, 1990), pp. 188–206, p. 203

31 Drew's Scriptorama. See: http://www.script-o-rama.com/movie_scripts/m/mona-lisa-script-transcript-jordan.html (accessed 10 October 2008).

32 Sarler, 'Thou shalt not…'.

33 Mills, Heather and Nick Cohen, 'Green's downfall rocks prosecution service', *The Independent*, 4 October 1991; Mullin, John, 'The street Mona Lisa turned her back on', the *Guardian*, 4 October 1991. Journalists Heather Mills and Nick Cohen describe the area in graphic terms: 'The square mile north of King's Cross is a squalid mishmash of dilapidated houses and derelict buildings. Used condoms and discarded syringes litter backyards'.

34 The song was re-released by Tracey Thorn in 2007 and has been set to images of King's Cross and the St Pancras Eurostar terminal on YouTube. See: http://uk.youtube.com/watch?v=XCIcAtjvsPI&feature=related (accessed 11 October 2008).

35 Tennant, Neil, 'Interviews: Actually, "King's Cross"', *Absolutely Pet Shop Boys: The Unofficial Website*. See: http://www.petshopboys.net/index.shtml (accessed 5 May 2009).

36 Similarly, in *Career Girls*, one of several films set in the area directed by Mike Leigh, the plot focuses on the lives of two women who met at college in the north-east, and who are reunited in London. The opening sequence sees one of the women arriving at King's Cross station. The contrast between the north-east of the mid-1980s, and London of the late 1990s, provides a backdrop for the exploration of the changing social statuses of the women and the dynamics of

their relationship: Leigh, Mike (dir.), *Career Girls*, Cinema Club, 283 minutes, VHS (1997).

37   Turner, Mark W., 'Gay London', in Joe Kerr and Andrew Gibson (eds), *London: From Punk to Blair* (London: Reaktion, 2003), pp. 48–59; Andersson, Johan, 'Consuming Visibility: London's New Spaces of Gay Nightlife', PhD dissertation, University of London, 2008. In 1988, The Bell was subjected to a heavy-handed police raid, involving 60 officers, for alleged licensing infringements. Andersson argues that King's Cross continued to have an association with subcultural gay nightlife, and gay and lesbian activism into the 1990s and 2000s. In 1992, Central Station, opened on Wharfdale Road. Shortly afterwards, 'indie' gay nightclub Popstarz began to be hosted at the Scala, a former cinema completed in 1921, and located at the lower end of Pentonville Road. 'Polysexual' house music club Fiction was later hosted in The Cross nightclub, located in one of the former coal drop warehouses (2000–7). The Cross closed in 2008 to make way for the King's Cross Central redevelopment.

38   Jarman, Derek (dir.), *Projections*, MVD Visual, VHS (2000).

39   See: http://uk.youtube.com/watch?v=jIcdlNvyRVI (accessed 4 October 2008).

40   In the Pet Shop Boy's film, *It Couldn't Happen Here*, the lyrics to 'King's Cross' are accompanied by scenes of a man and a car in flames, resonating with the nightmarish dystopian landscape of *Mona Lisa*, and with the later apocalyptic vision of King's Cross provided by Salman Rushdie in *The Satanic Verses*: Pet Shop Boys, *It Couldn't Happen Here*, Picture Music International (1987); Rushdie, Salman, *The Satanic Verses* (London: Viking, 1992, first published 1988), p. 461; see also Battista, Kathy, Brandon LaBelle, Barbara Penner, Steve Pile and Jane Rendell, 'Exploring an area of outstanding unnatural beauty: a treasure hunt around King's Cross, London', *Cultural Geographies* 12/429 (2005), p. 462.

41   Jarman, Derek (dir.), *The Last of England*, 1989, 87 minutes, Second Sight, DVD, 2003, 87 minutes.

42   Julien, Isaac (dir.), *Looking for Langston*, 1989, BFI Video, DVD, 2005, 45 minutes.

43   When, in 1993, Julien adapted the film into a performance piece set around Camley Street, he wrote explicitly of his intentions in using King's Cross as a location, and in doing so emphasised the area's 'reputation for sex and sleaze': 'Listen to the [*sic*]Pet Shop Boys singing. Because of the railway station, King's Cross is also a gateway into England, a doorway between north and south. The performance used Camley Street in particular, a street that is notorious as a cruising ground for straights – it has a special geography. The proposed redevelopment of the area also means that there are certain political ramifications to the location. The whole space is going to be knocked down and renovated into a kind of Covent Garden yuppie village. It's barbaric. I enjoyed the idea of putting my audience into these different and difficult spaces where they might not normally go and certainly might not feel safe at that time of night. I wanted people to go into these spaces and to think about their architecture and its relationship to different dynamic forms of power – public and private, micro and

macro. Making the film meant that I could explore those locations cinematically but actually putting people – performers and audiences – into these landscapes has a different kind of excitement': Julien quoted in Gilroy, Paul, 'Climbing the racial mountain: a conversation with Isaac Julien', in Paul Gilroy (ed.), *Small Acts: Thoughts on the Politics of Black Cultures* (London: Serpent's Tail, 1993), p. 167.

44 This scene reinforces the association of male homosexuality with 'the ruins of the urban landscape', a trope identified by John Binnie in his work on the sexual geographies of London: Binnie, John 'A geography of urban desires: sexual culture in the city', PhD dissertation, University of London, 1997. See also Andersson, Johan and Ben Campkin, 'White tiles. Trickling water. A man!: literary representations of cottaging in London', in Olga Gershenson and Barbara Penner (eds), *Ladies and Gents: Public Toilets and Gender* (Philadelphia, PA: Temple University Press, 2009). The St Pancras churchyard has also been a key site of inspiration for the apocalyptic and spectral musings of contemporary psychogeographers such as Salman Rushdie in *The Satanic Verses*; the poet Aidan Andrew Dun; the writer Iain Sinclair; and the photographer Marc Atkins. Atkins, Mark and Iain Sinclair, *Liquid City* (London: Reaktion Books, 1999).

45 hooks, bell, 'Seductive sexualities: representing blackness in poetry and on screen', *Yearning* (Boston, MA: South End, 1990), pp. 190–201.

46 Edensor, *Industrial Ruins*, p. 13.

47 Edensor, *Industrial Ruins*, p. 13. In this, Julien's film is more aligned with the conception of a melancholic poetics of ruin in the work of the art and architectural theorist, Jane Rendell. In Rendell's understanding, as they feature in certain recent works between art and architectural practice, ruins can operate critically through an allegorical mode, rather than being purely nostalgic, politically disengaged, retro- or introspective. See Rendell, Jane, *Art and Architecture: A Place Between* (London: I.B.Tauris, 2006), p. 85.

48 Nick Lowe's song, 'Who was that man?' (1990), also refers to Fallon's case: 'Among the crowd was a lonely soul / With a mission in mind and a place to go / Nobody knows where he was bound / When his fateful steps took him underground.'

49 Chambers, Paul, *Body 115: The Mystery of the Last Victim of the King's Cross Fire* (Chichester, UK: John Wiley, 2007), p. 1.

50 Fennell, Desmond, *Investigation into the King's Cross Underground Fire* (London: Her Majesty's Stationery Office, 1988). See: http://www.railwaysarchive.co.uk/documents/DoT_KX1987.pdf.

51 Beauregard, *Voices of Decline*, p. 9.

52 Page, Mike Paul Neuburg and John Wakefield (dirs), *The London Programme: King's Cross Fire*, ITV (1987).

53 Fennell, *Investigation into the King's Cross Underground Fire*.

54 If the fire had not happened, some of the costs might have fallen on the private developers leading the Channel Tunnel Rail Link terminus, and the regeneration of the King's Cross railway lands. Modernisation and increased capacity were

essential for both of these schemes because of the projected increase in population. Thanks to Michael Edwards for discussing this point with me.

55 Stafford, Julia and Geraldine Pettersson, 'Vandalism, graffiti and environmental nuisance on public transport', in *Literature Review of Graffiti*, Report,
Department for Transport (London, Her Majesty's Stationery Office, 2004).

56 Brown, Colin and Nicholas Pyke, 'Railtrack to charge operators for new tracks
and signalling', *Independent*, 22 October 2000. Prescott had previously been
critical of the 'limited terms of reference' set out by the Thatcher government
in initiating the Fennell Report, which 'prevented a fuller examination of the
real causes ... including the climate created in London Underground Ltd by the
obsession with reducing costs through the continuous reduction of manpower
and resources affecting safety': Prescott, John, 'King's Cross fire (Fennell
Report)', HC Deb, 10 November, House of Commons sitting, vol. 140,
cc498–512, Hansard (1988). Part-privatisation occurred in January 2003 in the
second term of the Blair government. Since then, the infrastructure and rolling
stock have been maintained by private companies under 30-year contracts, but
the London Underground remains publicly owned and operated by Transport
for London. David Harvey notes that the 'greatest testimony' to the successes
of the Thatcher–Regan project of neoliberalism lies in its continuation under
Blair and Clinton, and their inability to avoid this, 'even against their own better
instincts': Harvey, *A Brief History of Neoliberalism*, pp. 62–3.

57 Ross, Rebecca, *Mapping Changes: Visualizing King's Cross*, Department of
Geography, University College London, 2005, p. 27.

58 Crockford, Sue (dir.), *King's Cross: David and Goliath*, 11 January 1992.

59 Interview with Martin Coll, London Borough of Camden Homelessness Unit,
London, 4 September 2001.

60 Ross, Rebecca, *Mapping changes: visualizing King's Cross*, Department of
Geography, University College London (London: 2005), p. 27.

61 Agamben, Giorgio, *State of Exception* (Chicago: University of Chicago Press, 2005).

62 Payne, Carolyn (dir.), *Sex, Drugs and Video Tape: The Cleaning up of King's Cross*,
first edition, ZKK 9 (1999).

63 Quoted in Payne, *Sex, Drugs and Video Tape*.

64 Dunne, 'Goodbye King's Cross, hello Regent Quarter', *Hampstead and Highgate
Express* (2001), p. 22.

65 For example, in 2002, journalist Andrew Martin wrote: 'Around the junction of
Pentonville Road and Caledonian Road, it is the heart of darkness. Every facet of
urban demonology was – still is, for the time being – represented on its streets,
thunderous lorries, strip pubs, sex shops, fast-food joints, prostitutes, and sham-
bling armies of winos and junkies ... But this is all about to change. King's Cross
is to be made over': Martin, Andrew, 'A platform for progress', *Daily Telegraph*,
12 January 2002. See also Staffell, Andrew, 'On the move: King's Cross', *Time
Out*, 4 January 2006, p. 134.

66 Hubbard, Phil, 'Cleansing the metropolis: sex work and the politics of zero
tolerance', *Urban Studies* 41(9) (2004), pp. 1687–1702, 1693.

67 Edwards, Michael, 'King's Cross: renaissance for whom?', in John Punter (ed.), *Urban Design, Urban Renaissance and British Cities* (London: Routledge, 2009). See: http://discovery.ucl.ac.uk/14020/1/14020.pdf.

68 Interview with Inspector Gary Buttercase, Metropolitan Police/King's Cross Partnership, London, 15 August 2001; interview with Martin Coll, Camden Borough Council Homelessness Unit, London, 4 September 2001.

69 Haworth Tomkins, known for a number of theatre projects, were nominated for the prestigious Royal Institute of British Architects' Stirling Prize (2007) for their design for the Young Vic Theatre, Waterloo, London. The Almeida at King's Cross was shortlisted for an *Evening Standard* award (2002), and won a *Time Out* Live Award for 'Most Inspiring Venue' (2002). It was the practice's second commission for a temporary venue for the Almeida, the first being located in the derelict Gainsborough Studios in Shoreditch, east London.

70 Interview with Philip Nicholls, Almeida Theatre, 17 July 2001.

71 Anon, *The Art of Regeneration: Urban Renewal Through Cultural Activity* (Nottingham: 1996); Harris and Moreno, *Creative City Limits*.

72 Interview with Steve Tomkins and Roger Watts, Haworth Tomkins Architects, London, 6 August 2001. On the aesthetic processes of large-scale conversions of industrial buildings and manufacturing complexes to post-industrial cultural uses, see architect and theorist, Phoebe Crisman's, examination of four international museums in Europe and North America: Crisman, Phoebe, 'From industry to culture: leftovers, time and material transformation in four contemporary museums', *Journal of Architecture* 12/1 (2007), pp. 405–22.

73 The architects used the plant sedum, a cost-effective means of achieving heat and sound insulation: Dyson, Jonathan, 'Almeida Theatre: beyond the fringe', *The Independent*, 2001.

74 Interview with Steve Tomkins and Roger Watts, Haworth Tomkins Architects, London, 6 August 2001.

75 Tomkins, quoted in Rufford, Juliet, 'Out of site: Haworth Tomkins, Paul Brown, and the "Shoreditch Shakespeares"', *Journal of Architectural Education* 61/4, p. 34.

76 The architects originally applied for planning permission to place signposts to the theatre from the main (Caledonian) road, but their application was refused. In retrospect, they stated that they preferred the theatre to be partially hidden. Interview with Steve Tomkins and Roger Watts.

77 Interview with Philip Nicholls, Almeida Theatre, London, 17 July 2001.

78 Wedekind, Frank, *Lulu* (London: Nick Hern, 2001). The *Lulu Plays* were brought to a wider audience through the film *Pandora's Box* (1928), directed by Georg Wilhelm Pabst.

79 Interview with Philip Nicholls, Almeida Theatre, 17 July 2001.

80 Loveridge, Lizzie, Lulu, *CurtainUp* (2001). See: http://www.curtainup.com/lulu.html (accessed 11 November 2008).

81 Rendell, Jane, '"Bazaar beauties" or "pleasure is our pursuit": a spatial story of exchange', in Iain Borden, Joe Kerr, Jane Rendell and Alicia Pivaro (eds), *The Unknown City: Contesting Architecture and Social Space* (London: MIT Press,

2001), p. 106. Geographer Steve Pile writes: '[the prostitute and the *flâneur* in the nineteenth-century city] are also markers of the difficulties of locating people in their proper place: each moves between locations, turning up where they "should not be". Indeed they matter precisely because they are both "out of place" ... they are the "contents" of a nightmare that proves the urban has an unconscious, an underground erotic life': Pile, *The Body and the City*, p. 235.

82   Walkowitz, *City of Dreadful Delight*, p. 21.

83   'Down towards King's Cross and the railway termini we are promised a Channel Tunnel terminal, and the biggest shopping mall in Europe inside Gilbert Scott's Victorian Gothic hotel building. What will happen to the poverty-stricken working class, both white and Bangladeshi, in the estates behind the station, currently plagued by prostitution and racial attacks, when they have to make way for the developers? They will be shovelled out to even less desirable locations, while their flats and shops are upmarketed or pulled down to be replaced by hotels, offices and a privately owned park. What will happen then to our quiet streets with their little shops, local eccentrics and leafy squares?': Wilson, Elizabeth, *The Sphinx in the City: Urban Life, the Control of Disorder, and Women* (London: Virago Press, 1991), p. 159.

84   Listerborn, Carina, 'How public can public spaces be?', *City: Analysis of Urban Trends, Theory, Policy, Action* 9/3 (2003), pp. 381–4, p. 383; Sorkin, *Variations on a Theme Park*. This discussion chimes with Baeten's criticism of a tendency in the contemporary urban research agenda to 'problematize the city from a white, Western, male middle-class perspective': Baeten, 'Hypochondriac geographies of the city and the new urban dystopia', p. 103.

85   Lefaivre, Liane, 'Dirty realism in European architecture today', *Design Book Review* 17 (1989), pp. 17–20.

86   Staffell, 'On the move'; Blinkhorn, Amanda, 'It's all change at King's Cross. Once London's most notorious area, it's now home to inner-city chic', *Hampstead and Highgate Express* (1995).

87   Anon, *A Framework for Regeneration* (London: Argent St George, 2002), p. 11.

88   Sladen, Teresa and Gavin Stamp, *Opportunity or calamity? The King's Cross Railway Lands Development* (London: The Victorian Society, 1988).

89   The Cross, Canvas and Key nightclubs, which occupied the warehouses and coal drops next to the canal on Goods Way through the 1990s, were closed in 2008 to make way for Argent's redevelopment.

Chapter 6: Ornament from Grime

1   Douglas, Mary, *Purity and Danger: An Analysis of the Concepts of Pollution and Taboo* (London: Routledge, 2000, first published 1966), pp. xvii–xviii.

2   Douglas, *Purity and Danger*. Douglas writes: 'If we can abstract pathogenecity and hygiene from our notion of dirt, we are left with the old definition of dirt as

matter out of place' (p. 36). For an extended discussion of Douglas' theory see Campkin, 'Placing "matter out of place"'.

3 Francis Bacon, quoted in Turner, Chris, 'Chaos theory', *Tate Magazine* 26 Autumn (2001), p. 53. Bacon's studio is briefly described in Savonuzzi, Paolo and Chiara Wolter, 'So what's trash in architecture?', in Vergine, Lea (ed.), *Trash: From Junk to Art* (Milan: Gingko Press, 1997), p. 256: 'empty bottles, jars full of dried brushes, a layer of dust and a coat of colour on everything, as if each object touched by him had settled in that special place'.

4 Bacon had been an interior decorator before becoming an artist.

5 For example, see Bauman, Zygmunt, *Wasted Lives: Modernity and Its Outcasts* (Oxford, UK: Polity Press, 2004); Cousins, 'The ugly (Part 1)', 'The ugly (Part 2)', 'The ugly (Part 3)'; Forty, *Objects of Desire*; Thompson, Michael, *Rubbish Theory: The Creation and Destruction of Value* (Oxford, UK: Oxford University Press, 1979); Shonfield, Katherine, 'Dirt is matter out of place', in Hill, Jonathan (ed.), *Architecture–the Subject is Matter* (London: Routledge, 2001), pp. 29–44; Sibley, *Geographies of Exclusion*; and Wright, Patrick, *A Journey Through Ruins: The Last Days of London* (London: Radius, 1991).

6 Wolkowitz, Carol, 'Linguistic leakiness or really dirty? Dirt in social theory' in Campkin, Ben and Rosie Cox (eds), *Dirt: New Geographiess of Cleanliness and Contamination* (London: I.B.Tauris, 2007 and 2012), pp. 15–24, 15.

7 Biernoff, Suzannah, 'The art of rubbish', unpublished lecture, University College London, January (2003); Vergine, *Trash*. Updating Vergine's survey, Biernoff has argued that, in modernist art, rubbish is incorporated into the artwork as an index of the everyday; while in postmodern art, rubbish is used to represent the relics and ruins of modernism.

8 Bruno, Giuliana, 'Ramble city: postmodernism and *Blade Runner*', *OCTOBER* 41 (1987), p. 64.

9 Campkin, Ben, 'Degradation and regeneration: theories of dirt and the contemporary city', in Campkin, Ben and Rosie Cox (eds), *Dirt: New Geographies of Cleanliness and Contamination* (London: I.B.Tauris, 2007), pp. 68–79; Campkin, Ben, 'Placing "matter out of place"'.

10 Ryan, Raymund, *Gritty Brits: New London Architecture* (Pittsburgh: Carnegie Museum of Art, 2007).

11 As well as Adjaye Associates, the group includes Caruso St John Architects, FAT, Níall McLaughlin Architects, muf and Sergison Bates Architects.

12 Bruno, 'Ramble city: postmodernism and *Blade Runner*'; Foster, Hal, 'Why all the hoopla?', *London Review of Books* 23/16 (2001), pp. 24–26; Stallabrass, *High Art Lite*; Zukin, Sharon, *Loft Living: Culture and Capital in Urban Change* (London: Johns Hopkins University Press, 1982).

13 Allison, Peter (ed.), *David Adjaye Houses: Recycling, Reconfiguring, Rebuilding* (London: Thames & Hudson, 2005a); Allison, Peter (ed.), *David Adjaye: Making Public Buildings: Specificity, Customization, Imbrication* (London: Thames & Hudson, 2006).

14 Sudjic, Deyan, 'Building in London', in Peter Allison (ed.), *David Adjaye Houses: Recycling, Reconfiguring, Rebuilding* (London: Thames & Hudson, 2005), pp. 186–91.

15 These buildings combine and rework the conventional typologies of library and community centre.

16 See, for example, Allison, Peter, 'The house of the artist: David Adjaye designs a studio house for London's new generation of artists', *Domus*, December (2002), pp. 60–9; Booth, Robert, 'Star house loses face', *Building Design* 1540/05, July (2002), p. 1; Baillieu, Amanda, 'Mirror mirror on the wall. Building study: Dirty House, east London', *RIBA Journal*, November (2002), pp. 34–8; Long, Kieran, 'David Adjaye', *Icon* 17 (2004), pp. 84–92; Street-Porter, Janet, 'It's time to settle a score', *The Independent*, 3 July 2005.

17 See Roux, Caroline, 'The tale of a house', in Allison, Peter (ed.), *David Adjaye Houses: Recycling, Reconfiguring, Rebuilding* (London, Thames & Hudson, 2005), pp. 132, 135, for comment on Adjaye's training at the Royal College of Art and links to contemporary London artists, and particularly to those such as Chris Ofili and Jake and Dinos Chapman, who explore ideas about dirt and abjection in their work.

18 See: http://www.kultureflash.net/archive/136/default.htm#event3019 (accessed 6 July 2007).

19 See Harris, Andrew, 'The installation of Hoxton: culture and capital in 1990s inner London', in 'Branding urban space: the creation of art districts in contemporary London and Mumbai', unpublished PhD dissertation, University of London, 2005, pp. 123–66; 'Art and gentrification: pursuing the urban pastoral in Hoxton, London', *Transactions of the Institute of British Geographers* 37(2), pp. 226–41, April 2012; and Stallabrass, *High Art Lite*.

20 The practice has since relocated to Marylebone, West London.

21 Allison, Peter, 'Living in ruins', in Allison, Peter (ed.), *David Adjaye Houses: Recycling, Reconfiguring, Rebuilding* (London: Thames & Hudson, 2005), pp. 83–8.

22 Hall, Stuart, 'Negotiating architecture', in Allison, Peter (ed.), *David Adjaye Houses: Recycling, Reconfiguring, Rebuilding* (London: Thames & Hudson, 2005), p. 10.

23 Rosenblum, Charles, 'The Carnegie's Gritty Brits offers keen architectural minds at work', *Pittsburgh City Paper*, 8 February 2007. See: http://www.pittsburghcitypaper.ws/gyrobase/Content?oid=oid%3A22477 (accessed 6 July 2007).

24 Ryan, *Gritty Brits*, p. 11.

25 Ryan, *Gritty Brits*, p. 12.

26 Ryan, *Gritty Brits*, p. 11.

27 Ryan, *Gritty Brits*, p. 11.

28 Reyner Banham, quoted in Webster, Helena, 'Modernism without rhetoric: the work of Alison and Peter Smithson', in Helena Webster (ed.), *Modernism without Rhetoric: Essays on the Work of Alison and Peter Smithson* (London: Academy Editions, 1997), pp. 10–123, 24.

29 At the Institute of Contemporary Arts and the Whitechapel Art Gallery, respectively.

30 Walsh, Victoria, *Nigel Henderson: Parallel of Life and Art, London* (London: Thames & Hudson, 2001). See especially pp. 89–122.

31 Independent Art Space, London, 22 June–3 August 1996.

32 See: http://www.saatchi-gallery.co.uk/artists/noble_webster_articles.htm (accessed 22 June 2007).

33 Harris, Mark, 'Tim Noble and Sue Webster at 20 Rivington Street', *Art in America*, July (1998).

34 Deitch, Jeffrey, 'Black magic', in Noble, Tim and Sue Webster, *Wasted Youth* (New York: Rizzoli, 2006), unpaginated.

35 Deitch, 'Black magic'.

36 Interview with Tim Noble and Sue Webster, Dirty House, London, 12 July 2007.

37 Baillieu, Amanda, 'Mirror mirror on the wall. Building study: Dirty House, east London', *RIBA Journal*, November (2002), p. 34. Baillieu explains that developing the original factory building rather than demolishing it completely and rebuilding left the clients liable to an additional tax – the UK's Value Added Tax (VAT) – of 17.5 per cent at that time.

38 Baillieu, 'Mirror mirror on the wall', p. 36.

39 Allison, 'The house of the artist'.

40 This quotation is used by the practice on their website: Aspden, Peter, 'Rising star with a store of ideas'. See: http://www.adjaye.com (accessed 26 June 2007).

41 Roux, 'The tale of a house', p. 135.

42 Full details of the coating, known as PL13, can be found at: http://www.clean-streets.co.uk/PL13.pdf.

43 'Paints, sealants and finishes', 17 May 2005. See: http://www.building. co.uk/story.asp?sectioncode=482&storycode=3051188 (accessed 29 June 2007). I am grateful to Aeli Roberts, UCL Bartlett School of Construction Management, for this reference on the chemical composition of the paint. As a feature of the design, it can be attributed directly to Adjaye, who successfully persuaded his clients to choose it, even though they were keen to leave the walls exposed. Noble and Webster remark that this was important to Adjaye in taking the design a step further than existing industrial–residential conversions. Interview with Tim Noble and Sue Webster, Dirty House, London, 12 July 2007.

44 Interview with Tim Noble and Sue Webster, Dirty House, London, 12 July 2007.

45 The scaffolding covers a synagogue being converted into a house for a prominent London-based sculptress.

46 Wilson, Robin, 'At the limits of genre: architectural photography and utopic criticism', *The Journal of Architecture* 10/9 (2005), pp. 265–73.

47 Tagg, John, *Grounds of Dispute: Art History, Cultural Politis and the Discursive Field* (Minneapolis, MN: University of Minnesota Press, 1992), p.101.

48 Wilson, 'At the limits of genre', pp. 265–6.

49 This is true of some, although not all, of the other Gritty Brits.

50 'Page 3 girls' are so called in reference to the fact that British tabloid newspapers such as *The Sun* have traditionally featured images of semi-naked women on page 3.

51 Interview with Tim Noble and Sue Webster, Dirty House, London, 2007.

52 Baillieu, 'Mirror mirror on the wall', p. 34.

53 Bruno, 'Ramble city', p. 64.

54 Wilhide, Elizabeth, *New Loft Living* (London: Carlton Books, 2002), p. 92.

55 Zukin, *Loft Living*, p. 3.

56 Celebrated in the kind of coffee-table books one might expect to see accessorising such properties, this genre of prestige property development remains popular, but has attracted surprisingly little in the way of critical commentary within architectural discourse, despite its pastiche, and by now clichéd aesthetic. For two examples of publications that uncritically celebrate loft spaces and the lifestyles associated with them, see Vance, Peggy, *Loft Living* (London: Ward Lock, 1999); and Wilhide, *New Loft Living*.

57 Since the publication of Zukin's book, academic debates have ensued over the appropriate degree of analytic emphasis on the roles and levels of responsibility of individual agents, and broader structures and socio-cultural factors in contributing to 'loft living' as a form of gentrification. For a recent example, see Hamnett, Chris and Drew Whitelegg, 'Loft conversion and gentrification in London: from industrial to postindustrial land use', *Environment and Planning A* 39 (2007), p. 110.

58 Interview with Tim Noble and Sue Webster, 2007.

59 Harvey, 'Foreword', in Zukin, *Loft Living*, p. xii.

60 Stallabrass, *High Art Lite*, pp. 237–45; Stallabrass, Julian, 'Urban pastoral', *The Urban Pastoral, AHRC Landscape and Environment Programme* (London, 2008). Stallabrass draws on William Empson's writings on the pastoral ideal in working-class literature: Emson, William, *Some Versions of the Pastoral* (New York: New Directions Publishing, 1950, first published 1935). For recent uses of the pastoral in urban studies, see Harnack, Maren, 'London's Trellick Tower and the pastoral eye', in Gandy, *Urban Constellations* (Berlin: Jovis Verlag, 2011); and Gandy, *Concrete and Clay*, p. 275, n. 54.

61 Stallabrass, *High Art Lite*, p. 250.

62 Stallabrass, *High Art Lite*, p. 250; geographer Andrew Harris has taken up the pastoral, and work on gentrification by Ruth Glass, Zukin and others, in order to understand the role of artists in Hoxton's transformation in the 1990s. He concludes that art-led gentrification in Hoxton, has both peculiarities – it does not feature direct displacement, and the artists involved have capitalised on a relationship with the area's working-class and industrial heritage – but it remains a form of class-based transformation: Harris, 'Art and gentrification', p. 235.

63 Stallabrass, *High Art Lite*, p. 242.

64 Stallabrass, *High Art Lite*, p. 243.

65   Rendell, *Art and Architecture*, p. 89. Rendell discusses Blees Luxemburg's *Caliban Towers I and II* (1997) as part of her exploration of 'ruin as allegory' in art and architectural projects.
66   Adjaye, quoted in Aspden, 'Rising star with a store of ideas'. This quotation is used by the practice on its website: http://www.adjaye.com (accessed 26 June 2007).
67   Foster, 'Why all the hoopla?'.
68   '[Adjaye] has captured the imagination with a blend of postmodern architecture that has gone beyond the feeble first phase of that movement, all pastiches and literalism, to engage with the dominant social trends of the day: access, democracy, civic empowerment': Aspden, 'Rising star with a store of ideas'.

Chapter 7: Burial and Bioremediation

1   Iain Sinclair, quoted on Stephen Gill's website. See: http://www.stephengill.co.uk/portfolio/about (accessed 27 December 2011).
2   Buchli, Victor and Gavin Lucas, 'The absent present: archaeologies of the contemporary past', in Victor Buchli and Gavin Lucas (eds), *Archaeologies of the Contemporary Past* (London: Routledge, 2001), p. 3.
3   See *Hackney Wick* (2004); *Buried* (2006); *Hackney Flowers* (2007); *Archaeology in Reverse* (2007); *A Series of Disappointments* (2008); *Warming Down* (2008); *The Hackney Rag* (2009); and *Off Ground* (2011) – all published in London by Nobody.
4   Theorist of archaeological photography, Michael Shanks, defines 'photoworks' as explicitly interpretative photographs, where the photographer is aware of photography as an act of cultural production rather than of objective documentation: 'It is proposed that photography, far from being homogenous, is an unstable category, and that it is better to think less of photographs than of photoworks, with emphasis placed upon acts of cultural production: photowork is then one aspect of how the archaeologist may take up the remains of the past and work upon them. This is the positive moment of critique – finding the creative potential within particular modes of cultural production, a potential to express different interests in the material past': Shanks, Michael, 'Photography and archaeology', in Molyneaux, Brian (ed.), *The Cultural Life of Images: Visual Representation in Archaeology* (London: Routledge, 1997), pp. 73–107.
5   Rose, David, *Report to the Secretary of State for Trade and Industry. The Regional Development Agencies Act 1998, Acquisition of Land Act 1981, Application by the London Development Agency. For confirmation of The London Development Agency (Lower Lea Valley, Olympic and Legacy) Compulsory Purchase Order 2005, Public inquiry opened on 9 May 2006* (Bristol: The Planning Inspectorate, 2006).
6   See Borromeo, Leah, 'Local heroes: the Olympic unwanted' (2012). See: http://fryingpanfire.com/2012/07/local-heroes-the-olympic-unwanted/ (accessed 30

July 2012); Games Monitor, at: http://www.gamesmonitor.org.uk (accessed 31 July 2012); and Powell, Hilary and Isaac Marrero-Guillamón (eds), *The Art of Dissent: Adventures in London's Olympic State* (London: Marshgate Press, 2012).

7 Iain Sinclair, quoted in Hatherley, Owen, '*Ghost Milk: Calling Time on the Grand Project*, by Iain Sinclair reviewed by Owen Hatherley'. See: http://www.independent.co.uk/arts-entertainment/books/reviews/ghost-milk-calling-time-on-the-grand-project-by-iain-sinclair-2308549.html (accessed 7 November 2011). See also Sinclair, Iain, 'The Olympics scam', *London Review of Books* 30/12 June (2008), pp. 17–23. See: http://www.lrb.co.uk/v30/n12/iain-sinclair/the-olympics-scam (accessed 6 May 2012).

8 Interview with Paul Jennings, London 2012 Organising Committee, and Anthony Palmer, formerly Olympic Delivery Authority Filming and Events Manager, 21 December 2011, Canary Wharf, London. In 2009, the ODA responded to complaints about the lack of visual accessibility to the site by introducing a mesh for viewing through the blue fence.

9 This publicly funded archive has to date only been made partially accessible. It is now controlled by the London 2012 Organising Committee (LOCOG), a private company, who are negotiating with the National Archives and the British Film Institute with a view to depositing it with them.

10 See Wilson, 'At the limits of genre'.

11 Correspondence with Stephen Gill, 8 November 2011.

12 Stephen Gill (2004). See: http://www.stephengill.co.uk/portfolio/about (accessed 1 December 2011).

13 See page 48 and Chapter 2, note 46.

14 Stephen Gill (2004). See: http://www.stephengill.co.uk/portfolio/about (accessed 1 December 2011).

15 Slavin, Martin, 'Living through placemaking: the London Olympics 2012', unpublished seminar paper, Bartlett School of Planning London Planning seminar series, University College London, 3 November (London: 2011).

16 The allotments are described as 'temporarily demolished' on Wikipedia. See: http://en.wikipedia.org/wiki/Manor_Garden_Allotments#cite_note-0 (accessed 3 January 2012).

17 Wray and Higgott, *Camera Constructs*, p. 28.

18 See Gill's website: http://nobodybooks.com/shop/ (accessed 1 December 2011).

19 Correspondence with Stephen Gill, 8 November 2011.

20 Luckhurst, Roger, 'The contemporary London gothic and the limits of the spectral turn', *Textual Practice* 16/3 (2002), pp. 527–46.

21 See, for example, Patrick Wright's account of the social, physical and cultural landscape of London's Dalston area in the early 1990s: Wright, *A Journey Through Ruins*.

22 Derrida, Jacques, *Spectres of Marx* (Abingdon and New York: Routledge, 2006, first published 1993).

23 Derrida, Jacques, *Archive Fever: a Freudian Impression* (Chicago and London: The University of Chicago Press, 1996).

24   Luckhurst, 'The contemporary London gothic and the limits of the spectral turn', p. 532.

25   Luckhurst, 'The contemporary London gothic and the limits of the spectral turn', p. 530.

26   Luckhurst, 'The contemporary London gothic and the limits of the spectral turn', p. 532.

27   This figure was obtained from one of the companies used to process the soil, from a website article subsequently archived. See: http://www.deme.be/projects/belg_dec_london_olympics.html (accessed 5 December 2011).

28   'Gardeners exposed to 2012 Olympics construction radiation hazard'. See: http://www.lifeisland.org/ (accessed 3 January 2012).

29   Charman, Paul and Mike Wells, 'London 2012: legacy or liability' (London: Games Monitor, 2010). See: http://www.gamesmonitor.org.uk/node/911 (accessed 3 January 2012); Mike Wells, 'London 2012: a rubbish Olympics' (London: Games Monitor, 2010). See: http://www.gamesmonitor.org.uk/node/1108 (accessed 3 January 2012).

30   This product and its uses are detailed at: http://www.terram.com/products/geotextiles/standard-filterseparators-general-construction-highways.html (accessed 3 January 2012).

31   An example of distress aesthetics would be fashion designer Hussein Chalyan's 1993 collection, 'The Tangent Flows', in which he buried clothes in his back garden and dug them up again, turning dirt and decomposition into a luxury commodity. See Townsend, Katherine, 'The denim garment as canvas: exploring the notion of wear as a fashion and textile narrative, *Textile* 9/1 (2011), pp. 90–107.

32   Raco, Mike and Emma Tunney, 'Visibilities and invisibilities in urban development: small business communities and the London Olympics 2012', *Urban Studies* 47/10 (2010), pp. 2069–91.

33   Buchli and Lucas, *Archaeologies of the Contemporary Past.*

34   Pollock, Griselda, 'The image in psychoanalysis and the archaeological metaphor', in Griselda Pollock (ed.), *Psychoanalysis and the Image: Transdisciplinary Perspectives* (Oxford: Wiley-Blackwell, 2006), p. 10.

Conclusion

1   London Borough of Newham, *Newham London: Investment Prospectus*, (undated). See: http://www.newham.gov.uk/NR/rdonlyres/8AF0D6BC-7A8E-4625-85D1-2083502CB3D5/0/InvestmentProspectus.pdf (accessed 19 June 2012). The film was available online but has subsequently been taken down from Newham's website. Within the Greater London Assembly, the London Development Agency was responsible for 'sustainable economic growth' in London until 2012, when it was disbanded. Thanks to Alberto Duman for drawing the film and brochure to my attention.

2   They were made in collaboration with and partly funded by the London Development Agency, which at the time was the Regional Development Agency for London.

3   Klettner, Andrea, 'Regeneration Olympian', *Regeneration and Renewal*, 30 July 2010. See: http://www.regen.net/news/1018972/Regeneration-Olympian/?DC MP=ILC-SEARCH (accessed 19 June 2012).

BIBLIOGRAPHY

Archives and reports

Anon, *Opening of the Elephant and Castle subways by the Mayoress of Southwark (Mrs. A. J. Wilson) on Thursday the 1st June, at 3.0 pm. Programme* (London: Metropolitan Borough of Southwark, 1911). Southwark Local Studies Archive.

———, *Moving from the Slums: Seventh Report of the Housing Management Sub-Committee of the Central Housing Advisory Committee* (London: Her Majesty's Stationery Office, 1956).

———, *Elephant and Castle Comprehensive Redevelopment Scheme: New Shopping Centre: LCC Press Bureau,* press conference, 14 July 1960. Southwark Local Studies Archive.

———, 'The Elephant and Castle Shopping Centre, promotional brochure', Mathers Public Relations for the Willett Group (London: *c.* 1963). Southwark Local Studies Archive.

———, *Elephant and Castle Shopping Centre. Terms and Conditions of Lease for Standard Shop Tenant* (undated, *c.* 1963). Southwark Local Studies Archive.

———, *2nd Birthday Spring '67,* Elephant and Castle Shopping Centre (1967). Southwark Local Studies Archive.

———, 'Clear-slums drive gets underway' (undated, *c.* 1970). Southwark Local Studies Archive.

———, *Aylesbury Development Area, Opening Ceremony,* press release, 11 April, London Borough of Southwark (1970). Southwark Local Studies Archive.

———, *Elephant Shopping Centre Hooligans Warned,* London Borough of Southwark press release, 29 April 1977. Southwark Local Studies Archive.

———, *Metro Central: London SE1,* Knight Frank International and St George Developments Ltd (London: 1996). Metro Central Heights Residents' Association.

———, *Principles for a Human City* (London: Argent St George, 2001).

———, *A Framework for Regeneration* (London: Argent St George, 2002).

———, 'Wardens' good practice guidance notes: case study – Aylesbury Estate security patrol, Southwark', *Factsheet 7* (Great Britain Neighbourhood Renewal Unit, 2002).

———, *Elephant and Castle BME [black and minority ethnic] Traders' Newsletter,* August 2006.

Argent, *King's Cross Central – Quarterly Monitoring Report* (London, 2008).

Bartlett School, 'King's Cross second report', University College London (1990).

Blair, Tony, 'The will to win', Aylesbury Estate, 2 June (London: Office for the Deputy Prime Minister, Social Exclusion Unit, 1997).

Blunkett, David, 'Alexander Fleming House. Written answers', House of Commons debate 241, c177W, 13 April (1994). See: http://hansard.millbanksystems.com/written_answers/1994/apr/13/alexander-fleming-house (accessed 1 February 2009).

Cain, David, 'Mapping bed bug infestations in London', unpublished powerpoint presentation (London: 2008). Bedbugs Ltd.

Ennis, Nick and Gordon Douglass, 'Culture and regeneration – what evidence is there of a link and how can it be measured?', GLA Economics Working Paper 48 (2011).

Fennell, Desmond, *Investigation into the King's Cross Underground Fire* (London: Her Majesty's Stationery Office, 1988). See: http://www.railwaysarchive.co.uk/documents/DoT_KX1987.pdf

Haynes, Ralph and Anna Savage, 'Assessment of the health impacts of particulates from the redevelopment of King's Cross', *Environmental Monitoring and Assessment* 130/1–3 (2007), pp. 47–56.

Horn, Chris, 'Delivering sustainable communities: the challenge at the Elephant and Castle' (undated). See: http://www.resource05.co.uk/presentations/day3/Chris%20Horn.pdf (accessed 1 July 2012).

Hutchinson, R., 'Alexander Fleming House approval', News release (London: London Borough of Southwark, 1996). Southwark Local Studies Archive.

London Borough of Newham, *Newham London: Investment Prospectus* (undated). See: http://www.newham.gov.uk/NR/rdonlyres/8AF0D6BC-7A8E-4625-85D1-2083502CB3D5/0/InvestmendProspectus.pdf (accessed 19 June 2012).

London Borough of Southwark, 'Aylesbury Redevelopment Design Brief' (London: undated).

———, 'Aylesbury Redevelopment', brochure (London: undated).

Medical Research Council, *Report of the Committee on Bedbug Infestation* (1935–40).

New Deal for Communities National Evaluation (Sheffield Hallam University, 2009). See: http://extra.shu.ac.uk/ndc/ndc_data.htm (accessed 8 December 2012).

Ouseley, Lord Herman, *Independent Review of the Council's Equality and Diversity Framework*, February (London: London Borough of Southwark, 2005).

Prescott, John, 'King's Cross Fire (Fennell Report)', HC Deb, 10 November, House of Commons sitting, vol. 140 cc498–512, Hansard (1988).

Raw, G. J., 'Sick building syndrome: a review of the evidence on causes and solutions', *HSE Contract Research Report* 42 (London: Her Majesty's Stationery Office, 1992).

Rose, David, *Report to the Secretary of State for Trade and Industry. The Regional Development Agencies Act 1998, Acquisition of Land Act 1981, Application by the London Development Agency. For confirmation of The London Development Agency (Lower Lea Valley, Olympic and Legacy) Compulsory Purchase Order 2005, Public Inquiry Opened on 9 May 2006* (Bristol: The Planning Inspectorate, 2006).

Scott, Nigel (ed.), *House Happenings* 7 (1930). St Pancras Housing Association Collection, Camden Local Studies and Archives Centre.

————, 'A peaceable habitation', *House Happenings,* 8 (1931), pp. 20–2. St Pancras Housing Association Collection, Camden Local Studies and Archives Centre.

Southwark Council, *Cleared for action. Elephant and Castle Regeneration: A Guide to the Programme* (London: London Borough of Southwark, 2005).

————, *Regeneration Programme: Introduction* (London: London Borough of Southwark, 2009). See: http://www.elephantandcastle.org.uk/regeneration programme/Introduction (accessed 5 May 2009).

Stafford, Julia and Geraldine Pettersson, 'Vandalism, graffiti and environmental nuisance on public transport', in *Literature Review of Graffiti*, Report, Department for Transport (London, Her Majesty's Stationery Office, 2004).

Books and articles

Agamben, Giorgio, *State of Exception* (Chicago: University of Chicago Press, 2005).

Allison, Peter, 'The house of the artist: David Adjaye designs a studio house for London's new generation of artists', *Domus*, December (2002), pp. 60–9.

———— (ed.), *David Adjaye Houses: Recycling, Reconfiguring, Rebuilding* (London: Thames & Hudson, 2005a).

————, 'Living in ruins', in Peter Allison (ed.), *David Adjaye Houses: Recycling, Reconfiguring, Rebuilding* (London: Thames & Hudson, 2005b), pp. 83–8.

———— (ed.), *David Adjaye: Making Public Buildings. Specificity, Customization, Imbrication* (London: Thames & Hudson, 2006).

Andersson, Johan, 'Consuming Visibility: London's New Spaces of Gay Nightlife', PhD dissertation, University of London, 2008.

Anon, 'A record of the symposium held to celebrate the 150th birthday of photography', *Makers of Photographic History* (Bradford: National Museum of Photography, 1990).

————, *The Art of Regeneration: Urban Renewal Through Cultural Activity* (Nottingham: 1996).

Aspden, Peter, 'Rising star with a store of ideas'. See: http://www.adjaye.com (accessed 26 June 2007).

Ave, Gaston and Franco Corsico (eds), *Urban Marketing in Europe* (Torino: Incontra, 1994).

Baeten, Guy, 'Hypochondriac geographies of the city and the new urban dystopia', *City*, 6/1 (2002), pp. 103–15.

————, 'The uses of deprivation in the neoliberal city', in Nicholas Lakides (ed.), *Urban Politics Now: Re-Imagining Democracy in the Neoliberal City* (Rotterdam: NAi Publishers, 2007).

Banham, Reyner, *The New Brutalism* (London: The Architectural Press, 1966).

Barclay, Irene, *The St Pancras Housing Association in Camden: What It Is and Why: A History 1924 to 1972* (London: St Pancras Housing Association, 1972).

————, *People Need Roots: The Story of the St Pancras Housing Association* (London: St Pancras Housing Association, 1976).

Bataille, Georges, 'L'Abjection et les formes misérables', in George Bataille (ed.), *Essais de sociologie, Oeuvres complètes* (Paris: Gallimard, 1970).

Battista, Kathy, Brandon LaBelle, Barbara Penner, Steve Pile and Jane Rendell, 'Exploring an area of outstanding unnatural beauty: a treasure hunt around King's Cross, London', *Cultural Geographies* 12/429 (2005), pp. 445–6.

Bauman, Zygmunt, *Wasted Lives: Modernity and Its Outcasts* (Oxford: Polity Press, 2004).

Beauman, Katherine Bentley, *Women and the Settlement Movement* (London: Radcliffe Press, 1996).

Beauregard, Robert, *Voices of Decline: The Postwar Fate of U.S. Cities* (London: Routledge, 2003).

Beck, Bernard, 'Bedbugs, stench, dampness, and immorality: a review essay on recent literature about poverty', *Social Problems* 15/1, Summer (1967), pp. 101–14.

Bersani, Leo, *The Freudian Body: Psychoanalysis and Art* (New York: Columbia University Press, 1986).

Biernoff, Suzannah, 'The art of rubbish', unpublished lecture, University College London, January 2003.

Binnie, John, 'A geography of urban desires: sexual culture in the city', PhD dissertation, University of London, 1997.

Blake, Ernest George, *The Protection of Buildings Against Vermin. With a Comprehensive Description of the Most Effective Methods That Can Be Adopted for the Extermination of Rats, Mice and Various Insects* (London: Crosby Lockwood & Son, 1926).

Borden, Iain, 'Thick edge: architectural boundaries in the postmodern metropolis', in Iain Borden and Jane Rendell (eds), *Intersections: Architectural Histories and Critical Theories* (London: Routledge, 2000), pp. 221–46.

————, *Skateboarding, Space and the City: Architecture and the Body* (Oxford: Berg, 2001).

Borden, Iain and Jane Rendell (eds), *Intersections: Architectural Histories and Critical Theories* (London: Routledge, 2000).

Borden, Iain, Joe Kerr, Jane Rendell and Alicia Pivaro (eds), *The Unknown City: Contesting Architecture and Social Space* (London: MIT Press, 2001).

Borromeo, Leah, 'Local heroes: the Olympic unwanted' (2012). See: http://fryingpanfire.com/2012/07/local-heroes-the-olympic-unwanted/ (accessed 30 July 2012).

Bottoms, Anthony, 'Review of *Defensible Space* by Oscar Newman', *British Journal of Criminology* 14 (1974), pp. 203–6.

Brand, Stewart, *How Buildings Learn* (London: Viking, 1997).

Bridge, Gary and Sophie Watson (eds), *The Blackwell Companion to the City* (Oxford: Blackwell, 2000).

Bristol, Katharine G., 'The Pruitt–Igoe myth', *Journal of Architectural Education* 44/3 (1991), pp. 163–71.

Bruno, Giuliana, 'Ramble city: postmodernism and *Blade Runner*', *OCTOBER* 41 (1987), pp. 61–74.

Buchli, Victor and Gavin Lucas (eds), *Archaeologies of the Contemporary Past* (London: Routledge, 2001a).

Burgin, Victor, 'Something about photography theory', in Alan Leonard Rees and Frances Borzello (eds), *The New Art History* (Atlantic Highlands, NJ: Humanities Press International, 1988), pp. 41–54.

Campkin, Ben, 'Urban image and legibility in King's Cross', in Miles, Malcolm and Tim Hall (eds), *Interventions: Advances in Art and Urban Futures 4* (2004), pp. 63–79.

———, 'Finding treasure in "trash": representations of London's Aylesbury and Heygate Estates', e-proceedings of the day conference organised by Docomomo's International Specialist Committee on Urbanism and Landscape (2007b). See: http://www.archi.fr/DOCOMOMO/docomomo_electronic_newsletter7.htm (accessed 14 December 2008).

———, 'Dirt, blight and regeneration: a study of urban change in London', unpublished PhD thesis, University College London, 2009.

———, '"Terror by night": bedbug infestations in London', in Matthew Gandy (ed.), *Urban Constellations* (Berlin: Jovis Verlag, 2011), pp. 139–44.

———, 'Placing "matter out of place": *Purity and Danger* as evidence for architecture and urbanism', *Architectural Theory Review* 18(1), forthcoming 2013.

Campkin, Ben and Rosie Cox (eds), *Dirt: New Geographies of Cleanliness and Contamination* (London: I.B.Tauris, 2007).

Castoriadis, Cornelius, *The Imaginary Institution of Society* (Cambridge: Polity Press, 1987, first published 1975).

Catterall, Bob, 'Informational cities: beyond dualism and towards reconstruction', in Gary Bridge and Sophie Watson (eds), *A Companion to the City* (Oxford: Blackwell, 2000), pp. 192–206.

Chambers, Paul, *Body 115: The Mystery of the Last Victim of the King's Cross Fire* (Chichester: John Wiley, 2007).

'Charles', Elephant and Castle Shopping Centre, 'London destruction' blog (2007). See: http://www.geocities.com/londondestruction/ (accessed 5 May 2009).

Charman, Paul and Mike Wells, 'London 2012: legacy or liability?' (London: Games Monitor, 2010). See: http://www.gamesmonitor.org.uk/node/911 (accessed 3 January 2012).

Cherry, Bridget and Nikolaus Pevsner, *Buildings of England. London 4: North* (London: Penguin, 1998).

———, *Buildings of England. London 2: South* (London: Penguin, 2001).

Clarke, Linda, *Building Capitalism: Historical Change and the Labour Process in the Production of the Built Environment* (London: Routledge, 1991).

Cohen, William A. and Ryan Johnson (eds), *Filth: Dirt, Disgust, and Modern Life* (Minneapolis, MN: University of Minnesota Press, 2005).

Coleman, Alice, 'Design influences in blocks of flats', *The Geographical Journal* 150/3 (1984), pp. 351–8.

———, *Utopia on Trial: Vision and Reality in Planned Housing* (London: Hilary Shipman, 1990, first published 1985).

————, 'The psychology of housing'. See: http://www.singleaspect.org.uk/?p=2363 (accessed 30 January 2012).

Collins, Michael, *The Likes of Us: A Biography of the White Working Class* (London: Granta, 2004).

Colomb, Claire, 'Unpacking new labour's "urban renaissance" agenda: Towards a socially sustainable reurbanization of British cities?', *Planning, Practice & Research*, 22(1) (2007), pp. 1–24.

Connor, Steven, *Fly* (London: Reaktion, 2006).

————, 'Zoopoetics'. See: http://www.bbk.ac.uk/english/skc/ (accessed 5 May 2009).

Cousins, Mark, 'The ugly (Part 1)', *AA Files* 28 (1994), pp. 61–6.

————, 'The ugly (Part 2)', *AA Files* 29 (1995a), pp. 3–6.

————, 'The ugly (Part 3)', *AA Files* 30 (1995b), pp. 65–8.

Crisman, Phoebe, 'From industry to culture: leftovers, time and material transformation in four contemporary museums', *Journal of Architecture* 12/1 (2007), pp. 405–22.

Darling, Elizabeth, 'To induce humanitarian sentiments in prurient Londoners: the propaganda activities of London's voluntary housing associations in the inter-war period', *London Journal* 27/1 (2002), pp. 42–62.

————, *Re-forming Britain: Narratives of Modernity before Reconstruction* (London: Routledge, 2007).

Davidson, Mark, 'Love thy neighbour? Social mixing in London's gentrification frontiers', *Environment and Planning A*, 42(3) (2010), pp. 524–44.

Deitch, Jeffrey, 'Black Magic', in Tim Noble and Sue Webster, *Wasted Youth* (New York: Rizzoli, 2006), unpaginated.

Dennis, Richard, 'Review of Linda Clarke, *Building Capitalism: Historical Change and the Labour Process in the Production of the Built Environment*', *Journal of Historical Geography* 18/4 (1992), pp. 484–6.

————, *Cities in Modernity: Representations and Productions of Metropolitan Space, 1840–1930* (Cambridge, UK: Cambridge University Press, 2008).

Derrida, Jacques, *Spectres of Marx* (Abingdon and New York: Routledge, 2006, first published 1993).

————, *Archive Fever: a Freudian Impression* (Chicago and London: The University of Chicago Press, 1996).

Dillon, Brian (ed.) *Ruins* (London: Whitechapel Gallery, 2011).

Douglas, Mary, *Purity and Danger: An Analysis of the Concepts of Pollution and Taboo* (London: Routledge, 2000, first published 1966).

Dreher, Nan H., 'The virtuous and the verminous: turn-of-the-century moral panics in London's public parks', *Albion* 29/2 (1997), pp. 246–67.

Edensor, Tim, 'Waste matter: the debris of industrial ruins and the disordering of the material world', *Journal of Material Culture* 10/3 (2005a), pp. 311–32.

————, *Industrial Ruins: Spaces, Aesthetics and Materiality* (Oxford: Berg, 2005b).

Edwards, Michael, 'A microcosm: redevelopment proposals at King's Cross', in Andy Thornley (ed.), *The Crisis of London* (London: Routledge, 1992), pp. 163–84.

————, 'Community resistance? Yes. But community alternatives as well!', *Regenerating Cities* 6 (1993), pp. 34–7.

————, 'How should we manage the land resources of state railways? Lessons from London', in Gaston Ave and Franco Corsico (eds), *Urban Marketing in Europe* (Torino: Incontra, 1994), pp. 869–76.

————, 'Fear and loathing at King's Cross', unpublished paper, University College London, 2003.

————, 'The struggle against the development plan in the King's Cross area', in Shuli Hartman (ed.), *Planning and Human Rights, Civil Society and the State* (Jerusalem, 2008), pp. 51–5.

————, 'King's Cross: renaissance for whom?', in John Punter (ed.), *Urban Design, Urban Renaissance and British Cities* (London: Routledge, 2010), pp. 189–205

————, 'London for sale: towards the radical marketisation of urban space', *Urban Constellations* (Berlin: Jovis Verlag, 2011), pp. 54–7.

Emson, William, *Some Versions of the Pastoral* (London: New Directions Publishing, 1950, first published 1935).

England, Kathleen M. (ed.), *Housing: A Citizen's Guide to the Problem* (London: Chatto & Windus, 1931).

Fainstein, Susan, *The City Builders: Property Development in New York and London, 1980–2000* (Lawrence, KS: University of Kansas, 2001, first published 1994).

Falconer, Morgan, 'Up the Elephant: a review of *Bert Hardy: The Elephant and Castle. Vintage Photographs of London Life in the 1940s*' (London: James Hyman Fine Art, 2004).

Forshaw, John H. and Patrick Abercrombie, *County of London Plan. Prepared for the London County Council* (London: Macmillan and Co., 1943).

Forty, Adrian, *Objects of Desire: Design and Society since 1750* (London: Thames & Hudson, 1986).

————, *Words and Buildings: A Vocabulary of Modern Architecture* (London: Thames & Hudson, 2000).

————, 'Concrete and memory', in Mark Crinson (ed.), *Urban Memory: History and Amnesia in the Modern City* (New York: Routledge, 2005), pp. 75–95.

————, 'The material without a history', in Jean-Louis Cohen and Martin Moeller Jr. (eds), *Liquid Stone: New Architecture in Concrete* (New York: Princeton Architectural Press, 2006), pp. 34–45.

————, *Concrete and Culture: A Material History* (London: Reaktion Books, 2012).

Foster, Hal, 'Why all the hoopla?', *London Review of Books* 23/16 (2001), pp. 24–6.

Freud, Sigmund, 'The uncanny', in Gilda Williams (ed.), *The Gothic* (London: Whitechapel, 2007, first published 1919), pp. 168–73.

————, *Civilization and Its Discontents* (London: Penguin Classics, 2002, first published 1930).

Frizot, Michel (ed.), *A New History of Photography* (London: Konemann, 1998).

Furbey, Robert, 'Urban "regeneration": reflections on a metaphor', *Critical Social Policy* 19(4) (1999), pp. 419–45.

Gabrys, Jennifer, 'Sink: the dirt of systems', *Environment and Planning D: Society and Space* 27/4 (2009), pp. 666–81.

Gandal, Keith, *The Virtues of the Vicious: Jacob Riis, Stephen of the Slum* (New York: Oxford University Press, 1997).

Gandy, Matthew, 'The Paris sewers and the rationalization of urban space', *Transactions of the Institute of British Geographers* 24/1 (1999), pp. 23–44.

———, *Concrete and Clay: Reworking Nature in New York City* (Cambridge, MA: MIT Press, 2002).

——— (ed.), *Urban Constellations* (Berlin: Jovis Verlag, 2011).

Gandy, Matthew and Alimuddin Zumla, *The Return of the White Plague: Global Poverty and the 'New' Tuberculosis* (London: Verso, 2003).

Gautrand, Jean-Claude, 'Looking at others: humanism and neo-realism', in Michel Frizot (ed.), *A New History of Photography* (London: Konemann, 1998).

Gershenson, Olga and Barbara Penner (eds), *Ladies and Gents: Public Toilets and Gender* (Philadelphia, PA: Temple University Press, 2009).

Ghirardo, Diane, *Architecture after Modernism* (New York: Thames & Hudson, 1996).

Gill, Stephen, *Hackney Wick* (London: Nobody, 2004).

———, *A Book of Field Studies* (London: Chris Boot, 2005).

———, *Buried* (London: Nobody, 2006).

———, *Hackney Flowers* (London: Nobody, 2007a).

———, *Archaeology in Reverse* (London: Nobody, 2007b).

———, *A Series of Disappointments* (London: Nobody, 2008a).

———, *Warming Down* (London: Nobody, 2008b).

———, *The Hackney Rag* (London: Nobody, 2009).

———, *Off Ground* (London, Nobody, 2011).

Gilroy, Paul, 'Climbing the racial mountain: a conversation with Isaac Julien', in Paul Gilroy (ed.), *Small Acts: Thoughts on the Politics of Black Cultures* (London: Serpent's Tail, 1993), pp. 166–72.

Gissen, David, 'Atmospheres of Late-modernity: The Urban Production of Indoor Air in New York City, 1963–2003', unpublished PhD dissertation, Department of Geography, University College London, 2007.

———, *Subnature: Architecture's Other Environments* (New York: Princeton Architectural Press, 2009).

Godlewska, Anne and Neil Smith (eds), *Geography and Empire* (Oxford: Blackwell, 1994).

Goffmann, Erving, *Stigma: Notes on the Management of Spoiled Identity* (New York, Simon & Schuster, 1963).

Goldfinger, Ernö, 'Offices: Elephant and Castle, London', *Architectural Review* 127 January (1960), pp. 38–43.

———, 'A talk to the Architectural Association on the 21st February 1962 prior to a site visit', *Architectural Association Journal*, April (1962), pp. 244–9.

Gray, Robert, *A History of London* (London: Hutchinson, 1978).

Greater London Council, *Greater London Development Plan* (London: Greater London Council, 1972).

Hall, Stuart, 'The social eye of *Picture Post*', in Glenn Jordan (ed.), *Down the Bay: Picture Post, Humanist Photography and Images of 1950s Cardiff* (Cardiff: Bluetown History and Arts Centre, 2001), pp. 67–74.

————, 'Negotiating architecture', in Peter Allison (ed.), *David Adjaye Houses: Recycling, Reconfiguring, Rebuilding* (London: Thames & Hudson, 2005), pp. 8–11.

Hallett, Michael, *The Real Story of Picture Post* (Birmingham: ARTicle Press, 1994).

Hamburger, Leonard, 'A deliberate preference of ugliness', Unpublished dissertation, University College London, 1997.

Hamilton, Ian, Irene T. Barclay and Evelyn E. Perry, 'The truth about bugs', in Kathleen M. England (ed.), *Housing: A Citizen's Guide to the Problem* (London: Chatto & Windus, 1931), pp. 73–7.

Hamnett, Chris, *Unequal City: London in the Global Arena* (London/New York: Routledge, 2003).

Hamnett, Chris and Drew Whitelegg, 'Loft conversion and gentrification in London: from industrial to postindustrial land use', *Environment and Planning A* 39 (2007), pp. 106–24.

Hardy, Bert, *Bert Hardy: My Life* (London: G. Fraser, 1985).

Harnack, Maren, 'London's Trellick Tower and the pastoral eye', in Gandy, Matthew, *Urban Constellations* (Berlin: Jovis Verlag, 2011), pp. 127–31.

Harris, Andrew, 'The installation of Hoxton: culture and capital in 1990s inner London', in 'Branding urban space: the creation of art districts in contemporary London and Mumbai', unpublished PhD dissertation, University of London, 2005.

————, 'Art and gentrification: pursuing the urban pastoral in Hoxton, London', *Transactions of the Institute of British Geographers* 37(2), pp. 226–41, April 2012.

Harris, Andrew and Louis Moreno, *Creative City Limits: Urban Cultural Economy in a New Era of Austerity* (UCL Urban Laboratory and the Arts and Humanities Research Council, London, 2012).

Harris, Mark, 'Tim Noble and Sue Webster at 20 Rivington Street', *Art in America*, July (1998).

Harvey, David, *Spaces of Hope* (Edinburgh: Edinburgh University Press, 2000).

————, *A Brief History of Neoliberalism* (Oxford: Oxford University Press, 2005).

Hastings, Annette, 'Discourse and urban change: introduction to the special issue', *Urban Studies* 36/1 (1999).

————, 'Stigma and social housing estates: beyond pathological explanations', *Journal of Housing and the Built Environment* 19 (2004), pp. 233–54.

Hatherley, Owen, *Militant Modernism* (Winchester: O Books, 2008).

————, *A Guide to the New Ruins of Great Britain* (London: Verso, 2010).

Hebbert, Michael, *London: More By Fortune Than By Design* (Chichester: John Wiley and Sons, 1998).

Hill, Jonathan, *Immaterial Architecture* (London: Routledge, 2006).

Hirst, Paul, 'Modernism's fear of dirt', unpublished keynote lecture, *Cleanliness, Dirt and Women's Roles*, Symposium, The Women's Library (London: 2002).

Hodkinson, Stuart, 'Housing regeneration and the Private Finance Initiative in England: unstitching the neoliberal urban straightjacket', *Antipode* 43/2 (2011), pp. 358–83.

Holm, Lorens, 'eS aitcH eYe Tee', *The Journal of Architecture* 12/4 (2007), pp. 423–36.

Holmes, Malcolm J., *Somers Town: A Record of Change* (London: London Borough of Camden, 1989).

———, *Housing Is Not Enough: The Story of St Pancras Housing Association* (London: St Pancras Housing Association, 1999).

hooks, bell, 'Seductive sexualities: representing blackness in poetry and on screen', *Yearning* (Boston: South End, 1990), pp. 190–201.

Hopkinson, Tom, *Bert Hardy: Photojournalist* (London: Arts Council of Great Britain, 1975).

Hubbard, Phil, 'Cleansing the metropolis: sex work and the politics of zero tolerance', *Urban Studies* 41/9 (2004), pp. 1687–1702.

Humphrey, Stephen, *Southwark in Archives* (London: London Borough of Southwark, 2000).

Hwang, Stephen W., Tomislav J. Svoboda, Iain J. De Jong, Karl J. Kabasele and Evie Gogosis, 'Bed bug infestations in an urban environment', *Emerging Infectious Diseases* 11/4 (2005), pp. 533–8.

Imrie, Rob, Loretta Lees and Mike Raco (eds), *Regenerating London: Governance, Sustainability and Community in a Global City* (London: Routledge, 2009).

Jacobs, Jane, *The Death and Life of Great American Cities* (London: Pimlico, 1961).

Jameson, Fredric, 'Imaginary and symbolic in Lacan: Marxism, psychoanalytic criticism, and the problem of the subject', *Yale French Studies* 55/56 (1977), pp. 338–95.

———, *Postmodernism, or, the Cultural Logic of Late Capitalism* (London: Duke University Press, 1991).

Jencks, Charles, *The Language of Postmodern Architecture* (London: Academy Editions, 1977).

Jenkins, Simon, *Landlords to London: The Story of a Capital and its Growth* (London: The Trinity Press, 1975).

Jordan, Glenn, *Down the Bay: Picture Post, Humanist Photography and Images of 1950s Cardiff* (Cardiff: Butetown History & Arts Centre, 2001).

Kaïka, Maria, *City of Flows: Modernity, Nature and the City* (London: Routledge, 2005).

Kaïka, Maria and Erik Swyngedouw, 'Fetishizing the modern city: the phantasmagoria of urban technological networks', *International Journal of Urban and Regional Research* 24/1 (2000), pp. 120–38.

Kamvasinou, Krystallia, '"Vague" parks: the politics of late twentieth-century urban landscapes', *ARQ: Architectural Research Quarterly* 10 (2006), pp. 255–62.

Katz, Peter, *The New Urbanism: Toward an Architecture of Community* (London: McGraw-Hill Professional, 1994).

Kelly, Mike, *The Uncanny* (Cologne: König, 2004).

Kerr, Joe, 'Blowdown: the rise and fall of London's tower blocks', in Joe Kerr, Andrew Gibson and Mike Seaborne (eds), *London: From Punk to Blair* (London: Reaktion Books, 2003), pp. 189–97.

Kerr, Joe, Andrew Gibson and Mike Seaborne (eds), *London: From Punk to Blair* (London: Reaktion Books, 2003).

Kerr, Robert, *The Newleafe Discourses on the Fine Art Architecture* (London: Weale, 1846).

Koolhaas, Rem, 'Junkspace', *OCTOBER* 100 (2002), pp. 175–90.

Krauss, Rosalind, 'The destiny of the informe', in Rosalind Krauss and Yve-Alain Bois (eds), *Formless: A User's Guide* (New York: Zone Books, 1997).

Kristeva, Julia, *Powers of Horror* (New York: Columbia University Press, 1982).

———, 'Approaching abjection', in Oliver, Kelly (ed.), *The Portable Kristeva* (New York: Columbia University Press, 1997), pp. 229–47.

Lacan, Jacques, *Écrits: A Selection* (London: W. W. Norton, 2003, first published 1966).

Lahiji, Nadir and Daniel S. Friedman, 'At the sink: architecture in abjection', in Nadir Lahiji and Daniel S. Friedman (eds), *Plumbing: Sounding Modern Architecture* (New York: Princeton Architectural Press, 1997).

——— (eds), *Plumbing: Sounding Modern Architecture* (New York: Princeton Architectural Press, 1997).

Laporte, Dominique, *History of Shit* (Cambridge, MA: MIT Press, 2000).

Lees, Loretta, 'The urban injustices of New Labour's "new urban renewal": The case of the Aylesbury Estate in London' (undated manuscript). See: http://www.enhr2011. com/sites/default/files/Session4-PaperL.Lees-_0.docx (accessed 29 April 2012).

Lefaivre, Liane, 'Dirty realism in European architecture today', *Design Book Review* 17 (1989), pp. 17–20.

Listerborn, Carina, 'How public can public spaces be?', *City: Analysis of Urban Trends, Theory, Policy, Action* 9/3, 2003, pp. 381–4.

Littlefield, David (ed.), *Architectural Design: London (Re)generation* (London: John Wiley, 2012).

Loveridge, Lizzie, *A CurtainUp London Review, Lulu* (2001). See: http://www.curtainup.com/lulu.html (accessed 11 November 2008).

Luckhurst, Roger, 'The contemporary London gothic and the limits of the spectral turn', *Textual Practice* 16/3 (2002), pp. 527–46.

MacDonald, Stuart, 'Review of Lulu at the Almeida King's Cross', Hackwriters.com (2001). See: http://www.hackwriters.com/almeida.htm (accessed 5 May 2009).

Markus, Thomas A., *Buildings and Power: Freedom and Control in the Origin of Modern Building Types* (London: Routledge, 1993).

Marriott, Oliver, *The Property Boom* (London: Hamish Hamilton, 1967).

Marx, Karl, 'Economic and philosophical manuscripts', in Karl Marx, *Early Writings* (London: Penguin/*New Left Review*, 1992, first published 1844), pp. 359–60.

Mawby, R. I., 'Defensible space: a theoretical and empirical appraisal', *Urban Studies* 14 (1977), pp. 169–79.

Mayhew, Henry, *London Labour and the London Poor* (London: Constable, 1968, first published 1861).

Mayor of London, *The London Plan: Spatial Development Strategy for Greater London* (London: Greater London Authority, July 2011).

McClintock, Anne, *Imperial Leather: Race, Gender and Sexuality in the Colonial Contest* (London: Routledge, 1995).

McDonald, Sarah, '*Picture Post*' – Essay for *Encyclopaedia of Twentieth Century Photography* (2004). See: http://corporate.gettyimages.com/masters2/press/articles/BWP_Picture_Post.pdf#search=%22sarah%20mcdonald%20picture%20post%22 (accessed 1 August 2006).

McKee, Will, 'London 2062 housing symposium', University College London, 2012.

McManus, Ruth, 'Public utility societies, Dublin Corporation and the development of Dublin, 1920–1940'. See: http://www.ucd.ie/gsi/pdf/29-1/pus.pdf (accessed July 2012).

Minton, Anna, *Ground Control: Fear and Happiness in the Twenty-first Century City* (London: Penguin, 2009).

Molyneaux, Brian (ed.), *The Cultural Life of Images: Visual Representation in Archaeology* (London: Routledge, 1997).

Morgan, D., 'Brief encounter with Richard Wentworth', *Culture* (2002), p. 14.

Mutale, Emmanuel and Michael Edwards, *Monitoring and Evaluation of the work of the King's Cross Partnership: Final Report* (London: Bartlett School of Planning, UCL, 2003).

Newman, Oscar, *Defensible Space: People and Design in the Violent City* (New York: Macmillan, 1972).

Oliver, Kelly (ed.), *The Portable Kristeva* (New York: Columbia University Press, 1997).

Orwell, George, *Down and Out in Paris and London* (London: Penguin, 2003, first published 1933).

Penner, Barbara and Olga Gershenson (eds), *Ladies and Gents: Public Toilets and Gender* (Philadelphia: Temple University Press, 2009).

Picon, Antoine, 'Anxious landscapes: from the ruin to rust', *Grey Room*, 1/Fall (2000), pp. 64–83.

Pile, Steve, *The Body and the City: Psychoanalysis, Space and Subjectivity* (London: Routledge, 1996).

Pollock, Griselda, 'The image in psychoanalysis and the archaeological metaphor', in Griselda Pollock (ed.), *Psychoanalysis and the Image: Transdisciplinary Perspectives* (Oxford: Wiley-Blackwell, 2006).

Porter, Libby and Kate Shaw (eds), *Whose Urban Renaissance? An International Comparison of Urban Regeneration Strategies* (Abingdon/New York: Routledge, 2009).

Porter, Roy, *London: A Social History* (London: Hamish Hamilton, 1994).

Powell, Hilary and Isaac Marrero-Guillamón (eds), *The Art of Dissent: Adventures in London's Olympic State* (London: Marshgate Press, 2012).

Powell, Kenneth, *City Reborn: Architecture and Regeneration in London, from Bankside to Dulwich* (London: Merrell, 2004).

Power, Anne, *Estates on the Edge: The Social Consequences of Mass Housing in Northern Europe* (London: Macmillan, 1999).

Power, Emma R., 'Pests and home-making: depictions of pests in homemaker magazines', *Home Cultures* 4/3 (2007), pp. 213–36.

Punter, John (ed.), *Urban Design, Urban Renaissance and British Cities* (London: Routledge, 2009).

Raco, Mike and Emma Tunney, 'Visibilities and invisibilities in urban development: small business communities and the London Olympics 2012', *Urban Studies* 47/10 (2010), pp. 2069–91.

Rainwater, Lee, *Behind Ghetto Walls: Black Families in a Federal Slum* (Harmondsworth: Penguin, 1970).

Rathje, William and Cullen Murphy, *Rubbish! The Archaeology of Garbage* (New York: HarperCollins, 1992).

Reilly, Leonard, *Southwark: An Illustrated History* (London: London Borough of Southwark, 1998).

Reinhardt, Klaus and Michael T. Siva-Jothy, 'Biology of the bed bugs (Cimicidae)', *Annual Review of Entomology* 52 (2007), pp. 351–74.

Rendell, Jane, '"Bazaar beauties" or "pleasure is our pursuit": a spatial story of exchange', in Iain Borden, Joe Kerr, Jane Rendell and Alicia Pivaro (eds), *The Unknown City: Contesting Architecture and Social Space* (London: MIT Press, 2001), pp. 104–21.

———, *Art and Architecture: A Place Between* (London: I.B.Tauris, 2006).

Richardson, Tim, 'E&C CDA: Elephant and Castle: an analysis of the redevelopment of the Elephant and Castle 1955–1965', unpublished dissertation, Architectural Association (London: Architectural Association, 1979).

Riis, Jacob A., *How the Other Half Lives* (London: Penguin Classics, 1997, first published 1890).

Robinson, Jennifer, 'Feminism and the spaces of transformation', *Transactions of the Institute of British Geographers: New Series* 25/3 (2000), pp. 285–301.

Robson, Garry, 'Class, criminality and embodied consciousness: Charlie Richardson and a south London Habitus', *Critical Urban Studies: Occasional Papers* (London: Goldsmiths College, 1997).

———, *No One Likes Us, We Don't Care* (Oxford: Berg, 2000).

Rogers, Richard, *Towards an Urban Renaissance: The Report of the Urban Task Force Chaired by Lord Rogers of Riverside* (London: Urban Task Force, 1999).

———, *Towards a Strong Urban Renaissance: Urban Task Force* (London: Urban Task Force, 2005).

Romero, Alvaro, Michael F. Potter, Daniel A. Potter and Kenneth F. Haynes, 'Insecticide resistance in the bed bug: a factor in the pest's sudden resurgence?', *Journal of Medical Entomology* 44/2 (2007), pp. 175–8.

Ross, Rebecca, *Mapping Changes: Visualizing King's Cross*, unpublished dissertation, Department of Geography, University College London (London: 2005).

———, 'Picturing the Profession: the view from above and the civic imaginary in Burnham's plans', *Journal of Planning History*, forthcoming.

Rothenberg, Tamar Y., 'Voyeurs of imperialism: the *National Geographic Magazine* before World War II', in Anne Godlewska and Neil Smith (eds), *Geography and Empire* (Oxford: Blackwell, 1994), pp. 155–72.

Roux, Caroline, 'The tale of a house', in Peter Allison (ed.), *David Adjaye Houses: Recycling, Reconfiguring, Rebuilding* (London, Thames & Hudson, 2005), pp. 132–7.

Rufford, Juliet, 'Out of site: Haworth Tomkins, Paul Brown, and the "Shoreditch Shakespeares"', *Journal of Architectural Education* 61/4 (2008), pp. 34–42.

Rushdie, Salman, *The Satanic Verses* (London: Viking, 1992, first published 1988).

Rutherford, Jonathan (ed.), *Identity: Community, Culture, Difference* (London: Lawrence & Wishart, 1990).

Ryan, Raymund, *Gritty Brits: New London Architecture* (Pittsburgh: Carnegie Museum of Art, 2007).

Rydin, Yvonne, et al., 'Shaping cities for health: complexity and the planning of urban environments in the 21st century', *The Lancet* (London: The Lancet Commission and UCL, 2012).

Saville, Stephen J., 'Playing with fear: parkour and the mobility of emotion', *Social & Cultural Geography* 9/8 (2008), pp. 891–914.

Sennett, Richard, *The Uses of Disorder: Personal Identity and City Life* (London: Allen Lane, 1971).

Shanks, Michael, 'Photography and archaeology', in Brian Molyneaux (ed.), *The Cultural Life of Images: Visual Representation in Archaeology* (London: Routledge, 1997), pp. 73–107.

———, 'Archaeologies of the Contemporary Past'. See: http://traumwerk.stanford.edu:3455/ContemporaryPast/56 (accessed 1 September 2006).

Shields, Rob, *Places on the Margin: Alternative Geographies of Modernity* (London: Routledge, 1991).

Shonfield, Katherine, *Walls Have Feelings: Architecture, Film and the City* (London: Routledge, 2000).

———, 'Dirt is matter out of place', in Jonathan Hill (ed.), *Architecture – the Subject Is Matter* (London: Routledge, 2001), pp. 29–44.

Shove, Elizabeth, *Comfort, Cleanliness and Convenience: The Social Organization of Normality* (Oxford: Berg, 2003).

Sibley, David, *Geographies of Exclusion: Society and Difference in the West* (London: Routledge, 1995).

Sladen, Teresa and Gavin Stamp, *Opportunity or Calamity? The King's Cross Railway Lands Development* (London: The Victorian Society, 1988).

Slavin, Martin, 'Living through placemaking: the London Olympics 2012', unpublished seminar paper, Bartlett School of Planning London Planning seminar series, University College London, 3 November (London: 2011).

Sontag, Susan, *On Photography* (London: Penguin, 1979).

———, *Regarding the Pain of Others* (New York: Farrar, Straus and Giroux, 2003).

Sorkin, Michael, *Variations on a Theme Park: The New American City and the End of Public Space* (New York: The Noonday Press, 1992).

Stallabrass, Julian, *High Art Lite: British Art in the 1990s* (London: Verso, 1999).

———, 'Urban pastoral', *The Urban Pastoral, AHRC Landscape and Environment Programme* (London: Royal Academy of Arts, 2008).

Stallabrass, Peter and Allon White, *The Politics and Poetics of Transgression* (London: Methuen, 1986).

Stedman-Jones, Gareth, *Outcast London: A Study in the Relationship Between Classes in Victorian Society* (Oxford, UK: Oxford University Press, 1971).

Sudjic, Deyan, 'Building in London', in Peter Allison (ed.), *David Adjaye Houses: Recycling, Reconfiguring, Rebuilding* (London: Thames & Hudson, 2005), pp. 186–91.

Sutherland, Patrick (ed.), *Community: The Elephant and Castle* (London: London College of Communication, 2006).

———— (ed.), *Home: The Elephant and Castle* (London: London College of Communication, 2008).

Swyngedouw, Erik and Maria Kaïka, 'The environment of the city ... or the urbanization of nature', in Gary Bridge and Sophie Watson (eds), *The Blackwell Companion to the City* (Oxford, UK: Blackwell, 2000), pp. 567–80.

Tagg, John, *Grounds of Dispute: Art History, Cultural Politics and the Discursive Field* (Minneapolis, MN: University of Minnesota Press, 1992).

Tennant, Neil, 'Interviews: Actually, "King's Cross"', *Absolutely Pet Shop Boys: The Unofficial Website*. See: http://www.petshopboys.net/index.shtml (accessed 5 May 2009).

Thompson, Michael, *Rubbish Theory: The Creation and Destruction of Value* (Oxford, UK: Oxford University Press, 1979).

Thomson, John, *Victorian London Street Life in Historic Photographs* (New York: Dover Publications, 1994).

Thornley, Andy (ed.), *The Crisis of London* (London: Routledge, 1992).

Townend, Peter Norman, *Top Shed* (Shepperton, UK: Ian Allan Ltd, 1989).

Townsend, Katherine, 'The denim garment as canvas: exploring the notion of wear as a fashion and textile narrative', *Textile* 9/1 (2011), pp. 90–107.

Turner, Mark W., 'Gay London', in Joe Kerr and Andrew Gibson (eds), *London: from Punk to Blair* (London: Reaktion, 2003), pp. 48–59.

Urbach, Henry, 'Closets, clothes, disClosure', in Jane Rendell, Barbara Penner and Iain Borden (eds), *Gender Space Architecture* (London: Routledge, 2000), pp. 342–52.

Vance, Peggy, *Loft Living* (London: Ward Lock, 1999).

Venturi, Robert and Denise Scott-Brown, *Learning from Las Vegas: The Forgotten Symbolism of Architectural Form* (Cambridge, MA: MIT Press, 1977, first published 1972).

Vergine, Lea, *Trash: From Junk to Art* (Milan: Gingko Press, 1997).

Vidler, Anthony, *The Architectural Uncanny: Essays in the Modern Unhomely* (Cambridge, MA: MIT Press, 1992).

Wacquant, Loïc, *Urban Outcasts: A Comparative Sociology of Advanced Marginality* (Cambridge, UK: Cambridge University Press, 2008).

Walkowitz, Judith, *City of Dreadful Delight: Narratives of Sexual Danger in Late-Victorian London* (London: Virago Press, 1992).

Walsh, Victoria, *Nigel Henderson: Parallel of Life and Art, London* (London: Thames & Hudson, 2001).

Warburton, Nigel, *Ernö Goldfinger – the Life of an Architect* (Abingdon, UK: Routledge, 2004).

Ward, Colin, *Vandalism* (London: The Architectural Press, 1973).

Watanabe, Haruko, 'The Elephant and Castle post-war development: a critical analysis of the perceived failure', unpublished dissertation, University College London (1995).

Webster, Helena, *Modernism without Rhetoric: Essays on the Work of Alison and Peter Smithson* (London: Academy Editions, 1997).

Wedekind, Frank, *Lulu* (London: Nick Hern, 2001).

Weightman, Gavin, *Picture Post Britain* (London: Collins & Brown, 1991).

Weightman, Gavin and Steve Humphries, *The Making of Modern London* (London: Sidgwick & Jackson, 1983).

Wells, Mike, 'London 2012: a rubbish Olympics' (London: Games Monitor, 2010). See: http://www.gamesmonitor.org.uk/node/1108 (accessed 3 January 2012).

Welshman, John, 'The concept of the unemployable', *The Economic History Review* 59(3) (2006), pp. 578–606.

Wentworth, Richard, '"The accident of where I live" – journeys on the Caledonian Road. An interview with Joe Kerr', in Borden, Iain, Jane Rendell, Alicia Pivaro and Joe Kerr (eds), *The Unknown City: Contesting Architecture and Social Space* (London, 2001).

White, Jerry, *London in the Twentieth Century* (London: MIT Press, 2008).

Whiteley, Nigel, 'Banham and "otherness": Reyner Banham (1922–1988) and his quest for an architecture *autre*', *Architectural History* 33 (1990), pp. 188–221.

Wilhide, Elizabeth, *New Loft Living* (London: Carlton Books, 2002).

Williams, Raymond, *The Country and the City* (New York: Oxford University Press, 1973).

Williams, Richard, *The Anxious City: English Urbanism in the Late Twentieth Century* (London: Carlton Books, 2004).

Wilson, Elizabeth, *The Sphinx in the City: Urban Life, the Control of Disorder, and Women* (London: Virago Press, 1991).

Wilson, Robin, 'At the limits of genre: architectural photography and utopic criticism', *The Journal of Architecture* 10/9 (2005), pp. 265–73.

Wilton, Robert D., 'The constitution of difference: space and psyche in landscapes of exclusion', *Geoforum* 29/2 (1998), pp. 173–85.

Wolkowitz, Carol, 'Linguistic leakiness or really dirty? Dirt in social theory', in Ben Campkin and Rosie Cox (eds), *Dirt: New Geographies of Cleanliness and Contamination* (London: I.B.Tauris, 2007), pp. 15–24.

Wray, Timothy and Andrew Higgott (eds), *Camera Constructs: Photography, Architecture and the Modern City* (Aldershot: Ashgate, 2012).

Wright, Patrick, *A Journey Through Ruins: The Last Days of London* (London: Radius, 1991).

Young, Lola, 'A nasty piece of work: a psychoanalytic study of sexual and racial difference in "Mona Lisa"', in Jonathan Rutherford (ed.), *Identity: Community, Culture, Difference* (London: Lawrence & Wishart, 1990), pp. 188–206.

Zukin, Sharon, *Loft Living: Culture and Capital in Urban Change* (London: Johns Hopkins University Press, 1982).

Films and music

Adams, Marcus (dir.), 'David Guetta vs. the egg', *Love Don't Let Me Go* (*Walking Away*) (London: Colonel Blimp Productions, 2006).

Belmont, Gerard E. and Leonard A. Day, *Paradox City*, 22.34 minutes (London: St Pancras House Improvement Society, 1934).

Cranston, Ros, 'Paradox city' (London: BFI Screenonline, undated). See: http://www.screenonline.org.uk/film/id/1168236/ (accessed 1 May 2009).

Crockford, Sue (dir.), *Somerstown* (UK: People to People, 1984).

———— (dir.), *King's Cross: David and Goliath* (UK, 1992).

Elton, Arthur and E. H. Anstey (Dirs.), *Housing Problems*, 35mm, black and white, 13 minutes (1935).

Jarman, Derek (dir.), *Projections*, MVD Visual, VHS (2000).

———— (dir.), *The Last of England*, Second Sight, DVD, 87 minutes (1988/2003).

Jordan, Neil (dir.), *Mona Lisa*, Handmade Films, 104 minutes (1986).

Julien, Isaac (dir.), *Looking for Langston*, BFI Video, DVD, 45 minutes (1989/2005).

Leigh, Mike (dir.), *Career Girls*, Cinema Club, 283 minutes, VHS (1997).

Mansfield, John M. (dir.), *Horizon: The Writing on the Wall*, BBC video, 50 minutes approx. (1974).

Novello, Ivor, 'Keep the Home Fires Burning' (1914). See: http://www.firstworldwar.com/audio/keepthehomefiresburning.htm (accessed 21 April 2008).

Pabst, Georg Wilhelm (dir.), *Pandora's Box*, DVD, Criterion (1929).

Page, Mike, Paul Neuburg and John Wakefield (dir.), *The London Programme: King's Cross Fire*, ITV (1987).

Payne, Carolyn (dir.), *Sex, Drugs and Video Tape: The Cleaning up of King's Cross*, first edition, ZKK 9 (1999).

Pet Shop Boys, *It Couldn't Happen Here*, Picture Music International (1987).

Newspapers and periodicals

Allen, Richard, 'Blot is saved', *South London Press*, 7 July 1992.

Allison, Rebecca, 'Residents fight to block 24-hour work on channel link', the *Guardian*, 12 January 2004.

Anon, 'Improving the Elephant', *London*, 16 December 1897.

————, 'Dynamiting of slums by Lord Monk Bretton', *The Daily Chronicle*, 24 January 1930.

————, 'Interesting remarks on present day problem', *Litchfield Times*, 24 January 1930.

————, 'The rise and fall of Somers Town', *Estates Gazette*, 22 November 1930.

————, 'The "burning" of slumland', *The Sunday Times*, 25 January 1931.

————, 'Slum clearance in Somers Town', *The Times*, 30 January 1931.

————, '"Burning" down the slums, A miniature garden city arising in the heart of Somers Town', *St Pancras Chronicle*, 30 January 1931.

————, 'Clearing the slums: brighter homes in St Pancras', *Westminster Chronicle*, 6 February 1931.

————, 'L.C.C.'s big reconstruction scheme. Redevelopment of the Elephant and Castle area', *The Municipal Journal and Local Government Administrator*, 25 October 1946.

————, 'Another "Piccadilly Circus" at the Elephant', *Evening Standard*, 21 March 1947.

————, 'The environment of the building operative: psychological research in industry', *The Builder*, 176/5540 (1949), pp. 499–500.

————, 'Goldfinger's Italian piazza', *Manchester Guardian*, 14 July 1959.

————, 'Progress of a sort', *Time*, 30 March 1959b.

————, 'Italian piazza look for South London', *The Sunday Times*, 10 January 1960.

————, 'The Elephant and Castle', the *Guardian*, 28 January 1963, pp. 12–13.

————, 'The children of Walworth weep for their slums', *South London Press*, 12 December 1967.

————, 'Showpiece estate criticised', *The Times*, November 1970.

————, 'Future slum? Is the Aylesbury Estate our very own home grown Pruitt-Igoe?', *Building Design*, 17 May 1974, pp. 20–1.

————, 'Estate is not just an ugly duckling', *South London Press*, January 1975.

————, 'Systems swansong', *Building*, 10 September 1976, p. 745.

————, 'Tickled pink!', *The Trumpet*, advertising supplement, London, August 1990.

————, 'Alexander Fleming House – soon to go?', *Southwark Sparrow*, 12 April 1991, p. 7.

————, 'Green light for massive homes plan', *South London Press*, 11 October 1996.

————, '£20m urban village plan for Alexander Fleming House', *Architects' Journal*, 27 June 1996.

————, 'Minister attacks prison-like buildings', *Evening Standard*, 17 October 2001, p. 6.

————, 'Row over 24-hour rail link work', *BBC News*, 18 December 2003. See: http://news.bbc.co.uk/1/hi/england/london/3330363.stm (accessed 5 May 2009).

————, 'Bedbugs bounce back from oblivion', *BBC News*, 14 April 2004. See: http://news.bbc.co.uk/1/hi/health/3622833.stm (accessed 5 May 2009).

————, 'Howard: why I will keep all my pledges', *The Express*, 14 April 2005, p. 8.

————, 'The big smoke – readers' poll', *Time Out*, 7 June 2007.

————, 'Voice of the people: to hell and back', *The People*, 24 June 2007, p. 8.

Arnott, Jake, 'Jumbo plans for Elephant. Jake Arnott reports on a scheme to raze London's ugliest landmark', *The Sunday Times*, 30 September 2001.

Baillieu, Amanda, 'Mirror mirror on the wall. Building study: Dirty House, east London', *RIBA Journal*, November 2002, pp. 34–8.

Bar-Hillel, Mira, 'New threat over hated building', *Evening Standard*, 21 July 1988, p. 11.

————, 'New granite face of the Elephant and Castle', *Evening Standard*, 1 August 1991.

Barker, Paul, 'Ever get that sinking feeling?', *The Times*, 28 September 2005, p. 18.

BBC, 'Prince attacks flawed design', *BBC News*, 12 May 2009. See: http://news.bbc.co.uk/1/hi/uk/8046946.stm (accessed 12 May 2009).

Bishop, Claire, 'At the crossroads of a trend', *Evening Standard*, 10 September 2002.

Blackman, Oona, Gary Jones and Rosie Dunn, 'Poverty shock report: forgotten families; hungry and sick, Leah, 3, lives with her mother in abject poverty on a squalid, violent estate', *The Mirror*, 30 October 1998, pp. 33–5.

Blinkhorn, Amanda, 'It's all change at King's Cross. Once London's most notorious area, it's now home to inner-city chic', *Hampstead and Highgate Express*, 1995.

Blunden, Mark, 'Why pull down a perfectly good housing estate, asks its architect', *London Evening Standard*, 10 March 2011. See: http://www.thisislondon.co.uk/news/why-pull-down-a-perfectly-good-housing-estate-asks-its-architect-6575907.html (accessed 1 May 2012).

Booth, Robert, 'Star house loses face', *Building Design* 1540/05, July (2002), p. 1.

Boseley, Sarah, 'A public nuisance cruising slowly in a private car', the *Guardian*, 4 February 1985.

Brown, Colin and Nicholas Pyke, 'Railtrack to charge operators for new tracks and signalling', *Independent*, 22 October 2000.

Chester, Lewis, 'Inside story: high and mighty', the *Guardian*, 16 July 1004, p. 28.

Coren, Giles, 'Dragon castle', *Times Online*, 22 July 2006. See: http://www.timesonline.co.uk/tol/life_and_style/food_and_drink/eating_out/giles_coren/article690242.ece (accessed 5 May 2009).

Cozens, Claire, 'Levi's goes up the Elephant and round the Castle', the *Guardian*, 9 August 2002.

Deans, John and Nick Hopkins, 'The premier chooses one of Britain's bleakest housing estates to launch his drive to make the single mothers pay their way', *Daily Mail*, 3 June 1997, pp. 12–13.

Derbyshire, David, 'Rise of the rat as town halls end free pest control', *Daily Mail*, 5 April 2008.

Douglas, Frank, 'The Greatest Happiness of the Greatest Number', *The Architect's Journal*, 27 May 1970, p. 1288.

Duffy, Ellie, 'Dirty rotten scoundrels', *Building Design* 1556 (15 November 2002). See: http://www.duffydesign.com/downloads/hirst.pdf (accessed 1 July 2008).

Dunne, John, 'Goodbye King's Cross, hello Regent quarter', *Hampstead and Highgate Express* (2001), p. 22.

Dunnett, James, 'Save Centre Point, the tower we loved to hate', *The Independent* (1990), p. 19.

Dyson, Jonathan, 'Almeida Theatre: beyond the fringe', *The Independent* (2001).

Fisher, James, 'Goldfinger: he's the man with the modern touch', *The Independent*, 28 August 1998, p. 11.

Frank, Douglas, 'The greatest happiness of the greatest number?', *The Architects' Journal*, 27 May (1970), p. 1288.

Fulcher, Merlin, 'Spending cuts: Aylesbury estate regeneration loses £20m', *The Architects' Journal*, 21 June (2010). See: http://www.architectsjournal.co.uk/news/daily-news/spending-cuts-aylesbury-estate-regeneration-loses-20-million/8601822.article (accessed 2 February 2012).

Glancey, Jonathan, 'It's very clever, but it's still a concrete block', *The Independent*, 15 May 1991, p. 19.

———, 'Nice and sleazy: the Almeida brings a touch of class to vice-ridden King's Cross', the *Guardian*, 30 April 2001.

———, 'Let there be light', the *Guardian*, 23 September 2002.

Goffe, Leslie, 'Sixties' concrete complex loses plea for listed status', the *Guardian*, 6 August 1988.

Hamilton, Alan, 'Blair meets apathy walking on the wild side', *The Times*, 3 June 1997.

Hartley-Brewer, Julia, Colin Freeman and Saba Salman, 'Blair pledges to flatten "sink estates" that shame the nation', *Evening Standard*, 15 September 1998, p. 5.

Hastings, Rob, 'South London estate residents bar filming', *Independent*, 6 February (2012). See: http://www.independent.co.uk/news/uk/this-britain/south-london-estate-residents-bar-filming-6579551.html.

Hatcher, David, 'Save the last dance: what impact will Argent's redevelopment have on King's Cross's club scene?', *Property Week*, 8 February 2008.

Hatherley, Owen, '*Ghost Milk: Calling Time on the Grand Project*, by Iain Sinclair reviewed by Owen Hatherley'. See: http://www.independent.co.uk/arts-entertainment/books/reviews/ghost-milk-calling-time-on-the-grand-project-by-iain-sinclair-2308549.html (accessed 7 November 2011).

Hillier, Bill, 'In defense of space', *RIBA Journal* 80/11 (1973), pp. 539–44.

Holliday, Richard, 'Selling of the "cool" Elephant', *Evening Standard*, 23 June 1997, pp. 4–5.

Hughes, David, 'I'll lay foundations of hope in these ghettoes, says Blair', *Daily Mail*, 16 September 1998, p. 13.

Katz, Ian, 'Land of pink and white elephants', the *Guardian*, 16 August 1991.

Kay, Richard, 'How William sampled life in a tower block', *Daily Mail*, 13 February 1999, p. 29.

Kirk, Jon, 'Estate that came back from hell', *The People*, 24 June 2007, p. 22.

Klettner, Andrea, 'Regeneration Olympian', *Regeneration and Renewal*, 30 July 2010. See http://www.regen.net/news/1018972/Regeneration-Olympian/?DCMP=ILC-SEARCH.

Lambon, Henry, 'London illustrated: Manhattan, here we come?', *Independent on Sunday*, 27 April 2003.

Lauder, Lorraine, 'Resident's plea for derided estate', the *Guardian*, 15 August 1997, p. 4.

Long, Kieran, 'David Adjaye', *Icon* 17 (2004), pp. 84–92.

Lloyd, A. L. and Bert Hardy, 'Life in the Elephant', *Picture Post* 42/2, 8 January (1949), pp. 10–16.

Martin, Andrew, 'A platform for progress', *Daily Telegraph*, 12 January 2002.

McAuslan, Fiona, 'Elephant & Castle Shopping Centre – the elephant graveyard', *Time Out*, 6 September 2006.

McEwen, John, 'Dealers in the temple art', *Sunday Telegraph*, 15 September 2002, p. 6.

Mills, Heather and Nick Cohen, 'Green's downfall rocks prosecution service', *The Independent*, 4 October 1991.

Moyes, Jojo, 'Even the stairwells were perfumed for Blair's visit', *The Independent*, 3 June 1997, p. 3.

Muir, Hugh, 'Hugh Muir asks why, when the media visit a "sink" estate, does it ignore the good news?', the *Guardian*, 18 May 2005, p. 11.

———, 'End of London's most ambitious postwar housing project', the *Guardian*, 22 September 2005, p. 11.

Mullin, John, 'The street Mona Lisa turned her back on', the *Guardian*, 4 October 1991.

O'Neill, Paul, 'Leisure centre inquiry delay', *South London Press*, 5 July 1994.

Paget, Sarah, 'Beauty or beast?', *South London Press*, 4 November 1988, p. 4.

Parnell, Tom and Ryan Kisiel, 'Elephant and Castle regeneration: struggling but still open for trade', *South London Press*, 1 May 2007, pp. 12–13.

Pilger, John, 'A great betrayal: ordinary people had the right to expect that after 18 years of the Tories, Tony Blair would be different', *The Mirror*, 30 April 2002, pp. 6–7.

Porter, Henry, 'The uplifting power of ingenious design enhances our daily lives', the *Guardian*, 25 March 2012. See: http://www.guardian.co.uk/commentisfree/2012/mar/25/henry-porter-kings-cross-new-concourse (accessed 30 July 2012).

Powell, Kenneth, 'Sixties "monument" in mirror glass row', *Daily Telegraph*, 31 March 1989.

Powers, Alan, 'Small change', *Building Design*, 11 October 2002, p. 8.

Raban, Jonathan, 'My own private metropolis', *Financial Times*, 8 August 2008.

Raymond, Clare, 'Death of an urban dream', *The Mirror*, 29 September 2005, pp. 24–5.

Rosenblum, Charles, 'The Carnegie's Gritty Brits offers keen architectural minds at work', *Pittsburgh City Paper*, 8 February 2007. See: http://www.pittsburghcitypaper.ws/gyrobase/Content?oid=oid%3A22477 (accessed 6 July 2007).

Rusbridger, Alan, 'Guardian tomorrows: a place in Peckham – after the planners', the *Guardian*, 17 February 1988.

Sarler, Caroline, 'Thou shalt not…', *The Sunday Times*, 6 October 1991.

Sherwin, Adam, 'Foster to tackle ugly Elephant', *The Times*, 27 June 2000.

Sinclair, Iain, 'The Olympics scam', *London Review of Books* 30/12: June (2008), pp. 17–23. See: http://www.lrb.co.uk/v30/n12/iain-sinclair/the-olympics-scam (accessed 6 May 2012).

Staffell, Andrew, 'On the move: King's Cross', *Time Out*, 4 January 2006, p. 134.

Stewart, Heather, 'PFI under attack from both left and right', *The Observer*, 4 September 2011. See: http://www.guardian.co.uk/business/2011/sep/04/pfi-private-finance-initiative (accessed 2 February 2012).

Street-Porter, Janet, 'It's time to settle a score', *The Independent*, 3 July 2005.

Toller, Robert, 'Did Grouch Marx invent the cost yardstick?', *The Architect*, April (1975), pp. 30–3.

Turner, Chris, 'Chaos theory', *Tate Magazine* 26/Autumn (2001).

Turner, Lucy, 'Wills came to visit my council flat; but I didn't even recognise him', *The Mirror*, 13 February 1999, p. 18.

Warman, Christopher, 'Tenants welcome plan for more say on homes', *The Times*, 20 May 1987.

Wilson, James Q. and George L. Kelling, 'Broken windows', *Atlantic Monthly*, March (1982). See: http://www.theatlantic.com/doc/198203/broken-windows (accessed 25 June 2009).

Woodward, Tim, 'The Elephant reborn: a miraculous transformation in south London', *Radio Times*, 12–18 July 1997.

Young, Alf, 'Workers in the shadows', *The Herald*, 3 June 1997 (Glasgow), p. 17.

Websites

Anon, 'Elephant and Castle – a history of change', Southwark Council (2008). See: http://www.elephantandcastle.org.uk/history-of-change (accessed 5 May 2009).

Games Monitor. See: http://www.gamesmonitor.org.uk (accessed 31 July 2012).

Gill, Stephen. See: http://www.stephengill.co.uk/portfolio/about (accessed 27 December 2011).

King's Cross Railway Lands Group. See: http://www.kxrlg.org.uk/history/timeline.pdf (accessed 30 April 2007).

King's Cross voices, 'A brief history of King's Cross'. See: http://www.kingscrossvoices.org.uk/History_of_Kings_Cross.asp (accessed 2 October 2008).

Picturing Place. See: http://www.picturingplace.net

Southwark Film Office. See: http://www.southwarkfilmoffice.co.uk (accessed 14 December 2008).

Southwark Notes and Archives Group. See: http://southwarknotes.wordpress.com/ (accessed 1 September 2012).

INDEX

Abercrombie, Patrick 5, 37, 40, 74
abjection, theory of 13–14, 71, 165, 166
Adjaye, David 16–17, 128–34, 136, 138–42, 144, 147–48
'aesthetic of recycling' 128–29, 142
Alexander Fleming House 58
  art and architectural aesthetics of 61, 65
  construction of 62
  lease of 63
  negative public image of 59, 64
  redevelopment of 75
  sick building syndrome 63
Allison, Peter 130–31, 136
Almeida theatre, King's Cross 106, 121–24
Alsop, Will 96
anxious landscapes, Picon's concept of 109–10
Archaeologies in Reverse 156
Architectural Association 82
architectural modernism 6, 103, 132, 147
architectural photography 139, 150–51, 158
  sanitising conventions of 140
Aylesbury Estate 16
  ambition and infamy 80–86
  architectural history of 78
  Channel 4's ident of 101–2
  construction methods used for 77
  defensible space, lack of 86–90
  design characteristics of 82

  media spotlight on 95–100
  New Deal for Communities 95
  opening ceremony 78
  Oscar Newman's view of 88
  representation in TV and film 101
  'sink estate' label 99
  Tony Blair's tour of 97–98

Barclay, Irene 25–27, 31
Bartlett, Jean 102
Battle Bridge 105
Beauregard, Robert 8, 117
bedbugs 19, 21, 23–28, 31, 33–34
Bill, The (TV drama) 100
'bioremediation' 150, 156, 159
Blade Runner (1982) 142
Blair, Tony 80, 97–99, 103, 118–19
Blake, Ernest 20–21, 33
Blees Luxemburg, Rut 146–47
Boissevain, Paul 70
Book of Field Studies, A (2005) 157
Bottomley, Virginia 63–64
Bridge over a Pond of Waterlilies (1899) 156
Bristol, Katharine 93–94
Brit Art 100
British documentary cinema 42
British Rail 108, 112, 118
  privatisation of 110
  Property Board (BRPB) 108–9
British Rubbish (1996) 133
Bruno, Giuliana 128–29, 142
brutalism, notion of 65
Buried (2006) 149–52

Camley Street Nature Reserve 111–12
Catterall, Bob 111
Chambers, Paul 115
Channel Tunnel Rail Link (CTRL) 16,
    105, 109, 120
Chilvers, Mark 50–51, 53–54
Cimex lectularius (bedbug) 19, 21, 26
*CITY: Analysis of Urban Theory, Culture,
    Policy, Action* (journal) 111
city branding 8
City of London financial district 135,
    142
civil rights organisations 111, 126
Clean Air Act (1956) 45, 106
Collins, Michael 39
Commission for Architecture and the
    Built Environment (CABE) 2
compulsory purchase order (CPO) 82,
    86, 150
computer-generated images (CGI) 102,
    150
consumer capitalism 43, 134
Country and the City, The (1973) 48
County of London Plan (1943) 5, 40
Cranston, Ros 30
creative cities 8
creative industries 130
cultural capital 2, 145
culture-led regeneration 2, 8, 122

*David Adjaye Houses: Recycling,
    Reconfiguring, Rebuilding* (2005)
    131, 139
deconstruction, philosophy of 157
Defensible Space (1972) 86, 90–91, 93
defensible space, theory of 16, 79,
    86–95
degradation and the polarised city,
    theories of 12–17
Deitch, Jeffrey 135
Department of Health and Social
    Services (DHSS) 62–63
Derrida, Jacques 157, 161
'design against crime' 86, 87

'Dirty House' (2001–2) 16, 128–31,
    133–34, 143–48
    representation of 135–42
Dirty White Trash With Gulls (1998)
    133, 134
discourse, notion of 8
'Disneyfication' of the city 124
distress aesthetics 71–75
documentary photography 108, 151
Douglas, Mary 13, 60, 127, 140, 148
Down and Out in London and Paris
    (1933) 24
'dual city' of extremes 13

Edensor, Tim 110, 115
Edwards, Michael 6, 120
Elephant and Castle
    architecture and environment 62,
        73
    LCC's post-war reconstruction of 58,
        61
    post-war environment 74
    Shopping Centre 59, 68–71
        distress aesthetics 71–75
        as London's ugliest structure 72
        North American influence in
            design and conception 70
        planning of 70
    'regeneration' strategy 74
exhibition
    British Rubbish (1996) 133
    Gritty Brits: New London Architecture
        (2007) 128, 132, 139
    Life in the Elephant 1948 and 2005
        55
    New Homes for Old (1931) 30
    Parallel of Life and Art (1953) 133
    This is Tomorrow (1956) 133

Falling Apart (2001) 134, 135
Fennell Report (1988) 118
financial crisis of 2008 5
fire at underground station in King's
    Cross 115–18

Foraker, Brett 101
Forshaw, John 5, 40, 74
Forty, Adrian 26, 62
Foster, Norman 110, 118–20, 140
Fountain (1917) 128
'free running' 101
frugal pastoral, notion of 142–45, 147

Garden Cities Movement 32
Gehry, Frank 147
Gill, Stephen 17, 149, 151–52, 154,
    156–58, 162
Glasgow Gorbals 43, 49
Goldfinger, Ernö 58, 60, 62–65, 67, 75
graffiti 53, 90, 100, 102, 134–35, 140,
    142, 156
Gray, Robert 106
Greater London Authority 6, 120
Greater London Council (GLC) 5,
    108, 111
Greater London Development Plan
    (1972) 5
'Gritty Brit' architects 128–29
Gritty Brits: New London Architecture
    (2007) 128, 130–33, 139–40
*Ground Control: Fear and Happiness in
    the Twenty-First Century City*
    (2009) 94
grunge aesthetics 129, 142–45, 147
*Guide to the New Ruins of Great Britain,
    A* (2010) 7

Hackney Flowers 155
Hardy, Bert 37
    contribution to war photography
        51–55
    'A Ghost Strayed from old Greece' 44
    'Life in the Elephant' 44–46, 54
    'Maisie' 49–50
    working-class identity 44
Harrison, Arthur 39
Harvey, David 66, 69, 75, 92
hauntology, notion of 157–58
Haworth Tomkins Architects 121

Heritage Lottery Fund 2, 51
Heygate Estate 80–81, 94, 102, 105
    communal spaces and pedways 85
    design characteristics of 82
    see also Aylesbury Estate
Hillier, Bill 90–91
Hirst, Paul 1–2, 168
Horizon 88
Horizon Housing Group 96
Horn, Chris 72
House Furnishings Ltd 33
House Happenings magazine 31, 32
House of Lords Committee 109
Housing: A Citizen's Guide to the Problem
    (1931) 25
Housing Act (1932) 20
housing reform 10, 24, 34, 167
hygiene aesthetic 26, 33, 99

Imaginary Order 9
Index of Multiple Deprivation 5
industrial aesthetics 140–41
Industrial and Provident Societies Act
    (1893) 20
Industrial Revolution 39, 153
industry in London, decline of 108

Jellicoe, Basil 19, 26
Jespersen 12M (pre-cast reinforced
    concrete components) 81
John Laing Construction 80
Jordan, Neil 112

Kerr, Joe 11, 108
King's Cross 16, 105
    Almeida theatre 121–24
    'clean up' campaign 118–21
    culture-triggered regeneration 122
    Fennell Report (1988) 118
    fire 115–18
    Pet Shop Boys 112–13
    railway lands 109
    Railway Lands Group 110, 119
    railway station 105–6, 108, 120

King's Cross (*continued*)
  Regeneration Partnership 120
  reputation as a wasteland 111
  Single Regeneration Budget 120
  training and employment
      programmes 120
King's Cross Central 105, 120, 126
Kristeva, Julia 12–14

Labour Party Conference (1976) 11
Lacan, Jacques 9
laissez-faire Conservatism 11
large panel system (LPS) 81, 85
Last of England, The 114
laws and legislation
  Clean Air Act (1956) 45, 106
  Housing Act (1932) 20
  Industrial and Provident Societies Act
      (1893) 20
  Safe Streets Act (1968) 87
  Sustainable and Secure Buildings Act
      (2004) 79
  Town and Country Planning Act
      (1947) 40
Lea Navigation system 156
lesbian, gay, bisexual and transgender
      (LGBT) 113
Libeskind, Daniel 7
'Life in the Elephant' 42, 44–46,
      50–51, 55
lifestyle consumerism 143
Likes of Us, The (2004) 39
Littlefield, David 7
Lloyd, Albert L. 46
'loft living,' cultural phenomenon of
      143–44
*Loft Living: Culture and Capital in
      Urban Change* (1982) 143,
      145
London Borough of Camden 119
London and Continental Railways
      120
London County Council (LCC) 5, 10,
      38

Abercrombie and Forshaw plan 40,
      74
  post-war reconstruction 61
London Development Agency (LDA)
      150
London Docklands 110
London Plan (2011) 4–5, 96
London Regeneration Consortium
      (LRC) 110, 118–20, 124
London smogs (1952 and 1962) 108
'London's ugliest landmark' 57
London Underground 116–18
Looking for Langston (1989) 115
Lulu Plays 123
Lynn, Jack 84

Magdalen College Mission settlement
      19
Making Do and Getting By (1974–
      ongoing) 157
Mass Observation 41–42
Meet Me in Arcadia (1996) 146
Metro Central Heights 62, 65–67, 70,
      75
Minton, Anna 94–95
Mona Lisa (1986) 112, 114, 124
Monet, Claude 156
*Municipal Journal and Local Government
      Administrator, The* 40

National Freight Corporation 110
natural surveillance 88
New Brutalists 61–62, 65, 91, 132–33,
      143
New Homes for Old exhibition (1931)
      30
New Loft Living (2002) 143
Newham, London Borough of 163
Newman, Oscar 79, 86–94, 98, 103
Nobel Peace Centre, Norway 130

Odeon Cinema, Elephant and Castle
      63
Old Vic Theatre 123

Olympic Delivery Authority (ODA)
150, 156
'Demolish Dig Design' slogan 157
Olympic Games 10–11, 17, 149, 156,
163, 167
Omega Street 123
Origin Housing *see* St Pancras House
Improvement Society (SPHIS)
Orwell, George 24–25, 27

Paradox City (1934) 30, 31
Parallel of Life and Art (1953) 133
Park Hill Estate, Sheffield 84
'Patio and Pavilion' 133
pest control 20, 27–31
ritualistic use of fire for 29–31, 33
see also ritual burning, of vermin
effigies
Pet Shop Boys' 'King's Cross' 112–13
'photo-real' 150, 162
photoworks 149, 159, 161–62
Piccadilly Circus 71
Picon, Antoine 109–10
Picture Post 37, 41–43, 45, 50–51
place imaginaries, notion of 9
Power, Anne 95–96
Private Finance Initiative (PFI) 7, 104
Pruitt–Igoe project 88, 93–94
'pseudomodern' architecture 7
public–private partnerships 7, 78, 118
*Purity and Danger: An Analysis of
Pollution and Taboo* 127–28

Raban, Jonathan 11
railway lands 105–12, 114
Rainwater, Lee 88, 93–94
Rauschenberg, Robert 145
red-light districts 16, 124
registered social landlords 53, 96
'right-to-buy' policy 78
ritual burning, of vermin effigies 33
Robson, Garry 38–39, 71

Safe Streets Act (1968) 87

St Christopher's Flats 28–30
St Pancras House Improvement Society
(SPHIS) 15, 19, 20
'Chamber of Horrors' 30
films 30–31
'secured by design' 79, 86
Sennett, Richard 74
'sick building syndrome' 63, 67
sink estate, notion of 16, 73, 80, 99,
100–104, 166
'sink' schools 99
slum
clearances 10, 15, 20, 28, 30, 43,
45, 98, 165
housing 23, 28, 39, 99
landlords 103
pests 30
Smith, Ivor 84
Soft City (1974) 11
Somers Town 19
ceremonial pest control 27–31, 33
cleansing nature and urban
environment 32–35
house improvement and rehousing
programme 20
housing reform in 24
pests infestations 20–27
slum life in 30
Southwark
disorderly territory of 38–40
London Borough of 80
social deprivation and endurance
54
Trading Standards Unit 67
Southwark Council 51, 53–54, 65–66,
86, 100, 103
Spectres of Marx (1993) 157
Sphinx in the City, The (1991) 124
Stallabrass, Julian 100, 129, 146
Street Life in London (1877) 43
Sustainable and Secure Buildings Act
(2004) 79
Sydney Estate 28

tabula rasa redevelopment 5, 80, 153, 157, 161, 166–67
Tagg, John 139
Tennant, Neil 112–13
'territoriality,' theory of 88, 91–92
Thatcher, Margaret 11, 78, 92, 108, 113, 118
This is Tomorrow (1956) 133
Thomson, John 43
Tinker, Timothy 85
'Top Shed' 107
Towards a Peoples' Plan (1990) 110
Town and Country Planning Act (1947) 40
trade unions 111
Trellick Tower, West London 67
'trickle down' effect 5

urban degradation 4–5, 7, 12, 14–15, 43, 103, 128, 130, 148, 164
urban pastoral, notion of 146–48
urban regeneration
  concept of 4
  and cultural phenomenon of 'loft living' 143–44
  and its contradictions 4–12
  meaning of 4–5
urban renaissance 2, 5–6, 16, 120

urban restructuring 10, 33, 144
Urban Task Force 2
urban transformation 14, 162
  modes of 165
  rise of neoliberal approaches to 10
Uses of Disorder, The (1971) 74

Villa Savoye (1929) 99

Wolkowitz, Carol 128
Walkowitz, Judith 97, 124
war photography 43, 51–55
waste and recycling, art from 133–35
Wasted Youth (2006) 135
wasteland 16, 101, 103, 105–6, 108, 111, 114, 118, 166
Wedekind, Frank 123
Welfare State, expansion of 2, 10, 16, 77
Welwyn, Operation 119
Whitechapel Ideas Store 132
Wick, Hackney 11, 149, 153–54
Williams, Raymond 48
Wilson, Robin 139
Women's Library, The 1–3
Wray, Timothy 140
Wright and Wright architects 2

'Young British Artists' 146